AF560864

THE ATLANTIC CRITICAL STUDIES

WILLIAM SHAKESPEARE'S
Othello

THE ATLANTIC CRITICAL STUDIES

WILLIAM SHAKESPEARE'S

Othello

Jibesh Bhattacharyya

Published by

ATLANTIC

PUBLISHERS & DISTRIBUTORS (P) LTD

B-2, Vishal Enclave, Opp. Rajouri Garden,
New Delhi-110027
Phones : 25413460, 25429987, 25466842

Sales Office
7/22, Ansari Road, Darya Ganj,
New Delhi-110002
Phones : 23273880, 23275880, 23280451
Fax : 91-11-23285873
web : www.atlanticbooks.com
e-mail : info@atlanticbooks.com

Printed in India
at Nice Printing Press, Delhi

General Preface

The Atlantic Critical Studies, modelled on the study-aids available in England and America, among other places, are primarily meant for the students of English Literature of Indian universities.

However, in consideration of the local conditions and the various constraints under which our students have to study—non-availability of relevant critical books, dearth of foreign and Indian journals, inaccessibility to good, well-equipped libraries, just to mention a few of them—the models have been considerably improved upon, both qualitatively and quantitatively.

Thus, while these Studies are meant to be comprehensive and self-sufficient, the distinguished scholars who have prepared these study materials, have taken special care to combine lucidity and profundity in their treatment of the texts.

The Select Bibliography at the end is meant not only to acknowledge the sources used but also to help a student in the pursuit of further studies if s/he wants to.

Atlantic Publishers & Distributors believe in quality and excellence. These studies will only reconfirm it.

Mohit K. Ray
Chief Editor [English Literature]
Atlantic Publishers & Distributors,
New Delhi

Preface

A few words of apology are needed for attempting to produce another critical study of Shakespeare's tragic masterpiece, *Othello*, when so many of brilliant studies of the play by great Shakespearian scholars are already in existence. The author does not claim it to be an all-embracing exploration of the mysterious product of a genius of all times. *Othello* is one of the four great tragedies of Shakespeare. In order to have an idea of Shakespeare's conception of tragedy, we will have to peruse this play along with the other three tragedies, *Hamlet*, *Macbeth* and *King Lear*.

Othello is a tragedy of jealousy. Some consider it a tragedy of intrigue. Others characterize it as a domestic tragedy. Because of these divergent nature of the play, it has roused great interest among critics and scholars. Besides, Iago in this play is an enigmatic character. He is a revenger. But the real motive of his revenge is not very clear. This, too, has created a diversity of opinion. Coleridge says that it is the "motive-hunting of a motiveless malignity" that is found in Iago. Moreover, the play is based on a known story narrated by Giovannibattista Giraldi Cinthio, a Sicilian novelist, in his *Hecatommithi* (a hundred tales) published in Monteregale in Sicily in 1565. So, it is interesting to observe what use Shakespeare has made of the story in his play.

King Lear of Shakespeare has been considered by A.C. Bradley the greatest work of the dramatist. But, in its grip upon the emotions of the audience and the readers, *Othello* is more sustained than *King Lear* or any other tragedy by Shakespeare. The plot of *Othello* is quite simple. It moves round the schemes of a person who seeks revenge because he thinks he has been wronged. But, as the plot is concerned with one of the strongest and most distressing of human emotions, it is most powerful and highly dramatic. None of the other three great tragedies of Shakespeare has much of a plot in this sense. Besides, the intensity of the play is heightened by the compactness achieved with the help of the observance of the three unities, much less given attention to in other plays of Shakespeare, a comparatively small number of characters and the absence of any comic relief.

The present study is an attempt to examine some of the problems connected with the play and help not only the students but also the discerning readers to come to a reasonable solution to those problems. In order to arm a reader with a comprehensive idea of the master dramatist's mind at work, so that he may appreciate this great tragedy of all times, a brief survey has been made, in the introduction, of the various aspects of Shakespeare's mind and art. A broad and detailed critical analysis of the play has been given with a view to helping the readers in their proper comprehension and appreciation of this unique tragedy of Shakespeare. For the quotations from the text, the seventh Arden edition (1958) edited by M.R. Ridley, reprinted in 1976, has been consulted.

A Shakespearian play presents some language difficulties. Shakespeare has used words in a different sense from what they mean today. Hence, it will be helpful to a reader, not initiated in Shakespearian language, if some guidance for understanding the exact meanings of these words used in the play, are provided. With that aim in view, a brief glossary of such words is given at the end. Also, it is hoped that a careful study of Shakespeare's use of language in this play will help a reader towards a proper understanding of other plays by the dramatist. For the readers curious to know more about Shakespeare in general, and *Othello* in particular, a select bibliography has also been provided. The questions on the play given at the end of the book are meant not merely for the students preparing themselves for their examinations in this drama, but also for the discerning readers to stimulate their interest in the various aspects and problems of this wonderful drama which has not lost its relevance and popularity even today.

Jibesh Bhattacharyya

Contents

General Preface *v*

Preface *vii*

1. Introduction 1
2. Life and Works of William Shakespeare 10
3. Characters and Places 21
4. A Brief Synopsis of the Play 26
5. A Critical Analysis of the Play 32
6. Date of Composition 75
7. Sources of *Othello* 78
8. *Othello*: A Distinctive Shakespearian Tragedy 89
9. *Othello*: A Tragedy of Intrigue 95
10. *Othello*: A Domestic Tragedy 99
11. The Plot-Structure 102
12. Art of Characterization 108
13. Character-Sketches 112

    Major Characters:

    Othello 112

    Iago 126

    Cassio 139

    Desdemona 141

    Emilia 147

Minor Characters:
- Brabantio 150
- Roderigo 151
- Lodovico 153
- Gratiano 154
- Mortano 155
- Duke of Venice 156
- Bianca 156

14. Role of Chance and Accident 158
15. Double-Time in *Othello* 161
16. Images and Symbols in *Othello* 171
17. Shakespeare's Use of Prose and Verse 177
18. *Othello*: A Work of Art 180
19. Universal Appeal of *Othello* 184
20. A Summing-Up 187
21. Critical Reception of the Play 193

Some Important Questions 200

A Select Bibliography 203

A Brief Glossary 208

Index 215

1

Introduction

Shakespeare is considered the best poet and dramatist of England. Some critics give him even the highest place in the field of world literature. Shakespeare's plays impress everybody by their singular excellence. The superiority of Shakespeare to all other English writers lies in the fact that he has united powers and advantages of three great forms: the romance, pure poetry and drama. The first gives him variety, elasticity, freedom from constraint and limit. The second enables him to transport. The third at once preserves his presentations from the excessive vagueness and vastness which non-dramatic romance invites, and helps him to communicate actuality and vividness. Shakespeare is a past master in the art of characterization. His characters appear as real human beings of flesh and blood and not as puppets drawn by the strings. Besides, his plays are expressions of passions and not a mere description of them. His imagination, too, is of the same plastic kind as his conception of character or passion. His command of language and versification is admirable. Shakespeare is as deep and many-sided as life and thus it requires great courage to face and understand him. In fact, the only way to know him is to completely submit to his overwhelming power.

We have little biographical records of Shakespeare the man. Particularly his early days are shrouded with a mystery. But, for a great literary artist the absence of biographical details is not much to be deplored, as his literary works help us in understanding the man, although Matthew Arnold, in his sonnet on Shakespeare, observes: "Others abide our question—Thou art free! "We ask and ask—Thou smilest and art still,/ Out-topping knowledge!" Arnold denies that we can find the man Shakespeare in his plays. Shakespeare is a dramatic poet and poetry is nothing but feigning. He has given us a long procession of dramatic characters who may appear as real to us as our neighbours, and in this crowd he conceals himself and escapes. But, it should be remembered that no dramatist can create live characters except by transmitting the best of himself to the children of his art, scattering among them a largesse of his own qualities giving to one his wit, to another his philosophic doubt, to another his love of action, to another his simplicity and constancy that he finds deep in his own nature. In the plays we may learn the questions that interest Shakespeare most profoundly and recur to his mind with most insistence. We may note how he handles his borrowed story, what he rejects and what he alters changing its purport and fashion, how many points he is content to leave dark, what matters he chooses to decorate with the highest resources of his romantic art, how in every type of character he emphasizes what most appeals to his instinct and imagination. We also share the emotions that are aroused in him by certain situations and events, and are made to respond to the strange imaginative appeal of certain others. Thus, Shakespeare makes us acquainted with all that he sees and all that he feels and hence with Matthew Arnold we cannot complain that Shakespeare has hidden himself from our knowledge.

A close study of the plays of Shakespeare will make us aware that the dramatist is endowed with an acute power of observation. Nothing escapes his keen gaze and intent contemplation. Habits, character, countenance, costume, landscape, emotions, seasonal changes, state affairs, events witnessed, reports heard and chronicle read, misery and pomp, vice and honour, health and sickness, vigour and frailty, cunning and pity, birds, animals and games, and every shape and condition and element of his eager daily experience become a fixed and glowing image in his mind for use as his art should require.

Shakespeare is a child of the English Renaissance, and it is the books of his own age—the translations and imitations of the classics, which pour from the press during the second half of the sixteenth century, the poems, love-pamphlets and plays of the University along with the tracts and dialogues in the prevailing Italian taste, have been the favourite reading of Shakespeare. This will be evident from the plots and themes of many of the plays of Shakespeare. Shakespeare has been a person with a pleasing personality. J. Dover Wilson in *The Essential Shakespeare* writes: "He must have been a very fascinating person to meet. His manners were charming, while in respect of looks and conversation a good tradition which comes from the son of one of his fellow-players pictures us a handsome, well-shaped man, very good company, and of a very ready and pleasant smooth wit." Ben Jonson criticizes the art of Shakespeare fiercely, but expresses his love for the man Shakespeare.

Shakespeare has been an upright man. According to Dover Wilson, Shakespeare "is a marvel of restraint and self-respect." The most admirable quality of Shakespeare is, however, his humanity. All critics have testified to the generosity, catholicity of temper and tolerance of Shakespeare. The breadth and impartiality of Shakespeare's view of things has been recognized in that great commonplace of criticism which compares him with Nature. On the tablet under his bust in Stratford church he is referred to as, "Shakespeare, with whom quick Nature died." Ben Jonson enlarges this comparison by saying: "Nature herself was proud of his designs,/And joy'd to wear the dressing of his lines." And Dryden says of him: "All the images of Nature were still present to him and he drew them, not laboriously, but luckily; when he describes anything, you more than see it, you feel it too."

In *Hamlet* we find for the first time a full development of Shakespeare's conception of tragedy. There is a sensational external struggle of the hero with current material of the theatre like villains, ghosts, murders, insanity and the like, and the hero's disaster is caused not merely by external forces or circumstances or to evils working within, but also by an inherent unfitness of the hero. A further development of tragic art is exhibited by Shakespeare in *Othello*. The ingredients of the story were not unfamiliar in tragedy, but Shakespeare enlarges and interprets them to fit his earlier conception of tragedy in the presentation of a spiritual struggle in which goodness is attacked by evil at its point of vulnerability, which is, in this case, is too much credulity. The play has only a few persons and virtually a single action. The underplot is subordinated and closely united to the main action, and there are no delays and new excitements between crisis and catastrophe, as in *Hamlet* or *King Lear*. Nowhere, even in Shakespeare, are generosity and greatness of soul more admirable than in Othello, nowhere is villainy more inhuman than in Iago. Hypocrisy, cynicism, cruelty, the absence of human sympathy, the pride and malignity of intellectual superiority have henceforth their symbol in Iago.

The main point in Shakespeare's conception of tragedy is the fact that Shakespeare strives to display themes essentially stirring and often melodramatic, and that his primal thought is dramatic effectiveness. But within the external sensationalism he has placed a more subtle, a more poetical and less tangible tragic spirit. The varied manifestations of the inner spirit are largely responsible for the impression that each play is a symphony on some definite abstract theme. Thus, *Othello* may be called a drama of deception and self-deception, *Macbeth*, a drama of ambition, *King Lear*, a drama of headstrong passion and false pride, *Hamlet*, a drama of indecision. With this abstract atmosphere moves the inner conflict of Shakespeare's dramas. This inner conflict exists alongside outer conflict, but rarely coincides with it. *Othello* presents an outer struggle in the persons of Othello, Iago, Cassio and Desdemona. But, the inner conflict is to be sought for in the mind of Othello and also in the mind of Iago. This inner conflict, however, is normally confined to one figure. Thus, although there is some sort of conflict in Iago's mind, Iago is presented as too fully developed along his own particular lines to display anything of the passionate inner struggle perceptible in Othello's soul.

Shakespeare's heroes are great personalities. Thus, Othello

is no mere private person. He is the General of the Republic of Venice. At the beginning of the play we see him in the Council Chamber of the Senate. The consciousness of his high position never leaves him. Even when, at the end, he is determined to live no longer after the realization of his mistake, he is anxious not to be misjudged by the world. The suffering and calamity of such a hero are exceptional. They are, as a rule, unexpected and contrasted with previous happiness or glory. Moreover, a Shakespearian tragic hero does not remain alive at the end. The fall of the tragic hero leading to his death is brought about by the agency of chance or Fate as well as by a fatal flaw in the character of the hero himself. The mind of the hero is left free, but it finds itself incapable of dealing with the forces of fate. Chance happenings or accidents have an appreciable influence on the course of action in the play. Thus, Desdemona drops her handkerchief at the most fatal moment, which hastens the tragedy.

A profound sense of fate underlies all Shakespeare's tragedies. The classical irony which plays with the ignorance of man and makes him a prophet in spite of himself, is an essential part of Shakespeare's tragic method. Such an irony runs all through *Othello*, so that only a repeated reading of the play can bring out its full meaning. The joyful greetings of Othello and Desdemona in Cyprus are ominous. "If it were now to die," says Othello, "'twere now to be most happy." His words are truer than he knows. Without this sense of fate, tragedy would be impossible. *Othello* is, in many ways, Shakespeare's supreme achievement. In this play he has given tragic dignity to a squalid story of crime by heightening the characters and making all the events inevitable.

Poetic justice is absent from Shakespeare's tragic picture of life. Poetic justice means that prosperity and adversity are distributed in proportion to the merits of the agents. But, such poetic justice is in flagrant contradiction with the facts of life. In Shakespeare we find that the doer must suffer and that the villains do not remain victorious or prosperous at the end. But an assignment of amounts of happiness and misery, an assignment even of life and death, in proportion to merit, is not to be found in Shakespeare. We may not find poetic justice in Shakespeare, but there is always a moral order, which is not indifferent to both good and evil, or equally favourable to both, but shows itself akin to good and alien to evil. Thus, in a Shakespearian tragedy the main cause that produces suffering and death is never good. The main cause of convulsion is a moral evil. In *Othello*, Iago is the main source of convulsion. Evil exhibits itself everywhere as something negative, barren, weakening, destructive, a principle of death. It isolates, disunites and tends to annihilate not only its opposite but itself too. That which keeps the evil man prosperous or makes him succeed, even permits him to exist, is the good in him. When the evil in him gets the better of the good and has its way, it destroys other people through him, and destroys him also.

Shakespeare's first care in writing a play is to get hold of a story that might be shaped to the needs of the theatre. Then he dresses his characters and puts them in action, so that his opening scenes are often a kind of postulate which the reader or the spectator is expected to accept. In his great tragedies, story and characters are marvellously adapted to each other. Before we learn anything of Shakespeare's larger purpose we must pass beyond and see, first, how character influences the dramatic construction and secondly, how far it is itself determined by the preconceived plot or story of the play. Thus, the nature of Othello seems to have been conceived in its special term in order to make the dramatic representation of the fictional tale of Cinthio possible. Shakespeare is a master craftsman. There is, thus, in his mature plays, an inextricable interweaving of plot and character. Hence, to study a play by Shakespeare, a mere character-study is not enough. The character-study, necessary as it may be, must be related to the larger whole, to the emergencies of the drama, before it can prove of any definite value.

Apart from the handling of the plot, Shakespeare's excellence lies in his power of characterization. Shakespeare seems to identify himself with the character he wishes to represent and to pass from one to another like the same soul successively animating different bodies. So, his characters appear as real beings of flesh and blood. In presenting his characters he is highly tolerant. He does not take sides and pronounce any judgment. In the quality of tolerance he excels all other authors. He adopts a strictly impartial attitude towards everybody. Different critics have tried to interpret the characters in Shakespeare in their own ways. In fact, the interpretation of the characters in Shakespeare has had a long history reflecting the general intellectual tendencies of the time. But it is impossible to interpret Shakespeare's characters by any definite method, because they are the product of the poetic exploration of the hidden springs of human conduct. Shakespeare is particularly happy in drawing female characters and his women are superior to men. The most beautiful characters of his creation depend for their beauty on their imaginative response to the need of the moment. Through the whole of the dialogue appropriated to Desdemona there is not one general observation. Words are with her the vehicle of sentiment, and never reflection. The comparative simplicity of character, which distinguishes Shakespeare's women from his men is maintained throughout the plays. Love and service are as natural to them as breathing. They are the sun-light of the plays, obscured at times by clouds and storms of melancholy and misdoings, but never subdued or defeated.

Shakespeare's methods of drawing characters are numerous. The most obvious of them is the soliloquy. The function of a soliloquy is self-revelation. In the case of persons who are deeply contemplative and who are more busy in the world of thought rather than of action, it is difficult to understand their motives. The dramatist in such circumstances makes them speak out their inmost thoughts, so that the consistency between their nature and action may be perceived by the audience. The soliloquy, then, is the dramatist's means of taking us down into the hidden recesses of a person's nature and of revealing those springs of conduct which ordinary dialogue provides him with no adequate opportunity to disclose. In *Othello* Iago's soliloquies explain to the audience the real motives of his criminal actions. Soliloquies, in Shakespeare, also add an air of idealization to the play, as they are highly lyrical and magnificently poetic. Shakespeare is the greatest English dramatic poet. In general his poetic style is characterized by ease and fluency. His mind and hand go together and what he thinks he utters with perfect ease. His ease is so great that his wildest conceits hardly seem far-fetched. Shakespeare's descriptions, particularly those of storm and tempests, are highly poetic. In the beginning of the Second Act of *Othello* he makes personages on the stage describe with vivid effect what they see taking place behind the scenes—the struggle of vessel after vessel on a fiercely tempestuous sea.

Shakespeare is in the habit of using recurring or dominating images in his plays. These images play a part in raising, developing, sustaining and repeating emotions in his plays. The main image of *Othello* is that of animals in action, preying upon one another, mischievous, cruel or suffering and through these the general sense of pain and unpleasantness is much increased and kept constantly before us. More than half the animal images in the play are Iago's and all these are contemptuous and repellent like a plague of flies, a quarrelsome dog, leading asses by the nose, beating an offenceless dog, wild cats, goats and monkeys. To this Othello adds his pictures of foul toads breeding in a cistern, summer flies in the shambles, the toad in a dungeon, the ill-boding raven over the infected house. These images of insects and reptiles swarming and preying on one another not out of special ferocity, but just in accordance with their natural instincts, or the harmless innocent animals trapped or beaten, reflect and repeat the spectacle of the wanton torture of one human being by another, which we witness in the tragedy. Hence a study of Shakespeare's imagery helps us to realize fully and accurately one of the many ways by which the dramatist so magically stirs our emotions and throws a fresh ray of light on the significance of the play.

Othello is the most effective dramatic achievement of Shakespeare among his tragedies. Dr Johnson holds that the beauties of this play impress themselves so strongly upon the attention of the readers that they need draw no aid from critical illustrations. In no other play of Shakespeare are there two such leading and tremendous parts, each challenging the actor's utmost study, as those of Othello and Iago. According to Macaulay, *Othello* is perhaps the greatest work in the world. Notwithstanding the aspect of unexpectedness created by chance and unreason predominating everywhere in the play, Shakespeare has wonderfully built up the whole drama by means of scenes which follow one another in the most orderly and rational manner. *Othello* is a finished piece of dramatic art. Here the passion rises with a positively musical effect. Iago's devilish plan is realized step by step with consummate certainty. All details are knit together into one firm and well-nigh inextricable knot. The apparent carelessness with which Shakespeare has treated the necessary lapse of time between the different stages of the action has, by compressing the events of months and years into a few days, heightened the effect of strict and firm cohesion which the play produces. The secret of the dramatic power of *Othello* is in its sustained unity of interest, in the fact that the central theme is before us from first to last. Our interest is never distracted from the trials of the hero and the heroine. The plot of Iago, its progress and success, occupies our attention all the time. We sympathize with his victims and marvel at his malignity. No minor character is allowed to interfere with the central theme of the drama. Thus, *Othello* can be said to be the most perfectly constructed of all the tragedies of Shakespeare.

2

Life and Works of William Shakespeare

Shakespeare is so important and, therefore, so well-known a name in English literature, that a sketch of his life as an introduction to any of his plays is generally dispensed with as unnecessary. The more so, because the works of a transcendental genius like Shakespeare bear almost no relation to the facts and incidents of his life. Besides, the facts and incidents of his life, which have been ascertained by the laborious research of scholars and antiquarians through more than three centuries, are so meagre that they can hardly make what may be called a biography of Shakespeare. If we want to know and understand the man Shakespeare, his mind and art, his attitude to life and the world, there are of course the plays which confide to us more secrets of the inner life of Shakespeare than any, even the most detailed, biography can ever possibly do. But if we want to know the externals of his life, we are sorely disappointed. Not a single fact of his life can be ascertained beyond doubt or dispute. What exactly were the nature and range of his education or literary knowledge, why he left his native town Stratford and came to London, how exactly he began his life in London, what exactly were his steps to fame and popularity with the court and the theatre-going public, why he left London in the very height of his active career, how exactly he died—all are based on clever conjectures and not on dependable material upon which to work. So, there develop various theories which deny him the authorship of the plays and poems generally attributed to him. The reason alleged is that no one with Shakespeare's scanty education could have produced such magnificent plays.

Among the various theories which deny Shakespeare the authorship of his plays and poems, was, the one developed in the middle of the eighteenth century from the supposed internal evidence in his works and external circumstances, that Francis Bacon used this pen-name to write the plays and poems known as Shakespeare's works. Thus, this Baconian theory denies the very existence of a man named Shakespeare. Another theory promulgated in June 1955 by Colvin Hoffman, an American journalist, who says that Marlowe was Shakespeare. According to him Marlowe was not killed in a street-brawl as is commonly known. Rather he killed a person and absconded to avoid penalty. From his place of hiding he continued to write, gradually improving his mind and art. He sent his manuscripts to his patron, an earl, who, in his turn, gave them to Shakespeare to publish them in his name. Thus, the plays bearing the name of Shakespeare are actually the product of Marlowe's pen. Another interesting theory is made out in December 1988 by a Libyan leader Muammar Al-Gaddafi who proclaimed that Shakespeare was, in reality, an Arab named Sheikh Zbir. Gaddafi claimed that the Sheikh was falsely presented by the Western world as an Englishman named Shakespeare and that it was a sort of cultural theft by the West. It was asserted that Shakespeare's plays are either borrowings from or subtle transpositions of well-known works of Arab literature. Thus, *Romeo and Juliet* is a mixture of two Arab love stories—*Leila and Majnoon* and *Quys and Lubna*, *Macbeth* is based on a story from *Thousand and One Nights*, while *Othello* is the exact replica of a love poem on "Quamar Al-Zaman and His Mistress." The very name 'Othello' is mispronunciation of the Arab name 'Abdullah.' Scholars everywhere are busy to find out the real identity of Shakespeare. Thus, very recently, in April 2000, Professor Martino Iuvara claims that the playwright was a Sicilian born in Messina as Michelangelo Florio Crollalanza, and he fled to London, because of the Holy Inquisition, changing his name to its English equivalent. Crollalanza or Crollalancia literally translates as Shakespeare, Professor Iuvara asserts. Professor Iuvara states that in 1564, the year John Calvin died in Geneva, Michelangelo was born in Messina, of a doctor, Giovanni Florio and a noble woman named Guglielma Crollalanza, both of whom had Calvinistic sympathies. Young Michelangelo was educated by Franciscan monks, taking a diploma in Latin, Greek and history at a very early age displaying formidable intelligence and power of memory. The inquisition was on the trail of Dr Florio because of his heretical ideas and the family fled to Treviso near Venice. They bought Casa Otello, built by a retired Venetian mercenary called Otello (Othello?) who, to local legend, killed his wife out of misplaced jealousy. Michelangelo studied in Venice, Padua and Mantua and travelled in Denmark, Greece, Spain and Austria. He was befriended by the philosopher Giordano Bruno who was to be burnt at the stake for heresy in 1600. Bruno had strong links with William Herbert, the Earl of Pembroke, and the Earl of Southampton and under their patronage Michelangelo went to England in 1588 at the age of 24. His mother had an English cousin at Stratford, who took the boy in. The Stratford branch of the family had already translated their name from Crollalanza to Shakespeare and had a son called William who had died prematurely. Michelangelo, Professor Iuvara says, simply took over the name for himself, becoming "William Shakespeare." Professor Iuvara also points out that fifteen of Shakespeare's thirty-seven plays have an Italian background.

The debate on the real authorship of the plays attributed to Shakespeare has been raging like a tempest since the late 1990s. The debate actually started in 1920 by an English schoolmaster, J. Thomas Looney who claimed that it was Edward de Vere (1550-1604), the 17th Earl of Oxford, who wrote those plays under the pseudonym, Shakespeare. The Stratfordians who believed in the traditional Shakespeare of Warwickshire as the real author, described this reconstruction of a new persona by the Oxfordians as a farrago of misinformation based on evidences plucked from thin air. However, the new candidate, Edward de Vere, proved more credible than his predecessors such as, Christopher Marlowe, Francis Bacon, William Stanley, the Sixth Earl of Derby, Sir Edward Dyer, the Earl of Rutland, and William Pierce, each of whom as alternate Shakespeare has been set up by a number of scholars. The champions of Edward de Vere harp on the fact that the sort of life that Shakespeare led did not match his literary eminence. Besides, they claim that there are some links between the Earl's life and some episodes in the plays like *Hamlet*, *Love's Labour's Lost*, *Othello*, *Measure for Measure* and some others.

The plays which were written after 1604, after Edward de Vere's death, like *Macbeth*, *King Lear*, *Antony and Cleopatra*, *The Winter's Tale* and others, are claimed by the defenders of de Vere as misdated. The debate still continues, although to most people who love reading Shakespeare, the Bard of Avon remains the one and the only composer of the works.

Leaving aside these bizarre and fanciful attempts at finding the identity of Shakespeare, if we consider the matter gathered by the tireless efforts of the serious scholars till now, we will find it enough to satisfy our natural curiosity about the life of the man whose works mean so much for us. The following entry in the register of baptisms is relied upon in fixing Shakespeare's birth approximately: "1564, April 26, Gulielmus filius Johannes Shakespeare" (William son [of] John Shakespeare). At that time the practice was to baptize the child within a few days of its birth. So, 23rd April was fixed on as Shakespeare's birthday. His birthplace was Stratford-upon-Avon in Warwickshire. Round the town are more or less distant hills, and the view of it from the nearest Welcombe Hills shows the town nestling in the broad valley.

There is sufficient ground to believe that Shakespeare's ancestors were farmers of Warwickshire. His father, John Shakespeare, seems to have been in his early life a prosperous man of business. Besides being a farmer he was also a butcher, wool-dealer and trader in all kinds of agricultural produce. He was a man of importance holding various municipal offices, for one year being the municipal bailiff—the highest office in the corporation—and then its chief alderman. Thus he claimed a coat of arms as a gentleman. Shakespeare's mother was Mary Arden, daughter of a farmer of Walmote, who brought her husband some land and houses. William Shakespeare was their first son and third child. Not long after the birth of Shakespeare, his father ran into debt, had to sell and mortgage his properties and lost his position in the municipality. Shakespeare grew up with his two brothers and two sisters, all younger than himself.

It is usually held that Shakespeare went to the free Stratford Grammar School at the age of seven and stayed there till he was thirteen, when he was withdrawn from school as his father fell on evil days. Shakespeare then was obliged to help his father in his trade of a butcher, the only means to keep the family going. What Shakespeare actually did after he had left school is uncertain and must be left to the fancy of every reader. It is, however, on record that Shakespeare at the age of eighteen married Anne Hathaway, some eight years older than himself, by a special licence on November 28, 1582, to avoid a scandal as conjectured by many, as we learn that the issue of this marriage, a daughter, Susanna, was baptized on May 26, 1583. Next, his twins Hamnet and Judith were baptized on February 2, 1585. Thus, when he was hardly twenty-one, he was burdened with three children and a wife eight years older than himself, and it is suggested that he must have worried about them. Whether his marriage was a happy one must remain an open question.

In the meantime Shakespeare, falling in the company of his country-bred friends, took to their usual pastime of poaching, stealing rabbits and deer from the park of Sir Thomas Lucy of Charlecote. To avoid a threatened prosecution, he left home for London in 1585. He was bent on finding some useful occupation in the city and the first employment he could secure was in a theatre where he had to attend to the horses of the rich among the audience. Soon he managed to become an actor and a member of the Lord Chamberlain's Company of players. He was also entrusted with the task of copying, rewriting, revising and adapting plays written by other playwrights. Not satisfied to remain an actor only, he, thus, tried his hand at revising old plays with a view to their adoption on the stage. *Love's Labour's Lost*, which may have been composed in 1591, is supposed to be his first dramatic production. It was about this time that he won the patronage of Henry Wriothesley, Third Earl of Southampton. His dramas soon excited the envy and wonder of the learned dramatists of the time—the University Wits. Robert Greene, whose sight was sharpened by jealousy, warned his friends of the "new upstart crow beautified with our feathers, a Johannes factotum, [a Jack of all trades] the only Shak-scene in the country," in his pamphlet, *A Groatsworth of Wit bought with a Million of Repentance* (1592). It may be inferred from Greene's ill-natured allusion that Shakespeare must have been actively engaged in writing plays by 1592 and that some at least of them were based upon the works of other men.

In 1596, Shakespeare seems to have been well-off enough to apply for a coat of arms. On August 11, the same year, his only son Hamnet died and was buried at Stratford. This was a great blow to him. He, however, had been growing richer as he bought New Place, the largest house in his native town, for sixty pounds, and later made further investments in land in the neighbourhood. Both as actor and dramatist Shakespeare was now having a good income and in 1599, when the 'Theatre' was rebuilt as the 'Globe,' he was taken in as a partner. The admission as a partner into the profits of the New Globe marked definitely his success in London better than his purchase of New Place at Stratford.

In the beginning of the year 1601, Essex's rebellion broke out, and, for his share in it, Lord Southampton was imprisoned in the Tower whence he was not released until James I's accession in 1603. Shakespeare's fortunes thus suffered a temporary eclipse. On March 24, 1603 Queen Elizabeth died and on James's accession, Shakespeare's Company, originally entitled, "The Lord Chamberlain's Servants," assumed the title of "The King's Players." Shakespeare's life in London is an unbroken record of success and growing prosperity. In the worldly sense, at least, Shakespeare had become and remained till his death, a prosperous and wealthy man. The numerous documentary references to him that have come down to us are mainly concerned with property bought, money sued for in the courts, or plays of his which were acted or published.

In 1601, his father died. On May 1, 1602 he purchased one hundred seven acres of arable land which he added to New Place. In 1607, his daughter Susanna married John Hill. Next year her mother died. After that, in or about 1609, after the period of his great tragedies, Shakespeare was supposed to have left London for Stratford. Since his retirement to Stratford, he seemed to have been once suing for the recovery of his share in the tithes which he had bought in 1605, and to have purchased a house and a piece of ground near the Blackfriar's Theatre. This Blackfriar's House was part of a large property belonging to the Bacon family and when this was cut up and sold, Bacon's widow Anne (mother of Francis Bacon) retained the title-deeds. On April 26, 1615 Shakespeare associated himself with his fellow-buyers in a Bill of Complaint to recover the title-deeds, and the widow's heir Matthew Bacon was ordered by Lord Chancellor to bring the deeds to court.

Shakespeare made the Blackfriar's House his London residence and came there occasionally, but he lived mostly at Stratford. His health began to fail about 1616. He made out his will on January 25, 1616 and executed it on March 25, the same year, and died at New Place on April 23, 1616 and was buried in the chancel of Stratford Church on the 25th. The only report as to the cause of his death is in the *Diary* (printed in 1839) of the Reverend John Ward, who was appointed Vicar of Stratford in 1662, that "Shakespeare, Drayton and Ben Jonson had a merie meeting, and it seems drank too hard, for Shakespeare died of feavour there contracted." On his tomb was the epitaph, supposed to have been written by the poet himself:

> Good friend for Jesus' sake forbear
> To dig the dust enclosed here,
> Blest be the man that spares these stones
> And cursed be he that moves my bones.

Just as actual details of Shakespeare's life are not available, so also the exact dates of composition and first publication of his plays and poems are uncertain. But so far as the number of plays is concerned, we get a list of thirty-seven plays attributed to him. The period during which these plays were composed extended from 1591 to 1613 approximately and during these twenty-two years Shakespeare wrote all varieties of plays like comedies, tragedies, romances and historical plays. The chronology of these plays may be ascertained by external and internal evidences. External evidences may be had from the entry in the *Stationers' Registers* for six plays and allusions to five other plays in contemporary books and letters like Weever's *Mirror of Martyrs* (1601), Manningham's *Diary* (1601-02), Dr Forman's *Diary* (1611), Thomas Lorkin's letter to Sir Thomas Puckering (June, 1613), and John Chamberlaine's letter to Sir Ralph Winwood (July 8, 1613). Internal evidence consists of allusions in the plays to past or contemporary events and it also relies upon the style and temper of the works. Thus, there are allusion to the rebellion of the Earl of Essex against the monarch in *Henry V* and reference to the great earthquake of 1580 in *Romeo and Juliet*. For the rest of Shakespeare's plays we have to depend on the style and temper of the works. Shakespeare's early plays are characterized by frequency of rhyme in various arrangements, occurrence of rhymed doggerel verse, comparative infrequency of feminine or double ending, of weak ending, of unstopped line, regular internal structure of the line, frequency of classical allusions, frequency of puns and conceits, wit and imagery drawn out in detail to the point of exhaustion, employment of clowns who appear as outstanding persons in the play, the presence of shrewish women, soliloquies addressed rather to the audience to explain the business of the piece or the motive of the actors than to the speaker's self and a symmetry in the grouping of persons.

Proceeding from Shakespeare's early to later plays we can trace the changes in style and metre, which marked the progress of Shakespeare's mind and art. He soon gave up the doggerel, the excessive word-play, the quip and crank of his early plays, their puns, conceits and occasional bombast. He curbed his exuberant fancy by the control of the higher imagination and poetic creation. He subdued the rhetoric of his historical plays. He exchanged the playfulness of fancy, the verbal ingenuity, the farce of the early plays, for the death-struggle of the passions, the terror of his tragedies, laying bare the inmost recesses of the human soul. Finally, he passed, serene and tender, to the pastorals and romances of his later age.

Shakespeare's plays are generally classified into four groups. First, there are the plays of his apprenticeship period. Then comes the period when the excellent comedies are composed. After that we get the period of great tragedies. Finally, there is the period of dramatic romances. During the period of apprenticeship extending from 1591 to 1595 Shakespeare composed the following plays:

History	Tragedy	Comedy
Henry VI — Parts I to III	*Titus Andronicus*	*Love's Labour's Lost*
King John	*Romeo and Juliet*	*The Comedy of Errors*
Richard III		*Two Gentlemen of Verona*
Richard II		*The Taming of the Shrew*
		A Midsummer Night's Dream

Venus and Adonis, a poem in six-lined stanzas, and *The Rape of Lucrece*, a poem in seven-lined stanzas, both dedicated to Henry Wriothesley, Earl of Southampton, were also composed during this period.

The second period is covered by the years 1596 to 1601. Shakespeare's dramatic abilities had now considerably developed. His sonnet sequence comprising 154 sonnets dedicated to "W.H." was also composed during this period. The dramas produced during this period are:

History	Comedy
Henry IV — Parts I and II	*All's Well That Ends Well*
Henry V	*The Merchant of Venice*
	Merry Wives of Windsor
	Much Ado About Nothing
	As You Like It
	Twelfth Night

The third period extends from 1601 to 1608. This was pre-eminently Shakespeare's tragic period. In the tragedies, Shakespeare deals with the problems of life and fate, evil-doing or error or excess followed by punishment and also the wider net spread by evil, in which the innocent are often involved, with the suggestion of a dark power which crushes down the wicked and the innocent alike. The dramas composed during this period are:

Tragedy	**Comedy**
Julius Caesar	*Troilus and Cressida*
Hamlet	*Measure for Measure*
Othello	
Macbeth	
King Lear	
Antony and Cleopatra	
Timon of Athens	
Coriolanus	

The fourth period dates from 1608 to 1613. In this period Shakespeare passes from the storm and stress of the third period to a great peacefulness of light, a harmony of earth and heaven. There is a prevailing sense of quiet and happiness in the plays of this period, which seems to bear witness to a change in the mind of the dramatist. The plays of the period are:

History	**Comedy (Romances)**
Henry VIII	*Pericles*
	Cymbeline
	The Winter's Tale
	The Tempest

In this period Shakespeare returns to his original method of construction. Instead of concentrating the action in two or three main characters, as he did in his tragedies, he intermingles them, as in the first period, but paints them on a broader canvas. Although in many things like the pictures of country life, in the portraiture of girls, Shakespeare seems to have returned to the first period, we notice now that the handling of the material is finer, characterization is deeper and charity and forgiveness are everywhere.

Most of the plays of Shakespeare were published during his life-time or immediately after his death in Folio and Quarto editions. Folio means a book of long size, the pages of which are formed by a sheet of paper folded once only. In Quarto, a sheet of paper is folded twice. Most of the plays of Shakespeare with the solitary exception of *Pericles* were published in the Folio edition of 1623, known as the First Folio, issued by his friends and fellow-actors John Heminge and Henry Condell. The First Folio is of great value as it is more correct than the Quartos and contains seventeen plays of which no Quarto editions exist. Only seventeen of Shakespeare's plays were printed in Quarto during his lifetime. The Second Folio appeared in 1632, the Third, in 1663-64 and the Fourth, in 1685.

3

Characters and Places

Every drama provides us with a list of characters and the scene of action, at the beginning. A little bit of details about the characters and some note on the location will help a reader in his comprehension and appreciation of the drama better. With this aim in view some details about the characters and places in *Othello* are given below.

THE CHARACTERS—THEIR IDENTITY

The Main Characters

Othello: A Moor (a member of the Arab peoples who settled in North-West Africa and those who once lived in Spain) in the military service of Venice. Originally a straightforward, direct, not-too-subtle character, he becomes a monster of jealousy through the machinations of Iago. Because of his very nobleness, he is easily gulled by Iago. He has some of the almost animal savagery of the pagan. He leaps quickly from thought to deed but he is never merely a type. He is made to believe by his ensign, Iago, that his young wife, Desdemona, is unfaithful. It is only after he kills his wife that he learns that he has been duped by Iago. In deep anguish he kills himself. At the end of the play he appears as a truly tragic figure having been chastened by suffering and purified by the tragedy.

Iago: An ensign (lowest commissioned officer in the navy or an infantry officer who carried the regimental colours) of Othello and one of the great problem characters in Shakespeare. An aspirant for the position of the lieutenant, he is crestfallen when the position is given to Michael Cassio, by Othello. He vows revenge against Cassio and Othello. He seems to lack adequate motivation to carry him to the length he reaches. Despising Othello as stupidly good and hating Cassio for superseding him as lieutenant, Iago seems to be merely an opportunist. He has been often interpreted as a devil's representative, a satanic figure without conscience or remorse. Having once begun his mischief, he cannot extricate himself from the web he has spun.

Michael Cassio: An honourable Florentine lieutenant of Othello. He is young and handsome, honest and trustworthy and courteous to the ladies. In order to seem a good soldier and friend to Iago, he drinks too much, wounds Montano, Governor of Cyprus, and is dismissed from his post by Othello. He manages, by sheer luck, to escape being killed in a murder plot contrived by Iago. At the end he is appointed Governor of Cyprus. Although he is not a paragon of virtue, he is an admirable man.

Desdemona: She is daughter of senator Brabantio and wife of the Venetian General, Othello. She is one of Shakespeare's memorable women. Less shadowy than Ophelia, less strong-willed than Lady Macbeth, she is primarily a sweet-tempered woman deeply in love with her husband, Othello, whom she marries against her father's wishes. Her love for Othello is so deep that as she is dying, being killed by her own husband, she attempts to protect him from his crime. It is her pity for Cassio that leads to her death.

Emilia: She is Iago's wife. She is sharp-tongued, worldly-wise and a foil to Desdemona. She loves her husband sincerely and this blinds her to his real character and purposes. In one sense, she is an agent in the death of Desdemona. She has an opportunity to explain to Othello that his wife has not given a sentimentally prized handkerchief to young Cassio, but she remains silent. She, however, nobly redeems herself at the end, when she is dying being stabbed by her husband, by exposing her husband and convincing Othello that his wife, Desdemona, has been faithful.

Supporting Characters

Brabantio: A senator of Venice and father of Desdemona. He welcomes Othello to his home as an honoured guest, but objects to accept him as his son-in-law, because he is a Moor. He is outraged and heart-broken when he learns of the marriage of his daughter to the Moor.

Gratiano: He is brother of Brabantio and a noble Venetian. It is he who, with a kinsman Lodovico, discovers Cassio lying wounded after he has been attacked by Roderigo and surreptitiously wounded by Iago. With Lodovico he serves the purpose of officiating for the state of Venice in the capture of and meting out of proper justice to Iago.

Lodovico: He is a kinsman to Brabantio and Gratiano. He discovers Cassio lying wounded after being attacked by Roderigo and Iago, and comes to his help. He is a noble Venetian who is sent to Cyprus by the Venetian Senate to recall Othello. He finds out the letters in dead Roderigo's pocket, that reveal Iago's villainy.

Duke of Venice: He appoints Othello to lead the Venetian forces against the Turks at Cyprus and, because of his admiration for the Moor, tries to pacify Brabantio's anger against his daughter, Desdemona, and her newly wed husband, Othello.

Montano: He is Governor of Cyprus, whom Othello is sent to replace. He is a friend and loyal supporter of Othello and has previously served under Othello's command. He joins in the pursuit of Iago after Desdemona's death.

Roderigo: He is a Venetian who is deeply enamoured of Desdemona. Iago convinces him that if the latter pays him sufficiently, he will arrange, eventually, for the latter to have Desdemona. Roderigo is an absolutely stupid person. He does Iago's dirty work for him, while Iago keeps his hand in Roderigo's pocket by promising him to win Desdemona for him. He is like Sir Andrew Aguecheek of *Twelfth Night*. Finally, he is killed treacherously at the hand of Iago.

Clown: A domestic servant in the service of Othello and Desdemona. He dismisses the musicians hired by Cassio to play in front of Othello's window. He serves to provide light comic relief after serious incidents like Cassio's drunken brawl and the great temptation scene.

Bianca: She is a courtesan in love with Cassio. She chases Casaio about the streets, makes a public spectacle of her infatuation for him, flies into a raging temper and accuses him of double dealing. She is also shrewd and witty and does not allow herself to be bullied by Iago when he tries to implicate her in the midnight ambush. The basic purpose for which she has been introduced is to enable Othello to be properly duped. Cassio gives her Desdemona's handkerchief, not realizing whose handkerchief it really is, to copy its beautiful embroidery, and as Bianca returns it to him on the street refusing to do the work, Othello, remaining hidden, sees it.

Besides these characters there are a few senators of Venice, a sailor, a messenger, a herald, some gentlemen of Cyprus, musicians, soldiers, attendants and servants to help in the continuity of the story and give the play a realistic appearance.

THE PLACES—THEIR LOCATION

The action of the play, *Othello*, is laid against the historical background of the wars between the Venetian Republic and the Turkish Empire during the sixteenth century. The island of Cyprus is the scene of the action in the play. It should be noted that Cyprus was the key to the east coast of the Mediterranean. It came into the possession of Venice in 1487. Selim the Second of the Turks formed his design against Cyprus in 1569 and took it in 1571. Mustapha, Selim's General, attacked Cyprus in May 1570 and it is the historical time of the play. The scene of the First Act of the play is Venice and the rest of the play is set against the background of a seaport in Cyprus.

Venice: A maritime city in Italy situated on the Island in the lagoons at the head of the Adriatic sea.

Rhodes: An island in the Mediterranean at the south-west of Turkey.

Cyprus: An island in the Mediterranean sixty miles to the west of Syria. It is situated further east of Rhodes.

4

A Brief Synopsis of the Play

Othello has eloped with Desdemona, daughter of senator Brabantio, and has secretly married her. Iago has a deep grudge against Othello for appointing Michael Cassio instead of Iago as his lieutenant. So, to have revenge on Othello, Iago stirs up the foolish Roderigo, a suitor rejected by Desdemona but still longing for her, to go to Brabantio at night and call him up from sleep and report the elopement. Iago slinks away, lest he should be cited as witness against Othello, while Roderigo leads the distracted Brabantio to Sagittary, an inn, where Othello and Desdemona have been staying. As they proceed they call up others to help them in the pursuit.

Meanwhile Iago, who has sneaked away to join Othello, warns his chief that Brabantio is coming in search of him being incited by Roderigo. Just then Cassio arrives with the news that the Duke, who is in Council Chamber deliberating over the news of the Turkish attack on Cyprus, wishes to see Othello immediately. As the Moor is on his way to the Council Chamber, he meets Brabantio who accuses him of drugging his daughter and intends to arrest him. When Othello informs Brabantio that he has been sent for by the Duke, Brabantio proposes that the Duke be made to redress the wrong done to him by Othello, at once.

At the Council Chamber, the Duke has been having discussion on the Turkish threat to attack Cyprus when Othello, Brabantio and others arrive. Seeing Othello, the Duke orders him to lead the Venetian forces against the Turks at Cyprus. Before Othello can answer, Brabantio breaks in with his grief for his daughter's abduction by Othello and charges him with having used sorcery for the purpose. Othello is then called upon to say whether he has anything to urge on behalf of himself. After Othello nobly and simply defends himself from the charge of sorcery, Desdemona enters and confirms her husband's account of himself. In broken-hearted disappointment Brabantio gives his consent to the marriage. Othello now prepares to leave for Cyprus. It is now decided that Desdemona will follow Othello to Cyprus with 'honest Iago.' Iago than privately speaks with Roderlgo, tells him to raise more money and promises him that he will still have occasion to enjoy Desdemona although Othello has married her. Iago now remembers that there has been some talk about illicit relations between his wife, Emilia, and Othello. He decides that he will make the Moor suspect that Desdemona is having an affair with Casslo.

Near Cyprus the Turkish fleet has been destroyed by a storm which has also separated Othello's ship from Cassio's. But, by good fortune first Cassio, then Iago and Desdemona, and finally Othello arrive on the island safely. In his bid to destroy the happiness of Othello and Desdemona, Iago calls Roderigo's attention to a private conversation between Cassio and Desdemona, and suggests that Roderigo should provoke a quarrel with Cassio who has been made Captain of the Guard. The resulting brawl, Iago feels, will bring Cassio into disgrace. Iago makes Roderigo understand that in order to enjoy Desdemona, he must remove Cassio, first, who, he insists, has seduced her affections. Then by way of justifying his action to his own mind, he again refers to his suspicion of an affair not only between Othello and his own wife, Emilia, but also between Cassio and Emilia. Thus he intends to disgrace both Cassio and Othello.

A public rejoicing is proclaimed to celebrate the providential destruction of the Turkish fleet and the marriage of the general, Othello, and people are permitted to engage themselves in whatever merriment they like till the bell has tolled eleven o'clock.

At about ten o'clock Othello retires charging Cassio to look after the guard personally. Iago now prevails upon Cassio, much against Cassio's inclination, to engage in a drinking bout with some gallants of Cyprus. Soon Cassio is drunk and when Roderigo insults Cassio, Cassio strikes Roderigo and when Montano tries to pacify him and tries to stop the brawl, he too is wounded by Cassio. At Iago's instigation Roderigo now rings the bell so that the whole town is roused by the noise. Othello comes and, highly incensed at Cassio, deprives him of his offices. Iago now suggests to Cassio to apply to Desdemona to intercede with Othello, so that he may be restored to his post. Cassio falls into the trap and departs, highly pleased with Iago for his honest advice. Iago now intends to convince Othello that Desdemona's intercession for Cassio arises out of her love for the young man. Thus he wants to poison the mind of Othello against both Cassio and Desdemona. Roderigo comes and complains of his having so far got nothing for all his pains. Iago, however, cheers him with the news of Cassio's dismissal.

Next morning Cassio comes with a band of musicians to bid good morrow to the newly married couple, but the Clown sends the musicians away. Cassio, however, prevails upon the Clown to ask Emilia to go to Desdemona for him. Iago now comes and offers to draw Othello out of the way so that Cassio may talk to Desdemona without any fear of interruption. Desdemona, in turn, immediately pleads with Othello to restore Cassio's honour and good name, when Othello comes back from duty.

Othello despatches some letters to the Senate by the pilot and goes out to inspect the fortifications.

While Cassio talks to Desdemona about his problems, Othello enters secretly, being apparently led by Iago. Seeing Othello, Cassio slinks away almost unnoticed. Iago uses this occasion to pour the first drop of poison of jealousy into the Moor's ears. Unwilling to believe Desdemona unfaithful, Othello is troubled by Iago's innuendos. Othello insists that he will not believe without ocular proof. Iago's opportunity to furnish this proof comes when Othello unwittingly drops a handkerchief given to him by Desdemona to bind his head as he has been complaining of a headache. Emilia picks it up and gives it to her husband who has often importuned her to steal it. Iago takes the handkerchief from her and intends to leave it unnoticed in Cassio's chamber. He then returns to Othello who demands visual proof of Desdemona's unfaithfulness. Iago first tells the Moor that he has heard Cassio speak of Desdemona in his sleep. He then insists that he has seen Cassio wipe his beard with a handkerchief very like one which Othello first presented to Desdemona after marriage. This whips Othello's jealousy to such a pitch that the Moor swears to revenge himself on his wife. He vows the death of Cassio and Desdemona. Iago is appointed lieutenant in Cassio's place and he undertakes the murder of Cassio. Othello himself plans to kill Desdemona.

Othello comes and asks Desdemona to produce the handkerchief. She hesitates and then says that she has lost it. The Moor stalks out angrily. Cassio, who has found the handkerchief in his chamber and likes the beautiful pattern on it, gives it to his mistress, Bianca, and asks her to have the pattern copied for him.

Iago makes light of the whole affair between Cassio and Desdemona in such a devilish manner to Othello as to rouse the dazed man to a greater fury. His next move is to talk with Cassio about Bianca, having first placed Othello nearly out of earshot. The Moor hears just enough to be convinced that the two are talking about Desdemona. And while Iago and Cassio are talking, Bianca comes to return the handkerchief to Cassio and refuses to copy the pattern as she thinks it to be a token of love from some new mistress of Cassio. As Caasio departs, Othello comes out of his hiding full of murderous thoughts. He is fully convinced of his wife's guilt and intends to murder her that very night. It is now decided that while Iago undertakes to despatch Cassio by night, Othello proposes to strangle Desdemona in her bed. Lodovico, who now appears with letters recalling Othello to Venice and making Cassio Governor in his place, is startled at the queerness of the Moor's behaviour.

In a room of the castle Othello questions Emilia about his wife's relations with Cassio and Emilia swears that Desdemona is chaste. But Othello remains unconvinced by her words. He sends for Desdemona and as Desdemona enters Emilia is asked to guard the door from without as if she were in-charge of a brothel. Othello now accuses Desdemona of being a whore and a strumpet. Desdemona is tremendously upset. In distress she sends for Iago who seeks to console her by saying that Othello has been put into this strange humour by state affairs. Roderigo now enters and complains of his patience and money both being exhausted, while to his enjoying Desdemona, he is everyday put off with some plausible excuse. In his desperation he demands satisfaction from Iago who, however, by coaxing and fair promises, succeeds once more in bringing him round and engages him to kill Cassio in the dark, for, he makes Roderigo understand that unless Cassio is removed, Roderigo's quest for Desdemona will be fruitless.

Supper over, Othello accompanies Lodovico to his lodgings bidding Desdemona to bed unattended. As she undresses for the night she sings snatches of a pathetic ballad learned in her distant girlhood from her mother's maid. It is the "Willow song" describing a woman who loved a man who went mad. Desdemona questions Emilia, who is with her, as to whether there can really be any woman disloyal to her husband. Emilia says that there are such women and the fault is due to their husbands not doing their duty to their wives. Desdemona finds it hard to believe her words and chooses rather to be wronged than to do wrong in retaliation.

Late that same night on a street in Cyprus, Iago and Roderigo are waiting for an opportunity to murder Cassio. As Cassio is returning after his dinner with Bianca, Roderigo attacks him, but his thrust at Cassio fails, as Cassio, having a mailcoat on, is not wounded at all, while Roderigo, in his turn, is fatally wounded by Cassio. Iago now suddenly comes up from behind and wounds Cassio in the leg, severes it, and disappears. When Gratiano and others arrive on the scene, Iago reappears from his hiding place and pretending to be indignant kills the wounded Roderigo before he has a chance to talk. Iago feigns great sympathy with Cassio and when Bianca enters he tries to implicate her, since Cassio has just dined with her. Cassio and Roderigo are carried off. Now Emilia comes and Iago sends her to tell Othello what has occurred.

Othello, carrying a lighted taper, finds his wife asleep in their bedchamber in the castle. He extinguishes his candle and, filled with regret, gives her a last kiss. Desdemona awakens and realizing her husband's intent pleads for mercy. But Othello will not be stopped and he smothers her. Emilia pounds at the door, trying to bring news of Cassio, but Othello does not let her in to deliver Iago's message until Desdemona is apparently dead. Emilia then enters and discovers Desdemona in her last gasp. Desdemona tells Emilia that she has been falsely murdered and takes the guilt upon herself and expires commending herself with her last breath to her beloved husband. Othello, however, openly declares his guilt and tells Emilia that he has murdered her following authenticated reports from Iago of her affair with Cassio. Horrified, Emilia tells him that Iago has told him lies and then she is about to rush out to announce the crime, when Montano, Gratiano and Iago enter. Othello now tells of his suspicion based upon the handkerchief and Emilia, realizing her part in all this, confesses that it was she who found the handkerchief and gave it to Iago. Infuriated, Iago kills Emilia. Iago is caught while escaping and he is brought along with Cassio in a sedan chair. Othello and others learn from Cassio how the handkerchief was found in his room, while Lodovico produces documents discovered in the pockets of the slain Roderigo, which fully prove the depth of Iago's villainy. Convinced of his wife's innocence, Othello kills himself, while Iago is led out to torture.

5

A Critical Analysis of the Play

Act I, scene 1

The play opens late at night on a street in Venice. Iago, an ensign in the Venetian navy, and Roderigo, a wealthy Venetian gentleman, are found discussing about the recent elopement of Desdemona, a woman Roderigo hoped to marry, with Othello. Iago professes hatred of Othello who, he argues, has treated him unfairly in the matter of promotion by making Michael Cassio, a less efficient person, as his lieutenant. He and Roderigo arrive below the house of Desdemona's father, create an uproar and wake up her father, Brabantio, and tell him that his daughter has eloped with Othello. Brabantio becomes furious and demands vengeance. He sets off with Roderigo and a search party to find his missing daughter and Othello, while Iago slips away to join his master, Othello, as soon as possible.

Shakespeare's opening scenes are all important. Besides explaining preliminaries, they often strike the keynote of the whole play. The drama begins with a rush into the main subject. Desdemona has escaped from her father's house. The disgruntled ancient, Iago, and the disappointed lover, Roderigo, have knowledge of this elopement. They at once raise a hue and cry and rouse the sleeping father, Brabantio. The old father appears in his night-gown and hurries forward in quest of his daughter. This is the tumultuous opening of the tragedy and it suggests the storm-swept atmosphere of human passion in which we are to live from Act 2 until the end. The tragic atmosphere is cast right from the beginning of the action of the play.

According to Professor Raleigh, Shakespeare's opening scenes are often a kind of postulate which the spectator or reader is asked to grant. At this point of the play improbability is of no account. The intelligent reader will accept the situation as a gift and will become alert and critical only when the next step is taken. In this drama there is a *prima facie* improbability in Desdemona's love for Othello. The natural, indeed the rational feeling of the world is against such an affection. And Shakespeare makes everyone in the play, except Desdemona, feel how odd it is, how out of the natural way of things. But once this improbability is granted, subsequent development seems eminently probable.

The first scene in a Shakespearian drama is the most important part and is called the exposition. It puts the audience in possession of all information that is essential for the understanding of the play. In *Othello* it introduces at once, Iago, who is to contrive the tragic harms and is to work out the hero's undoing. It gives a brief, vivid glimpse of his two principal victims—Roderigo and Cassio. The exact relationship between Iago and his dupe Roderigo is one of purse. Iago is handsomely paid to further Roderigo's suit to Desdemona. At a late hour of the midnight, Iago takes Roderigo to Desdemona's house and makes him the witness to her escape to Othello's place at the Sagittary. This incenses Roderigo against Othello. The news of the abduction is broken into the ears of Brabantio who is kindled into white heat of anger against the "thick-lipp'd Moor."

Far more important, however, than catching our interest and establishing Iago's basic character, this opening scene sets forth the key elements of the tragedy's conflict. It reveals Iago's deep resentment toward Othello. Iago, the master-plotter, has suffered signal humiliation at the hands of Othello. He has been wrongly deprived of the lieutenancy. His sense of power has met with an affront. His resentment against Othello becomes lively because he supposes that he has been superseded by a "mere arithmetician—man of straw and an interloper." His malicious portrait of Cassio gives the audience a preliminary notion of his principal tool in the ruin of his commanding officer. But he is fully aware of Othello's high prestige in Venice. So, with the coolness of a pre-conceived experimenter he prepares to work in the dark. Shakespeare makes a strong case for Iago's anger toward Othello and for his motive for revenge. Here, we have a clear-cut picture of a man who is professionally wounded. His self-esteem has been insulted and we must, of necessity, realize how deeply he has been offended if we are to understand the full extent of his revenge upon Othello.

The tragic hero is kept out of sight. But the forces arranged against him hint that the shadow of fate already rests upon him. Professor Raleigh has observed in this connection: "The subdued voices talking earnestly in the street, of money and preferment, and ancient grudges, are the muttering of the storm which breaks with tropical violence in the sudden night-alarm and is lulled into quiet again in the Council Chamber of the Duke. But this cloud is only the vanguard of the darkness that is to follow, and of the winds that are to blow till they have wakened death." Although Othello is not present in this scene, we learn from Iago that he is an important public figure upon whom the Venetian state depends for its safety. And that is why Iago will manage to stay in Othello's good graces.

Iago stands supreme among Shakespeare's evil characters. In the opening scene he shows himself as a man of remarkable powers of intellect and will, of great intensity and subtlety of invention. He has a high opinion of himself and contempt for others. He scoffs at his successful rival as "mere prattle, without practice, is all his soldiership." He is fully aware that Roderigo is a simpleton and he exploits him to gain his end. He has little regard for Brabantio and flings insult at him. He has a keen sense of superiority. His egotism is absolute. Conscience, honour or any kind of regard for others is an absurdity to him. The disappointment at the loss of the lieutenancy touches him on the raw. His thwarted ambition wants satisfaction. But he is no rash fool like Roderigo. He knows that his commanding officer, Othello, is too great to be cast with safety by the Venetian senate. He knows also that it will be foolish to break with him openly. So, he slinks away and he must "show out a flag and sign of love" to his commander. But from behind the scene he sets in motion the disappointed lover and the angry father against the object of his hatred. His remarkable powers of intellect and will, his cool, calculated hypocrisy and utter disregard for humanity make him an artist in mischief-making.

Roderigo is a young man torn in the purple. He has sued Desdemona for some time and has been jilted and is not likely to succeed in his suit for the hand and love of Desdemona. He can be easily imposed upon. His intemperance of mind stands in sharp contrast with Iago's coolness. Such a simple, credulous young man becomes a convenient tool in the hands of the consummate artist in intrigues.

Brabantio is clearly among the "great ones" of Venice. He can call at every house and "may command at most." He is conscious of his blue Venetian blood. So, he receives a mortal shock when he learns of Desdemona's elopement and marriage with the Moor. This treason of the blood strikes him as quite unnatural. He is thus incapable of understanding Desdemona's love for Othello. But all the same, his love for his daughter is deep.

The opening scene has its function in the economy of the drama. It serves to bring about the conditions from which the tragic action is to spring. The abduction of Desdemona and the loss of lieutenancy by Iago and follies of "honest fools" are the conditions from which the tragic action is to emerge. Iago's thwarted sense of superiority wants satisfaction. This keen desire for satisfaction is to make the course of action irresistible and its issue inevitable.

Act I, scene 2

Shortly afterwards on another street Iago has just joined Othello, when Cassio delivers a message from the Duke of Venice that summons Othello immediately to a military council. Then, as Brabantio and Roderigo enter, accompanied by armed officers, the scene nearly erupts into violence. Brabantio accuses Othello of having bewitched Desdemona and demands that he be thrown at once to prison. He cannot believe that his daughter, of her own accord, has given up the fashionable Italian youths to marry a dark-complexioned Moor. With dignity Othello manages to pacify others and persuades Brabantio to take his complaint to the Duke.

This scene thickens the tragic atmosphere of the previous scene. It is a mêlée of passion and noise and is again an outward prologue to the inward and dreadful turmoil in the soul of Othello and the spirit of Desdemona. The elopement of Desdemona which forms the starting point of the play is taken a step further. The angry father confronts Othello and threatens to prefer his complaint to the Duke in Council. This scene introduces for the first time the tragic hero and discloses the noble and romantic nature of the central figure. Othello appears in the most glorious aspect as the support of Venice and the terror of the Turks. His birth is fetched from men of royal siege. He enjoys high prestige at Venice and at every national crisis his services are imperatively needed. Something from Cyprus requires his post-haste appearance before the Council Chamber at dead of night. This scene reveals that there is something mysterious in Othello's descent from men of royal siege. Romance hangs over his wanderings in an unhoused free condition. According to Bradley, Othello is the most romantic figure among Shakespeare's heroes. Othello is also the greatest poet among the tragic heroes of Shakespeare. "Keep up your bright swords, for the dew will rust them," is the first hint of Othello's brilliant romantic imagination. Othello's frankness, quiet dignity, self-control and confidence in his "perfect soul" are some of the essential qualities of his heart. Further, in his union of perfect self-command, instant resource and repugnance to needless violence, we recognize the finest type of soldier. Thus, in this scene the tragic hero comes before us dark and grand, with a light upon him from the sun where he was born.

Iago is again the dominating figure in this scene. He appears as a damnable double-dealing rogue. In the first scene he heartily abuses the "thick-lipp'd Moor" and incites the jilted lover and the stunned father against his commanding officer. In this scene he wheels over and becomes the trusted officer and honest friend of Othello. He acts his part to such perfection that Othello has not the least suspicion of Iago's duplicity. It presages his complete success in making a dupe of Othello later. The consummate villainy of Iago is now clearly manifest.

This scene is immediately connected with the preceding one, no digression being allowed between the two. Desdemona's flight with Othello is the starting point of the action. It is further complicated by the trouble at Cyprus. If the senate decides to deal severely with Othello in the present circumstances, the nation will be in danger. So, it will have to come to terms with him. Thus, Othello seems to be the master of the situation. But as Iago, with his diabolical purpose, seems partly to control the action and pursues Othello with covert hostility, the reader can anticipate the tragic results of his intrigues. Iago's brief acknowledgment of the Moor's character, his swearing softly "by Janus," is almost a throwaway line, one that might go unnoticed, but he could not have selected a more proper or ironical god to swear by, for Janus was the two-faced god of the Romans.

The source of the tragedy is clearly indicated in the scene. Such a romantic simple character like that of Othello can be easily misled and excited. Desdemona, like Othello, has married under the impulse of a sudden attachment. Such romantic impulsive natures can easily be betrayed. And the tragic action springs largely from the characters of the hero and the heroine.

Act I, scene 3

Later the same night, the Duke and his senators, in council, are discussing discrepancies in the several reports about the threatening Turkish fleet. Othello, Brabantio, Iago, Roderigo and others enter and interrupt the discussion. Brabantio accuses Othello of sorcery, as nothing but witchcraft could have induced his daughter to marry Othello. Othello denies the charge and proceeds to relate the whole story of his love, how he courted his newly-wed wife and how he fascinated her with accounts of his travels and adventures. The Duke sends attendants to fetch Desdemona. Desdemona is called to speak for herself. She confirms Othello's story. Brabantio bitterly rejects his daughter and also the Duke's attempts to console him. The Duke now asks Othello to leave for Cyprus. As others leave, Iago and Roderigo are left alone. Iago persuades Roderigo to get together all his money and accompany him to Cyprus where Roderigo, as Iago promises, will have possession of Desdemona. For, Desdemona will soon get tired of Othello and Othello too will prove inconstant. Left alone, Iago admits to himself that money and amusement are his real reason for befriending Roderigo. Then he begins to plan the deception of Othello, which will afford him revenge for his many grievances against the Moor.

This great scene—a little drama in itself—completes the preliminary and puts us in possession of the most important data of character and incident involved in the tragic sequel. Elopement of Desdemona is the starting point of the play. In the first scene the despised and jilted lover and the aggrieved father are roused only in full cry against the tragic hero. In the second scene the hero is confronted and threatened with action. In the third scene the action comes to a head. Brabantio makes his complaint and insists upon hearing of his grievances. The verdict of the Council Chamber goes in favour of Othello. In a preliminary contest between the hero and Brabantio, the hero wins. Indications in the previous scenes prepare us for such an easy victory in the senate. In the first scene Iago says that the state "cannot with safety cast him [Othello]." In the second scene Othello is conscious of the high prestige he enjoys in the state of Venice. He is confident that his services "shall out-tongue his [Brabantio's] complaints," though the complainant "hath in his effect a voice potential/As double as the Duke's." On the top of these Fortune plays into the hands of Othello. His trial coincides with a national crisis—the impending Turkish invasion of Cyprus. Thus, Othello is not only acquitted of all charges but receives a commission to conduct the Cyprus wars. Everything that follows up to this point helps to raise Othello to the top of admiration, and to fix him in the affections of the readers.

Ominous indications of the coming disaster are, however,

not wanting. Desdemona's hasty action has thrown cloud over the desolate home of her father. Even on the wedding-day man and wife are separated by the urgency of war. Othello is to make an instant start for Cyprus, and Desdemona is to follow under the escort of Othello's ancient, Iago. These untoward circumstances of their marriage do not presage well. Brabantio's solemn warning to his son-in-law is also significant ook to her, oor, have a uick eye to see he has deceiv'd her father, may do thee. These ominous words dimly foreshadow the tragic issues of a union upon which, from its outset, there lies the heavy load of a father's malediction.

This scene is very important so far as the principal characters Othello, Desdemona and Iago are concerned. The keynote of Othello's character is his free and open nature. e looks on men with a ga e too large and royal to suspect them of malignity and fraud. e is a man at once grandly and simply built. e is trustful and his trust is thorough. y life upon her faith honest Iago are the words of absolute dependence on the love of Desdemona. e is not observant. e does not understand Iago 's devilish intention. o, he puts entire confidence in the honesty of Iago. e entrusts Iago with the task of escorting Desdemona to Cyprus. is speeches in his own defence against Brabantio's charges are the finest hakespearian e ample of natural and finished elo uence. They earn for Othello the renown of being the noblest man. They at the same time show a man not subtler or shrewd. is defence is full of self-confidence, and yet there is in it a curious simplicity of a child. The tragic issue is inherent in a hero of this e traordinary character. Othello suffers for his very virtues and the noblest ualities of his mind are made the instruments of his crucifi ion. is un uestioning faith in Desdemona is his life. Iago knows this weakness in his commanding officer. o he is sure that the oor will as tenderly be led by the nose ... s asses are.

Desdemona, the heroine, appears for the first time in this scene. eference to her in the first two scenes indicate her gentle birth and grace of form. he is the centre of attraction to both oderigo and the oor. er father describes her tenderness and gentleness in the beginning of the scene: "A maiden never bold of spirit,/So still and quiet, that her motion/Blush'd at her self." But there is a large romantic element in her composition. She hears Othello's strange story and feels the sudden impulse of a deep attachment to the Moor. It is not a temporary infatuation of the senses. Her heart is subdued even to the very quality of her lord. "I saw Othello's visage in my mind," says she. To his honours and valiant parts she consecrates her soul and fortunes. She is utterly trustful. Such a nature so simple, gentle and romantic is capable of singularly bold action. In the first scene she takes independent action in leaving her father's house and marrying the man of her choice. She is put to her final choice in the Council Chamber in this scene. But she neither falters nor fumbles. She is, however, a child of nature in a large sense, and is unaware of the crooked ways of everyday existence. Such a woman naturally carries her own doom.

The complex character of Iago receives further clarification in this scene. Bradley has rightly remarked: "Iago stands supreme among Shakespeare's evil characters." This preeminence is due to union of absolute evil with supreme intellectual power. He has little faith in the honesty of man or in the honour of woman. Nobility of character is a myth to him. "Virtue? a fig!" says he to Roderigo. He is incapable of appreciating the spiritual value of love. It is to him "merely a lust of the blood, and a permission of the will." But he has immense faith in his own powers. He tells Roderigo, "'tis in ourselves, that we are thus, or thus." Such a man is capable of great mischief in life. His sense of superiority has received a sharp affront. He has been kept out of lieutenancy by Othello. His thwarted ambition wants satisfaction. He therefore plans a double knavery—the ruin of both Cassio and Othello. He has a remarkable power of insight, within certain limits, into human character. He knows the open unsuspecting nature of Othello. So, he will be able to lead him by the nose like an ass. He knows that Roderigo is a snipe. He can use him for his sport and profit. Thus, he engineers his plot against Othello. In this scene he discloses his plot at the end in a soliloquy. In this soliloquy Iago introduces a second motive for his hatred of Othello. He says that it is common gossip that "'twixt my sheets/He's done my office;" and for him "mere suspicion in that kind,/Will do, as if for surety." It need hardly be pointed out here that we are listening to a man whose mind is poisoned. For, there is not the slightest bit of evidence anywhere in the play that Othello has had an affair with Emilia.

Othello is the most masterly of tragedies in point of construction. The entire First Act is devoted to exposition. The nature of the tragic conflict is clearly indicated and the foundation of the whole play is firmly laid here. All the characters are drawn not only in the clearest outline, but the outline is filled up with a multitude of subtle touches like those of a great painter. Nor can the politic and human character of a great council, such as the Senate of Venice, be better indicated than Shakespeare has done it in this scene.

Act II, scene 1

Several weeks have passed and the scene opens at the harbour of Cyprus. A fierce storm at sea has crippled the Turkish fleet and has also delayed the course of Othello's voyage. At Cyprus, Governor Montano greets Cassio whose ship arrives first. Shortly afterward Iago's ship arrives with Desdemona on board. To assuage Desdemona's anxiety for Othello's safety, Cassio tries to distract her attention in amiable conversation. Iago privately notices Cassio's behaviour toward Desdemona and plans to entrap him later by spreading gossip about him and Desdemona. Finally, Othello arrives and joyously united with Desdemona. When the others have left the stage, Iago convinces Roderigo that Desdemona actually loves Cassio and urges Roderigo to pick a fight with the lieutenant that night. When he is alone, Iago discloses in a soliloquy that he has vague suspicions about both Othello's and Cassio's affairs with Emilia.

In this scene the action of the play moves from Venice to the island of Cyprus. Montano, the Governor of the island, is anxiously awaiting word of Othello's ship. Othello will replace Montano as Governor, but the Moor's ship is somewhere at sea, battling a great storm. The storm in this scene has more than its obvious significance. It destroys the Turkish fleet. Be it noted that Othello is sent specifically to deal with the Turkish invasion of Cyprus. It becomes now a minor issue. The storm is a prelude and setting to the tragedy of Othello's love, which is wrought out on this island by fate and Iago's machination. The storm atmosphere of the First Act is carried into the first scene of the Second Act. The impression of a great tragedy to come falls like a shadow on the soul. The great storm at sea gives awful warning of the mighty tragedy that is shaping within the minds of men. On the chafing Adriatic Othello's fleet has been molested by the gale. In this atmosphere of tempest Othello and Desdemona step on this island of their misfortune. Othello's rapturous delight in the reunion with Desdemona gives the first intimation of the terrible torture that will rack his soul in future. Othello tells Desdemona: "If after every tempest come such calmness,/May the winds blow, till they have waken'd death," and that, "My soul hath her content so absolute,/That not another comfort, like to this/ Succeeds in unknown fate." Othello, thus, becomes the unconscious prophet of the fate that will overtake him.

The Second Act marks a stage of transition from the First Act which is a stage of preparation, where the motive force of action appears only in a rudimentary stage. In the Second Act Iago feels that his scheme of ruining Othello and Cassio is complete. He arranges and outspreads the events which enable him to make safe and probable his attack on Othello. Cassio is made the object of Othello's jealousy. The suggestion this time is not that Cassio loves Desdemona, but that Desdemona is directly in love with him. The saintliness of Desdemona to him is "Blest fig's-end!" The "poor trash of Venice," Roderigo, becomes a convenient tool in the "double knavery" of Iago. Cassio is to be caught on the hip and Othello's peace and quiet are to be disturbed even to madness. Iago's scheme is near completion, but it is yet confused, for, "Knavery's plain face is never seen, till us'd." The seed of the conflict of action is sown in the very first scene of the First Act. In the Second Act the seed of conflict germinates.

The long first scene of the Second Act is largely occupied with mere conversation, artfully drawn out to dimensions, which can scarcely be considered essential to the plot. These expedients are fully justified by their success. These conversations give the reader deeper insight into the characters of the principal figures. They also fill up the interval before the arrival of Othello. Cassio's personal devotion to Othello, which goes far beyond the claims of loyalty to a military chief, prepares us for his overwhelming grief at dismissal. His unfeigned but honourable admiration for Desdemona gives material for the plot woven by Iago. His warm-hearted generous nature overflows into hyperbolical looseness and fervid colouring of his speech. In sharp contrast the native cynicism of Iago expresses itself in close-packed logical speech. While Iago is critical, Cassio is enthusiastic. It is also clear that Cassio is touchy and can be easily incited to anger by speaking too loud or tainting his discipline.

In the long conversation between Desdemona and Iago, her true womanly sympathy stands out in contrast to the distasteful wit of the professed hater of man and despiser of woman. Desdemona is no Rosalind and lacks the latter's intellectual capacity or experience of life. It is evident that such a 'womanly woman' may fall an easy victim to the wiles of a villain. The love between Othello and Desdemona, though romantic in origin, had called forth in both a deep mutual devotion. But plot is shaping in Iago's brain to invade this love and ruin both. Roderigo is the poor trash of Venice and has importance only as a convenient tool in the hands of Iago. The only thing steady is Iago's supremacy as a master plotter. Thus, the long conversation in this scene may not actually advance the interest of the plot, but it yields to other effects of characterization.

The asides and soliloquies are an important part of Shakespeare's technique. They are so many explanations to the audience. The complex character of Iago and the obscure workings of his heart are clearly defined and presented to the readers and the audience through these soliloquies. Iago is not very certain about the purpose of his villainous actions. In his soliloquy he is, therefore, engaged in motive-hunting. Not because he is ever troubled by scruples, but because he feels that in playing the part of a villain some explanation is due to the audience. His self-examination is after all a make-believe, which, he is inclined to suppose, may satisfy the audience.

Act II, scene 2

Othello's herald proclaims a night of feasting to celebrate the destruction of the Turkish fleet and also to celebrate the wedding of Othello and Desdemona. The time fixed for such rejoicings is between five and eleven o'clock. The herald concludes with a general blessing upon Othello and upon the isle of Cyprus.

This is the shortest scene in the play. But it has a dramatic necessity. It helps Iago in maturing his plot. The proclamation of festivity in jubilation of the destruction of the Turkish fleet by the storm, and of the marriage of the general, gives the excuse for conviviality. The people have full liberty of feasting till eleven in the night. The revelry may easily result in a quarrel. Iago's idea is to engineer a rising among the people of Cyprus. Nothing could have given him a better opportunity than this public festival, when men's judgment would be muddled by wine and mirth. If there is a fracas, Iago will get his chance. He will at once throw the blame on Cassio and thereby secure his disgrace and dismissal. Moulton has rightly commented on this scene: "Then comes Othello's proclamation of a festival, and with it Iago's idea of making Cassio drunk; the action has now made progress, and the lesser intrigue against Cassio is successful."

Act II, scene 3

Othello retires for the night with Desdemona leaving Cassio in-charge of the night watch. In a hall of the castle, against the background of the night's merry-making, Iago succeeds, with wine and song, in making Cassio drunk and quarrelsome. Urged by Iago to start an altercation, Roderigo follows Cassio offstage. Quickly the two men reappear fighting. Governor Montano interferes in an attempt to stop them and accuses Cassio of being drunk. Enraged, Cassio turns on him and wounds the governor as Roderigo hurries to sound the general alarm. Disturbed by the alarm bell, Othello comes onstage and halts the fighting, demanding to know what caused it. After Iago's seemingly reluctant description of the disturbance, Othello finds Cassio at fault and immediately relieves him of his rank. Iago and Cassio remain behind as the wounded Montano is led off and the others follow. Cassio, sobered, regrets the loss of his military status and reputation, but Iago persuades him that perhaps he can regain Othello's favour with Desdemona's help. After Cassio leaves, Iago gloats over his successful, although seemingly innocent, scheming. Roderigo returns, sore and full of complaints after his beating. Iago soothes his patron's impatience with platitudes and points out that their success has caused Cassio's discharge. Dawn is coming and it promises good things for them. The two men part as day breaks. While alone, Iago resolves to get his wife Emilia to ask Desdemona to plead Cassio's cause. When Cassio waits upon Desdemona and urges his suit, he will bring Othello on the scene and will arrange things in such a manner as to arouse the Moor's suspicion.

The scene opens on the night of revels in Cyprus. People have the full liberty of feasting. Suddenly at the dead of night the "dreadful bell" of the town begins to ring. It frightens the isle from her propriety. The sense of wild disturbance serves to thicken the tragic atmosphere.

The interest of the plot deepens in this scene. The whole sweep of Iago's plot is revealed here. In the First Act it was merely a 'monstrous birth.' In the first scene of the Second Act it was still confused. In the present scene Iago's intrigue ripens. The first step in it is taken. The disgrace of Cassio is carried out with consummate success. Nothing is left to chance. No loop-hole is left open for suspicion. Cassio is made to drink to excess. Iago acts perfectly the part of a boon companion. Montano is made a witness to the "ingraft infirmity" of the lieutenant. Roderigo picks a quarrel with touchy Cassio and is hotly chased with a drawn sword into the guard room. Montano intervenes and is attacked and "hurt, to the death." Roderigo under Iago's instruction slips away, shouts mutiny and rings the "dreadful bell" of the town. Thus, the dupe, Roderigo, is told to raise a general alarm while Iago assumes the role of a peace-maker. Othello is roused from sleep, hears Iago's report of the disturbance, believes it and cashiers the lieutenant. Thus, Iago's intrigue against Cassio has become partially successful. But the moment of its success is the great moment of advance in the movement, when the scene, already busy enough, culminates in an emotional shock. Desdemona unexpectedly appears on the scene. Othello is, in an instant, transformed. The master-thought is flashed in Iago's mind of utilizing Desdemona's intervention. Under the garb of a shrewd and sympathetic comrade he counsels Cassio to seek redress. He observes that Desdemona is kind-hearted and that she may be easily induced to intercede with Othello on Cassio's behalf. Desdemona can easily influence Othello to take the lieutenant back into his favour. Cassio at once accepts the advice. But the real motive of Iago is to show that behind the intervention there is Desdemona's guilty love for Cassio. In this way he wants to poison Othello's happiness and take revenge on him. Thus the two separate trends of action—intrigue against Cassio and intrigue against Othello—are linked together by his "Divinity of hell." He now feels that his scheme is complete and he speaks not of plotting but acting.

This scene shows Iago as a supreme artist in villainy. With Mephistophelean coolness he makes Othello, Cassio, Roderigo and Montano, his dupes. All of them are taken in by his appearance of honesty and plausibility. "And what's he then, that says I play the villain," he exclaims in a rhapsody of self-appreciation. The inner workings of the arch-villain's mind are nowhere more clearly disclosed than in the soliloquy in which he says this. For the first time the whole sweep of his plot is revealed to himself as he thinks over the complications to which Desdemona's honest mediation can be made to lead, and he sees that his net will be big enough to enclose all his victims at once. Such an idea could have arisen only from the pit of hell. Iago, it must be allowed, gives the devils their full share of the glory. His exhilaration breaks out in the ghastly words with which he greets the sunrise after the night of the drunken tumult, which has led to Cassio's disgrace: "by the mass 'tis morning; / Pleasure, and action, make the hours seem short:" As the Act ends Roderigo, the simple gull, comes and complains of having little money left and that he has been "well cudgel'd." He is ready to go back to Venice. But Iago's thoughts are ever on Roderigo's bountiful purse, and so he promises him that morning will bring things. Alone again, he reveals two more of his machinations. Emilia must ask Desdemona to speak to the Moor about Cassio, and Iago will try to position the Moor so that he sees his wife and the young courtly lieutenant in close conversation.

This scene reveals the inherent weakness in the character of the tragic hero. Othello lives all his life by faith, not by sight. He is not observant. He cannot observe and interpret trifles. He cannot see through the hypocrisy of Iago. Moreover, there is an element of excitability in his character. His hot Mauritian blood mounts quickly to the boiling point. There is a great source of danger in such a character.

Act III, scene 1

In order to try to win back Othello's favour, Cassio, early the following morning, arranges for a group of musicians to play beneath the Moor's window. The Clown pays the musicians and sends them away, saying that Othello prefers peace and quiet. As Cassio asks the Clown to fetch Emilia in order to have an access to Desdemona, Iago arrives and helps Cassio arrange a private meeting with Desdemona, by drawing Othello out of the way. Emilia enters and reports that Desdemona has already pleaded Cassio's case with Othello and Othello has assured her that he will reinstate Cassio at an opportune moment. But as Cassio insists that he should have an interview with Desdemona, Emilia takes him inside the castle.

This short scene brings us several steps nearer to the solicitation of Desdemona by Cassio. Events are shaping according to the plan indicated by Iago towards the end of the last scene of the Second Act. The solicitation will enable Iago to throw in the first suggestion of suspicion about the relation between Desdemona and Cassio. This short scene is an important link in the chain of events. There are indications that Cassio's restoration would have taken place in the ordinary course after an interval. Desdemona has already spoken stoutly to Othello. Othello is ready "To take the safest occasion by the front,/To bring you Cassio in again." But here again good luck favours Iago. Cassio, tortured by disgrace, cannot wait for a favourable turn of events. He seeks Desdemona's intercession in the very morning after the night's brawl. The music arranged by Cassio in front of Othello's castle is a silent appeal to the general's clemency.

This scene serves as a kind of comic relief. It gives the emotions of the audience a brief pause from the tension of the preceding acts and offers the audience some respite before it is plunged into the highly emotional scenes that follow very swiftly. There are the musicians and in addition to them there is a clown or jester, a figure that appears in many Renaissance plays and could be counted on to entertain the audience with his physical nimbleness and his witty double *entendres*. Here the clown makes humorous reference to 'wind' instruments and purposely confuses 'tails' and 'tales' in several coarse puns before he pokes fun at the musicians' performance.

Dramatic irony has been very subtly used by Shakespeare in this scene. As the clown exits, Iago enters and notes that Cassio has not been to bed yet. Cassio confirms it. He has decided to follow Iago's suggestion and talk with Emilia and see if she can convince Desdemona to speak with him. Iago is obviously pleased and offers to keep the Moor lousy so that the "converse and business" of Cassio and Desdemona "may be more free." The dramatic irony here is that Iago hopes to keep Othello 'busy' while Cassio and Desdemona are talking together, meaning that the Moor will be 'busy' observing his wife and his courtly ex-lieutenant exchanging serious conversation. Upon Iago's exit, Cassio remarks that he "never knew/A Florentine more kind and honest." The irony here is self-evident. Hopefully many Florentines are more honest than Iago and hopefully, most Florentines are not as naïve as young Cassio.

Act III, scene 2

Othello gives some letters to Iago to be posted to the Venetian senate. Then he goes to inspect the fortifications asking Iago to meet him there later.

Dramatically this scene is not of much importance. It does not advance the plot. It is a restful scene in between the scenes that precede and follow. But it throws light on one aspect of Othello's character. He is every inch a soldier. Though the Turkish menace is gone for the time being, he is not sitting idle. He is strengthening fortifications against future Turkish assaults. He sets about strengthening the defence of the island. It is also a strange coincidence that Iago, who is contriving the undoing of Othello, is always at his elbow to help and advice.

This scene gives Iago an opportunity to have Othello out of the way. Desdemona is now free and if Iago can make the necessary arrangements he can bring Cassio and Desdemona together so that Cassio can plead his case. Moreover, the possibility exists that Iago can even arrange to have Othello secretly witness a meeting between his wife and his ex-lieutenant.

Act III, scene 3

A little later in the gardens of the castle Cassio talks to Desdemona in Emilia's presence. Although Desdemona has assured Cassio that she will do all she can on his behalf, he is afraid that once Othello has appointed a new lieutenant, he may forget Cassio's former services. Desdemona promises to do her best for him and give her husband no peace until Cassio is reinstated. Othello and Iago return now from their tour of inspection. As they enter Cassio leaves hurriedly. Iago takes advantage of the occasion and slyly mutters as if to himself, "Ha, I like not that." He tells Othello that the man they have just seen stealing away could not possibly have been Cassio, as he would not, on seeing them coming, hurry off so guilty like. But Desdemona confirms that the man was indeed Cassio and immediately urges her husband to reconsider the case of Cassio. Her very urgency is misinterpreted and her obstinacy irritates Othello. With ill-concealed impatience Othello finally dismisses her. As soon as Othello is away from Desdemona and Emilia, Iago begins to assail Othello with a series of innuendoes, hesitant, unfinished sentences and repetitions of Othello's own words. Iago implies that Cassio's behaviour is not at all that it seems. Iago's insinuation works up Othello's passion. He carefully prepares the ground by begging to be excused to keep his own thoughts to himself, supposing they are not proper to be communicated to Othello, for, it may be fatal to his peace of mind. Thus he fully arouses Othello's curiosity about Cassio. Then he cunningly warns Othello against jealousy, the "green-ey'd monster." Praising the importance of a good name, he has already told Othello that a man, who robs another of his good name, makes him poor indeed. Thus he aims directly at Othello's heart and plants in it the first surmise of his wife's infidelity. He adds that the husband who suspects his wife of disloyalty and cannot resign his love is an unfortunate man. Thus he presses the dart firmly and securely into the wound of Othello by mockery. Othello now surrenders himself to the power of Iago. His mind is so poisoned that he stoops to the meanness of appointing Emilia to act as a spy to watch Desdemona's conduct. Iago now leaves and Desdemona enters to remind Othello that his dinner is waiting and his guests are expecting him. But Othello complains of a headache. Desdemona attempts to bind his head with her handkerchief, but he says irritably that it is too small and pushes it and it drops to the ground. Desdemona stoops to pick it, but Othello forbids, and both of them leave for dinner. As they depart Emilia picks up the strawberry-embroidered handkerchief, Othello's first intimate gift to Desdemona, gives it to Iago, and exits. Othello now re-enters with his mind fermenting with the doubts planted by Iago. In deep anguish he abuses Iago for opening his eyes, and fiercely demands ocular proof of Desdemona's guilt. He appeals to Iago's honesty and forces Iago on to his knees to give out the whole truth. He demands proof, immediate and positive, that his wife is guilty of infidelity. Iago claims that while spending a night with Cassio he himself overheard Cassio talking in a dream about making love to Desdemona saying, "Sweet

Desdemona,/Let us be wary, let us hide our loves;" and then Cassio kissed Iago very hard, taking him to be Desdemona, and sighed, "Cursed fate, that gave thee to the Moor!" Iago also says that he has seen Cassio wipe his beard with a handkerchief embroidered in a strawberry pattern. Othello now blazes forth into a passion of having bloody revenge. He is joined by Iago and together they vow sacred revenge. Othello charges Iago to murder Cassio within three days. He himself decides to slay Desdemona, and appoints Iago his lieutenant.

This scene consists, in reality, of six scenes: (i) interview between Desdemona and Cassio (lines 1–34), (ii) Desdemona's first pleading with Othello (lines 35–90), (iii) Iago's first colloquy with Othello (lines 91–283), (iv) second meeting of Othello and Desdemona—the handkerchief scene (lines 284–293), (v) interview between Emilia and Iago (lines 294–338), (vi) Iago's second meeting with Othello (lines 339–486).

This is the cardinal scene in the play. The actual conflict begins in this scene. It is called the 'suggestion scene' by Moulton. It is also the great temptation scene. Iago shows here the most devilish ingenuity in tempting Othello. He plays well the role of "honest Iago." The more the peace of Othello's mind is disturbed, the more he believes that Iago means him well. It is in this seeming friendship and loyalty that his principal villainy consists.

This scene is Shakespeare's finest display, not of knowledge or passion separately, but of the two combined, of the knowledge of character with the expression of passion, of consummate art in the keeping up of appearances with the profound workings of nature and the convulsive movements of uncontrollable agony, of the power of inflicting torture and of suffering it. The two antagonists, Othello and Iago, are brought into direct conflict in this scene. The victim and the victimizer, the tempter and the tempted, are seen in a grim struggle for mastery. With a skill that defies analysis the villain throws out suggestions after suggestions and poisons the happiness of Othello and kindles bloody thoughts in him.

Iago's sense of superiority receives a slight at the hands of Cassio who was preferred to him for the post of the lieutenant. So he vows by the "Divinity of hell" to "enmesh them all" in his net. With extraordinary skill he succeeds in getting the satisfaction he seeks. Othello writhes in agony of soul and decides to slay his wife he loves so dearly. Iago is made the lieutenant and is charged with murdering Cassio within three days. Thus "knavery's plain face" is seen in execution.

Bradley says that *Othello* is a tragedy of character. It is Othello's nature that makes him an easy prey to villainy. This scene shows that Othello is at once grandly and simply built. He is free from introspection and is not given to reflection. Emotion excites his imagination, but it confuses and dulls his intellect. He has no faculty of curious enquiry into complex facts. Thus his hot Mauritian blood mounts quickly to the point of extremity. If he be infected, the poison hurries through his veins, and he rages in his agony. He is of a trustful nature and his trust is absolute. His open unsuspecting nature leads him to believe in the exceeding honesty of Iago. He accepts Iago as his friend and guide for his superior knowledge of men and the world. His love for Desdemona has all the traits of genuine deep passion except insight into the childlike simplicity of her nature. This scene shows to full advantage the combination of greatness and simplicity that brings about the tragedy. Iago builds his case on flimsy grounds. These are Cassio's sudden departure from Desdemona on Othello's arrival, Desdemona's special pleading for Cassio's reinstatement, Cassio's supposed dreamy talk and a reference to Cassio's possession of Desdemona's handkerchief. A man of average intellect would have easily seen through the game. But Othello is so constituted that he falls a victim to it.

This scene brings into full relief the very remarkable powers both of intellect and of will of Iago. Iago is not an ordinary rogue. His insights, within certain limits, into human nature, his ingenuity in working upon it, his quickness and versatility in dealing with sudden difficulties and unforeseen opportunities, have probably no parallel among dramatic characters. Equally remarkable is his strength of will. All these features of his character are clearly in evidence in this scene. With extraordinary skill he builds his case out of nothing. He raises a cloud of suspicion to confuse Othello and ensure his undoing. He recalls to Othello, Brabantio's own warning: "Look to her, Moor, have a quick eye to see: She has deceiv'd her father, may do thee" (I.3. 292-93) as he reminds Othello: "She did deceive her father, marrying you." Then Iago plays upon his inferiority complex. Othello must have been conscious that Desdemona has done him a favour by marrying him—an alien, different in colour, temperament and nationality. So, Desdemona's love for him may be followed by the reaction of dislike and almost repulsion. Iago also incites Othello against Cassio by reminding Othello how Desdemona and Cassio have known each other for some time as Cassio used to play the role of an intermediary between Othello and Desdemona. Then again playing the reluctant confidant, he begs, as it were, not to be pressed about certain of his dark thoughts. It is interesting to note how skilfully Iago makes use of his public reputation for honesty. It is for this reason that Othello is alarmed by Iago's hesitation to open his mind to him. Othello believes that Iago is not a "false disloyal knave" and that he is "full of love and honesty." If Iago fears something, it must be a concern "working from the heart." What Iago is doing, of course, is making Othello believe that Iago's honour is at stake if he confesses his fears. Thus he lies to Othello, saying that he is unwilling to speak further because he may be "vicious in my guess." But one will never doubt that Iago will speak the "worst of thoughts." First, he speaks only the word "jealousy" aloud, fixing it in Othello's imagination and then sanctimoniously he warns his general against this evil, this "green-ey'd monster." Iago then proceeds to a glorification of reputation. One may recall that earlier (Act II, scene 3) he has told Cassio, "reputation is an idle and most false imposition, oft got without merit, and lost without deserving (lines 260–62)." But here Iago seemingly holds reputation in the highest esteem. And Othello has began to suffer the aching pangs of jealousy. Iago knows that man, being human, is flawed and subject to fears and irrational suspicions. So he asks the Moor to use his "free and noble nature" to determine for himself the truth of the behaviour between Desdemona and Cassio. He, however, reminds Othello that Desdemona is a Venetian lady and "In Venice they do let God see the pranks/They dare not show their husbands." In other words, the faithless wife is a well-known member of the Venetian society. The logic of Iago's arguments is forceful and he is astute enough to pause now and then, begging his superior's forgiveness, and, at the same time, attributing his own frankness to his devotion and regard for Othello. When we hear the Moor say, "I am bound to thee for ever," we feel that indeed he has been irrevocably trapped. He is now obsessed with the need to prove or disprove Desdemona's fidelity. His mind and soul are torn with irrational images of Desdemona's infidelity and his own unworthiness. To complete his scheme of making Othello suspicious about his wife's fidelity, Iago concocts the story of Cassio's dream in which Cassio is supposed to have been talking about his secret love with Desdemona, and of Desdemona's handkerchief with which he has seen Cassio wiping his beard. Othello becomes mad with rage and demands the death of both Desdemona and Cassio. Iago's plan is accomplished.

In *Othello,* chance or unreason, blind and deaf, is at the centre of human life. It is chance that brings Othello to find Cassio soliciting his wife. It is chance again, that leads Desdemona to intercede for Cassio's reinstatement with fatal obstinacy. It is chance that causes the loss of the handkerchief. Emilia finds it by chance and hands it over to Iago. Thus, chance plays an important part in the shaping of the tragic action.

The scene illustrates the remark of Herford that, "the great distinctive feature of this drama, among the mature tragedies, lies not in the hero, magnificent creation as he is, but in the external agency by which the tragic situation is brought about." It is the situation invented by Iago, which becomes tragic as the hero supposes it real. It is the tragedy of fatal misunderstanding.

Act III, scene 4

In front of the castle, Desdemona and Emilia come upon the Clown. Desdemona urges the Clown to find Cassio and inform him that all goes well with her suit to Othello, on his behalf. Speaking to Emilia, Desdemona laments the loss of her handkerchief. Emilia denies any knowledge of it. Desdemona is sure that her husband is not subject to jealousy and therefore he will not be upset when she tells him of the loss. When Othello enters she again pleads with him to reinstate Cassio as his lieutenant, but Othello's only concern is with the lost handkerchief. Pretending to be suffering from a distressing cold in the head, the Moor asks her for her handkerchief, insisting on the one he had given her. He speaks of the history and magic virtue of the handkerchief.

Desdemona is seriously alarmed. She is unable to produce the handkerchief. Othello leaves her in a fit of anger. Now Iago and Cassio enter. They too are at a loss to explain Othello's moodiness. Desdemona comforts herself with the thought that some state affairs must have upset Othello, as Iago has suggested to her. Desdemona bids Cassio wait, while she goes to seek her husband and move him again for Cassio. When others have left, Cassio meets Bianca, his current mistress, who charges him with a whole week's absence. Cassio promises to make up for it and gives Desdemona's handkerchief, which he has picked up in his chamber without knowing to whom it belongs, to Bianca to have the pattern copied. Bianca is disturbed at his neglect for her, but she nevertheless agrees to do what he asks.

At the beginning of the scene there is a brief exchange between Desdemona and Othello's clown. The broad comedy provided by this conversation tends to relieve the tension of the last scene and provide a short respite before Desdemona and Othello confront each other again. Yet, the comedy here is not particularly amusing. It is too brief and its humour depends on wordplay involving the verb 'lie.'

The two lines of Iago's plot meet in this scene in a focus of unsurpassed dramatic intensity. Cassio is disgraced and cashiered.

He is advised by Iago to appeal to Desdemona. With engaging and dangerous frankness Desdemona presses Othello for his immediate restoration, and thus irritates him. Othello is worked into a jealous passion by Iago. He comes to test his wife about the handkerchief. Desdemona chooses this unlucky moment to press Cassio's suit. The delay in the restoration of Cassio leads to Desdemona's chivalrous importunity at the wrong moment. The mysterious disappearance of the handkerchief confirms the worst suspicion of Othello about his wife's fidelity and leads him to demand it fiercely. Thus, the tactless but chivalrous importunity of Desdemona and the impetuous resolve of Othello to know the worst concur with deadly effect. The unlucky handkerchief that causes so much mischief, accidentally passes into the hands of Bianca. Thus everything seems to be working into Iago's hands.

This scene shows that Desdemona is as simple as a saint. From first to last, while she is unconsciously knotting the cords around her, there is no trace, in any speech of hers, of caution or self-regard. She is tactless, it is said, in her solicitations on behalf of Cassio, but it is the tactlessness of unfaltering faith. When anger and suspicion intrude upon her paradise, she cannot deal with them reasonably. Feeling so secure in Othello's love she counts a lost handkerchief, for all its magic virtues, as a mere trifle in comparison. The guiltlessness of Desdemona renders her more womanly. She is, in a sense, a child of nature. She seems to know evil only by name. Her falsity about the disappearance of the handkerchief ("It is not lost, but what an if it were?") shows the momentary child's fear and the deathless woman's love, according to Bradley.

Emilia's silence over the loss of the handkerchief in this scene has led critics to charge her with bad faith towards her mistress. Bradley remarks that we rightly resent her unkindness in permitting the theft of the handkerchief. But she is, in minor matters, far more scrupulous, blunt in perception and feeling and quite destitute of imagination. She is the first gull of her husband. She does not know the extent of his wickedness. But she is well aware of her impotence to control him and she is terribly afraid of him. She knows that she will provoke his instant wrath if she discloses that the handkerchief is in Iago's hands. Moreover, she cannot suspect that Othello's jealousy is intimately connected with the loss of the handkerchief. She feels for the distress of her mistress in her dull worldly fashion. Thus the scene does not show any bad heart in her. Her silence shows her stupidity, a certain coarseness of nature. It contributes its share in the enactment of the tragedy. Her disclosure of the secret about the handkerchief at this critical stage might have averted the tragedy.

This scene shows that Othello is simple as a hero. He is writhing in suspicion and jealousy. He does not know how to watch and wait. He is a master of simple commanding action. He asks for the handkerchief in the spirit of 'hands up and deliver the goods'. Evasive replies of Desdemona confirm his worst suspicion. And her doom is sealed. But an unpleasant trait develops in this scene under the sudden impulse of suspicion and jealousy. He acts as a spy upon his own wife and plays the hypocrite with her.

Bianca, Cassio's mistress, berates her lover for neglecting her bed. Cassio asks to be forgiven and asks the girl to copy the embroidery pattern of a handkerchief he found in his chamber. This becomes a variation of the jealousy theme. For, the girl suspects that it is "some token from a newer friend;" who has replaced her in Cassio's affection. Cassio scoffs at this and mildly upbraids Bianca for becoming jealous without a cause. Clearly this is meant to be a miniature mirror of Othello's raging jealousy toward Desdemona. To Bianca, Cassio's admiration of the handkerchief and its unusual embroidery pattern, is proof that Cassio loves someone else.

The handkerchief, indeed, seems to have special powers. Othello tells Desdemona a fantastic story about an Egyptian giving a certain handkerchief to his mother. It is a magical handkerchief. It carries the power of love, but it also carries a curse. If it is ever lost or given away, disaster will damn its owner. Othello swears that the legend is true and that a sibyl herself embroidered it with silk that was spun from sacred worms and dyed with a precious liquid. The handkerchief, then, is no mere piece of cloth. It is a part of Othello's past. It was important to his mother. It helped her subdue her husband's love. It is a symbol of love of Othello's parents and Othello believes that it is a symbol of the purity of Desdemona's love for him. Desdemona is ready to acknowledge the handkerchief's magic. Iago is so fascinated by it that he insists that his wife steal it. Cassio, too, finds it irresistible, and it causes even him misfortune. This thread of the supernatural would especially interest an Elizabethan audience who believed in magic, charms, and even witchcraft. This employment of the supernatural element adds an air of mystery and suspense to the tragedy.

Act IV, scene 1

The scene opens with a conversation between Othello and Iago. Iago sees that Othello has fallen into a dazed lethargic state and thinks that he must be quickened into action. So, Iago renews his attack on Othello. He tells over again all the charges against Desdemona and Cassio. But he professes to make light of the whole affair and gives Othello false consolation. This time Iago does not talk by indirect hints and subtle insinuations, rather he confronts Othello with open direct lies. He tells Othello that Cassio has admitted that he has lain with Desdemona. The accumulating evidence—the handkerchief and then the dream and now the confession—proves too much to the already shattered nerves of Othello and he falls into a trance. Just then Cassio enters but Iago asks him to withdraw and to return in a short time, since Othello has just suffered an epileptic seizure. Soon Othello recovers and agrees to hide so that he can watch Cassio as Iago draws him out in a conversation apparently about Desdemona. Iago is, of course, going to question Cassio about Bianca. Cassio now comes along. As Iago expected, Cassio laughs outright to hear that he is going to marry Bianca. Othello, who cannot hear him, misinterprets his laughter and his gesture when Cassio explains to Iago how Bianca once fell upon his neck and wept in public in Venice. At this moment Bianca arrives and angrily returns the handkerchief to Cassio, saying that she refuses to copy another woman's present. Othello sees it and naturally imagines that it is the handkerchief that he gave to

Desdemona. Cassio is afraid that Bianca might make a public scene, and runs after her. Othello now needs no further proof of Desdemona's guilt. At Iago's suggestion he agrees to strangle Desdemona in her bed. Iago, in turn, promises to murder Cassio. Lodovico meanwhile has arrived on a ship from Venice with the order of the Duke asking Othello to return to Venice and appointing Cassio as Governor of Cyprus. Desdemona expresses her delight at the news. In the overzeal of her innocence she frankly professes her love for Cassio and expresses her joy in his promotion. Othello's worst suspicions are thus confirmed from his lady's own lips. Othello loses his self-control and strikes Desdemona in the presence of Lodovico, insults her in the foulest language and expresses no regret for his conduct. Desdemona withdraws from the place broken-hearted. Othello flings himself out of the room in intolerable rage.

This scene is only a continuation and working out of the previous Act. In all probability there is a perceptible interval between Act III and Act IV. But, Shakespeare imaginatively brushes aside this interval to produce an effect of cumulative horror. This scene is, in reality, the second temptation scene, and is but a prolongation of the last scene of the Third Act.

In the fourth scene of the Third Act Othello gets startling confirmation of Desdemona's guilt. He gets confused and bewildered with the wreck of faith and love. In this second temptation scene Iago renews the attack to stimulate Othello into action. He repeats his old evidence and adds more monstrous proofs. Cassio has now 'confessed' and Othello is made to 'overhear' Cassio boasting of his conquest. From dark hints and indirect insinuations Iago comes to direct charge of unchastity against Desdemona. He says that he cannot regard her as innocent. Othello's mind reels and he swoons. The conversation between the victim and the victimizer takes place before the castle where Cassio blunders into the presence of Othello. With smooth excuses Iago gets rid of him. But he hits upon his audacious device of making Othello 'overhear' his conversation with Cassio. Othello regains consciousness. Iago again plies him with false consolation. He tells Othello that the latter is making much ado about nothing. Most husbands have faithless wives. Othello has the advantage over others that he knows of the unchastity of his wife. Othello is maddened to desperation.

Just at this point Iago asks Othello to stand apart and play the eavesdropper to a conversation between Cassio and himself. Iago questions Cassio about Bianca in a way that makes him laugh aloud. Othello, who cannot hear their conversation but can only see the gestures and facial expressions of Cassio, is fully gulled as he thinks that Cassio is talking about Desdemona. At this psychological moment Bianca comes with the fatal handkerchief and returns it to Cassio angrily. Both Cassio and Bianca now withdraw. Othello can no longer contain his fury. The plan of double murder is mooted and settled. Iago will be Cassio's undertaker and Desdemona will be strangled in her bed by Othello himself. Time is hastened. It is to be 'to-night' and not within 'three days.' Thus, Othello is brought back to the position reached at the end of the temptation scene in the third scene of the Third Act.

Another event now takes place, which makes a fresh turn of affairs and leads up to the tragic climax. It hurries on the final catastrophe. A Venetian envoy arrives with letters recalling Othello and deputing Cassio in his place. Lodovico, a cousin of Desdemona, questions about the ill-will between Othello and his successor. Desdemona expresses her keen desire to atone it in Othello's presence. Her frank profession of love for Cassio ("I would do much/To atone them, for the love I bear to Cassio.") and her joy in his promotion sting Othello to fury. Othello takes all these as open confession of Desdemona's guilty passion. He strikes her in public. His degradation is now complete. All dignity and self-control have now deserted him.

This scene shows Othello in his fall. It is the wreck of Othello. He is maddened into savagery. He loses public sympathy by striking a blow on his innocent wife. But even in the wildness of grief and rage, glimpses of his deep love for Desdemona can be seen. Her gentleness, her beauty and her grace give at times a brooding pause in his mad career. Even when he is greatly infuriated he admits: "the world has not a sweeter creature." As his heart burns in rage and despair he laments: "Iago: O Iago, the pity of it, Iago!"

This scene reveals Desdemona in her most lovely and adorable form. She tends to become to us predominantly pathetic, the sweetest and most pathetic of Shakespeare's women, as innocent as Miranda and as loving as Viola, yet suffering more deeply than Cordelia or Imogen.

This scene shows that Iago is an absolutely evil creature. But this absolute evil is united with supreme intellectual power. He uses his exceptional powers of will and intellect for the ruin of Othello. His sense of superiority leads him to feel contempt for "credulous fools" like Othello. He succeeds in leading Othello by the nose. Breach of faith is the real kernel of crime in all genuine crimes. This is Iago's crime against Othello—the greatest crime which can be committed. He knows that Desdemona is innocent. But by his devilish art he shows her up as a false woman and maddens Othello to do the terrible deed.

Lodovico finds Othello's conduct inexcusable. He is stunned by the actions of the "noble Moor," the man whose character "passion cannot shake," whose "solid virtue" has always had a reputation for being invincible. These are the virtues which were used to describe Othello before Iago began his evil machinations. Othello has permitted passion to "shake" him and it has destroyed his "solid virtue." In a word, he has not survived the supreme test which a hero in high tragedy must undergo. On the other hand, to the emissary from Venice, as to all others, Iago seems cool, honest, concerned, fair and trustworthy—noble, even.

Act IV, scene 2

Othello has made up his mind to kill Desdemona. But before taking any action he subjects his wife's attendant, Emilia, to a mock trial with regard to her mistress's suspected infidelities with Cassio. Emilia replies that she saw nothing wrong between them. But Othello will not believe her. He assumes that she connives at her mistress's amours and is paid for it. He sends Emilia to fetch her mistress. As Desdemona comes Othello asks Emilia to shut the door and stand in watch outside. Othello accuses Desdemona of being a whore and a strumpet. Othello's gestures and words alike terrify Desdemona. In vain she protests herself "his true and loyal wife." But Othello does not believe her protestation. He calls back Emilia and goes out. Desdemona is stunned and speechless. In her extreme distress she sends for Iago, relates the incident to him and seeks his advice. Emilia loudly and resolutely maintains that Othello's mind has been poisoned by some crafty villain. Iago rejects the supposition and believest that state affairs have something to do with it. He consoles Desdemona by saying that all will be well. Desdemona and Emilia leave as Roderigo enters and charges Iago with unfair dealing. He has paid Iago handsomely. He has given jewels to him in order that they may be used as presents to Desdemona. As no progress has been made in his love-suit, he threatens to go to Desdemona himself and demand back the jewels which, he has been led to believe, have passed to her through Iago. Iago tactfully turns him round with smooth excuses and fair promises. He tells Roderigo that Othello has been recalled to Venice and Cassio has been appointed in his place. If Cassio is not murdered, Desdemona will leave the place with her husband. Roderigo is thus asked to murder Cassio as the only means of detaining Othello and Desdemona to Cyprus. The murder is to be effected on Cassio's way back from Bianca's house at night. Iago promises to be an aid of Roderigo in this act.

This scene is naturally divided into three parts: (i) the interview between Othello and Emilia and Othello and Desdemona (lines 1–111), (ii) the conversation between Desdemona, Iago and Emilia (lines 112–173) and (iii) the encounter between Roderigo and Iago (174–244). This scene is a continuation of the previous scene. Chaos has come upon Othello. Horrible fancies have transformed him. He is not prepared to listen to argument or accept anything contrary to his agonized but undoubting conviction of Desdemona's guilt. Emilia is subjected to a sort of mock trial. Her protestations of Desdemona's innocence only confirm Othello's suspicion.

Othello summons Desdemona to his presence. He brings the charge of unchastity directly home to his wife. He has made up his mind to kill her. But he does not like to kill her "unprovided." He gives her the last chance to confess and to save at least her soul. Desdemona pleads innocence. But Othello turns a deaf ear to her pleading. Thus events are moving apace towards the tragic end.

Nothing can now undeceive Othello. Nobody can open his eyes to truth sufficiently jaundiced by Iago's insinuations. Cassio might have clinched the deceit, but he has been cleverly put out of the way in the last scene. Roderigo might have exposed Iago's game. But Iago's skilful coup disposes him of. He is told off to murder Cassio. Desdemona and Cassio will be dead in the night and the proofs of their innocence will then perish. Self-preservation now forces Iago to finish what he has begun. Emilia is the one person who can upset Iago's calculations, but she rouses no concern in him. In the end, however, she discloses the whole truth, but it comes too late to save the life of Desdemona. At this stage she does not have the shrewdness to understand what use Iago made of the lost handkerchief. Her silence on these vital points despite her warm defence of her mistress contributes largely to the tragic conclusion.

This scene is full of intense pathos. Othello is seen in his fall, but glimpses of his noble spirit have not entirely left him. He is overpowered for a time by the innocence and loveliness of Desdemona. But a compelling sense of justice leads him to banish all softness towards her. The agony of his suffering soul is full of intense pathos.

This scene shows the effect of the overwhelming blow upon Desdemona's innocent but rather hapless soul. She appears passive and defenceless. She has infinite endurance and forgiveness of a love that knows not how to resist or resent. It is a strange irony of fate that in her extreme distress she turns to her greatest enemy Iago and on bended knees entreats him to help her.

Iago is seen caught in his own web. No turning back is

now possible. He has egged Othello on to advance to conclusions of which he did not dream at the outset. He is afraid of the premature leakage of the plot. He dislikes the warm defence of Desdemona by Emilia. He asks her to speak within doors. If her words reach Othello, his whole scheme may be upset. While Othello is raging somewhere else in the castle and Desdemona is numbed and Iago is wailing in mock horror at what has happened, Emilia stands back and expresses her conviction that, "some eternal villain,/Some busy and insinuating rogue,/Some cogging, cozening slave" ambitious "to get some office" has slandered Desdemona. Her insight is remarkably on the target. Emilia curses any man who would label Desdemona a whore, reminding Iago that Desdemona is a strong woman who defied "Her father, and her country, all her friends," for the man she loved.

When Desdemona pleads with Iago to tell her how she may win back the trust and love of Othello, we realize that this is a dark parallel to the incident that initiated Desdemona's plight. Earlier Cassio asked her to speak to Othello and effect a reconciliation; now Desdemona asks Iago to speak to Othello and effect a reconciliation. In both cases Iago is the villain who is responsible for the breach of love.

The scene ends as Iago once more dupes the gullible Roderigo. Roderigo is a hot-tempered fool. He may also disclose Iago's plot. So, on false promises Iago engages him in the murder of Cassio. His ingenuity and skill in inventing lies and creating situation are shown to full advantage. Bradley says that, "against his will Iago is a little better than his creed." Indeed he does not show any sign of pleasure in Desdemona's distress as he does in Othello's misery. On the contrary, a certain discomfort, a faint touch of shame and remorse may be perceived in him, for, against Desdemona he has no ground of resentment or excuse for cruelty.

Act IV, scene 3

Supper is just over. Othello offers to attend Lodovico to his quarters. He bids Desdemona go to bed at once dismissing her attendant. As Emilia prepares her friend to bed,

Desdemona's mind wanders, preoccupied with sad thoughts. She sings the "Willow song," a song she learned from her mother's maid, Barbara, who died singing the song when her lover had forsaken her. Suddenly her mind returns to Othello's charge of infidelity against her. She asks Emilia whether there are women who are capable of deceiving their husbands, and whether Emilia would do it for the world. Emilia replies that she does not mind doing it for the world, though the world will be too great a price for it. Then she airs her own views about the rights of wives to return good for good and ill for ill. Desdemona swears that she could never dishonour her husband for any price. She then dismisses Emilia and retires to bed.

This scene does not advance the progress of the action. It is a quiet but pathetic scene. It may be described as the lull after the storm of the second scene of the Fourth Act. Such a quiet scene affords some dramatic relief. Such a scene of tender and pathetic beauty can often be seen shortly before the catastrophe in a Shakespearian tragedy. Such scenes are the meeting of Lear and Cordelia (IV.1.), the talk of Lady Macduff with her little son (IV.2.), the madness of Ophelia (IV.5.).

This scene adds material traits to the characters of Desdemona and Emilia. Desdemona is stunned by the consciousness that she has lost the love of her husband. The simple and innocent nature that provoked her brave intervention for Cassio is now gone. She is oppressed by a vague dread she cannot formulate. She has a dim intimation of the impending evil, but she does not know the nature of it. A question about the lost handkerchief to Emilia might have brought about the truth in time to save her. But she is so much weighed down in spirit that she never thinks of such a question. She moves helplessly to her doom. The deep poignancy of pathos is expressed in her willow song.

The talk between Desdemona and Emilia on the fidelity of women shows the difference in tone and temper between the two women. Desdemona's purity of soul is so absolute that it can never entertain any thought of infidelity to her husband under any circumstance. Emilia has known the world. She has also a vulgar conception of wedded fidelity as a bargain. "But I do think it is their husbands' faults/If wives do fall," says Emilia. But Desdemona's conception of the sacred married relations stands on a much higher level. She refuses to "pick bad from bad." The sinless innocence of her character comes out in clear light in her conception of wifely duty. She loves Othello with the love which is her doom. The angelic purity of her character comes out in bold relief in her attitude to married relation. The purpose of all the chatter between Desdemona and Emilia, of course, is to keep before us the theme of infidelity.

Rather oddly, Shakespeare inserts here a brief reference to Lodovico. Desdemona praises him as a man who "is a proper man" and who "speaks well." Emilia is no less approving in her remarks. Exactly what Shakespeare intended here is hard to imagine. It may be that the young wife, Desdemona, feels for the moment abandoned, and is comparing her moody, raging husband, the Moor, with the Venetian she once knew.

At the end of the scene the mood changes and with Desdemona's short prayer that she should never be guilty of returning evil for evil, she says good night to her friend. The contrast between Desdemona's young innocence and the worldliness of Emilia intensifies our pity for the young bride as she prepares for bed and for Othello's return.

Act V, scene 1

It is dark midnight. On a street in Cyprus, Iago and Roderigo are waiting for an opportunity to murder Cassio. As Cassio enters Roderigo hits at him, but Cassio is saved by his shirt of mail. He, in return, draws his sword and wounds Roderigo. Iago then darts out of his hiding place, wounds Cassio in the leg and exits. Othello hears Cassio cry out the word "murder" and believes that Iago's plot has been successful. He hastens to kill Desdemona. Cassio's repeated cries for help bring on the scene Lodovico and Gratiano. Iago comes onstage with a light. Both the wounded men, Cassio and Roderigo, are still alive. Iago comforts Cassio and then stabs Roderigo in the darkness as if to take revenge on Cassio's assailant. Bianca now appears on the scene. Iago charges her with being involved in the plot to murder Cassio, since Cassio just dined with her. She is, therefore, arrested. Emilia also comes in to see what has happened.

She is at once sent to the castle to inform Othello and Desdemona what has occurred. Cassio is borne away in a chair for medical aid to his wounds.

In this scene which precedes the final and climactic one, Shakespeare provides exciting physical action. This scene shows the working of the plot hatched between Iago and Roderigo. The plot formed between Othello and Iago in the first scene of the Fourth Act partially succeeds. Cassio is to be killed by Iago. Roderigo is employed for the purpose. He fails to kill Cassio and is, on the contrary, mortally wounded by him. Iago wounds Cassio in the leg from behind. On return from his hiding Iago dispatches Roderigo as the possible assailant of Cassio. Iago's intention as disclosed at the beginning of this scene, is to remove both Roderigo and Cassio. A crisis in his affairs has come. Roderigo cannot be deceived any further. He might disclose Iago's treacherous action. By stabbing Roderigo to death Iago removes this danger. Cassio is a standing peril to the success of his plot. He may reveal the truth about the lost handkerchief and thus expose his game. So he hurts Cassio from behind, when Roderigo fails, intending to kill him. But unfortunately Cassio is wounded only, but he lives to clinch the demonstration of Iago's guilt later on.

Iago's murderous attack on Cassio is noticed by Othello. He is convinced that Iago has such noble sense of his friend's wrong. He is then tightened in his resolution to kill Desdemona. Thus Iago's action moves forward the action of the drama towards the catastrophe.

Iago's calculation at one point proves wrong. He sends Emilia to the castle to inform Othello and Desdemona about the murders of Roderigo and Cassio who, according to him, is fatally wounded. He hopes that Emilia will discover that Othello has murdered Desdemona and will give alarm. Emilia, however, proves the means of revealing the whole truth. Iago's miscalculations on two points prove his undoing. Cassio is not dead. He lives to bear testimony against Iago. Emilia exposes Iago's game by telling everything about the lost handkerchief.

This scene throws light on the character of Iago. His power of dissimulation is remarkable. His resourcefulness is wonderful in a difficult situation. He wins credit for his honest and loyal intervention, from Othello. Lodovico and Gratiano are impressed by Iago's courage and wisdom. Iago plays his game successfully. He turns aside all suspicion from him to Roderigo and Bianca. The crowning act of treachery he does is to deal the death-blow on Roderigo. Iago gives the final impression of a man of extraordinary intellectual powers with knavery of the deepest dye. It will be noted that Emilia still finds no reason not to believe that her husband is basically "honest" in respect of this particular violence.

Act V, scene 2

Othello, carrying a lighted taper, enters the bedchamber of Desdemona and finds her asleep. He has come to murder her. The beauty and innocence of sleeping Desdemona charm him for a moment and seem to shake his purpose. He kisses her repeatedly. But he persuades himself that he is but executing justice. The worst of his anguish is that he must kill one whom he loves. Desdemona wakes up. Othello tells her brusquely, before she dies, to ask God's forgiveness for any unconfessed sins. Desdemona is amazed to hear him talk of killing. She does not know how she could have offended him, unless it were an offence to love him much. For the first time Othello makes the charge against her in precise terms. He refers to the handkerchief he gave her and which was found in Cassio's possession. Desdemona denies having given it to Cassio. Her protestation of innocence enrages Othello and he declares that Cassio has publicly admitted adultery with her. Desdemona begs her husband for mercy. But Othello has already seized her throat and he smothers her. Emilia rushes in and reports Roderigo's death and Cassio's injuries. Othello is dismayed to hear that Cassio is still alive. With her dying breath Desdemona now tells Emilia that she dies guiltless and that she has killed herself. Emilia is frantic with grief and her piercing cry brings to the chamber Montano, Gratiano, Iago and others. She tells everybody that her mistress has been murdered in bed. Othello begins to tell of his suspicions based upon the handkerchief and Emilia, realizing her part in all this, confesses that it was she who found the handkerchief and gave it to Iago. Othello begins to discern the horrible truth of Iago's treachery, but before he can fall upon the villain, he is disarmed by Montano. Iago stabs Emilia to death and flees. Montano and others run in pursuit of Iago. Othello is disarmed and made a prisoner. Now, Lodovico, Montano and the attendants come in with Iago as a prisoner, and Cassio in a sedan chair. Othello now lunges at and wounds Iago with a sword tempered in Spain found in the room. Iago is wounded and not killed and is reserved for still more cruel tortures. Cassio explains how the handkerchief came into his possession. Letters found in the pockets of slain Roderigo further corroborate Iago's guilt. Othello is fully convinced of his gigantic mistake. Drawing a dagger from beneath his gown he stabs himself, before the horrified onlookers can stop him, and dies beside his beloved Desdemona. Lodovico takes charge of the affairs. Before departing for Venice to report these sad events, he confirms Cassio's appointment as Governor of Cyprus and instructs him to see that Iago is condemned and tortured for his crimes.

This last scene opens in a bedchamber in the castle. It falls into some natural divisions: (i) the murder of Desdemona, (ii) the unmasking of Iago by Emilia and Othello's realization of the fatal mistake, (iii) the murder of Emilia, Othello's agony and death, (iv) Iago wounded and imprisoned for further punishment and Cassio made Governor of Cyprus. This closing scene opens with the catastrophe of the tragic action. Desdemona is smothered to death. Emilia is struck dead by Iago. Iago is wounded but not killed. He is made over to Cassio for further punishment. Iago is unmasked and the agony of discovery fills Othello with hopeless despair. He stabs himself to death to atone for the crime. Desdemona, Emilia and Othello lie dead upon the same bed. This tragic loading of the bed is the most harrowing scene in all literature.

This murder scene is the most painful scene and provides us with an intensely moving climax to the great tragedy in the life of Othello. The Othello who enters the bedchamber of Desdemona with the words, "It is the cause, it is the cause, my soul," is a composed man free from the mounting tension that he had in the Fourth Act. Irving Ribner expresses the view that as the madness of Othello grows in intensity, owing to jealousy, there grows alongside of it a grotesque solemnity. Othello enters his wife's bedchamber to strangle her in her bed, as Iago has suggested to him. He stands for a long time by the bed in which his wife lies sleeping, staring down at her and shaken by his love and anguish. He utters a soliloquy explaining why he must kill, the implication being that it is her unchastity which has doomed her to die at his hands. He must not spare her because then she might live to betray more men. The murder to which his delusion leads him is converted into a ceremonial act of sacrificial justice. He is to save Desdemona from herself, not in hate, but in honour, and also in love. His anger has passed, a boundless sorrow has taken its place and "this sorrow's heavenly,/It strikes when it does love." Even when at the sight of her apparent obduracy, and at the hearing of words which, by a crowning fatality can only reconvince him of her guilt, these feelings give way to righteous indignation and not to rage.

When Iago suggests: "Do it not with poison, strangle her in her bed, even the bed she hath contaminated (IV.1.)," Othello's reply is an assertion not of revenge, but of justice: "Good, good, the justice of it pleases (IV.1.)." According to Ribner, Othello's grotesque parody of justice is expressed in the terrible second scene of the Fourth Act where he arraigns Desdemona and Emilia as in a court of law, cross-examining each in a tone of official inquiry. But the court-room is a 'brothel,' and Desdemona is the "cunning whore of Venice,/ That married with Othello: (IV.2.)." Othello's very questions are a perversion of justice, for, his mind can now admit no true verdict. The grotesque perversion of this mock judicial inquiry recalls the simple grandeur of Othello's answering to justice before the Venetian Council in the First Act. These two judicial scenes reflect the two poles of Othello's development, the madness of the later scenes recalling the reason of the earlier. They focus also upon the theme of justice: reason causes it to reflect the law of God, but madness perverts it to the very opposite.

Some critics are of opinion that it is in this mock judicial mood that Othello approaches the bed where Desdemona is to be murdered. Othello declares to himself that Desdemona must die, otherwise she would betray more men. Desdemona is asleep and a lighted candle lies beside her bed. Strangling the delicate Desdemona would be as easy as extinguishing the candle, and yet Othello's mind is suddenly filled with the great difference between the consequences which the two actions would entail. Blowing out the candle is like extinguishing the fire of life in Desdemona. Moreover, the candle can be re-lighted, but if once the light of Desdemona's life is extinguished, he does not know from where he would get the original Promethean fire to restore her to life again. Kissing her, her fragrant breath almost persuades him to break the sword of justice, that is, spare her the punishment which he believes to be the demand of justice. Moreover, he soon recovers himself to destroy love in a pose of self-sacrificing duty. Othello blinds himself to reality by the very calmness of the ritual of execution. But no sooner had the deed been completed than the world of reality intruded with the sound of Emilia's voice.

Othello now comes to recognize the delusion under which he has laboured. He sees the true Iago for the first time, and he rushes at him in fury and Desdemona becomes not only an angel of divine mercy, but also a spirit of heavenly justice who will demand his damnation: "O ill—starr'd wench,/Pale as thy smock, when we shall meet at count,/This look of thine will hurl my soul from heaven,/And fiends will snatch at it." Othello dies accepting damnation as his just desert, but the audience knows that in his renunciation of evil, he has his penance and expiation.

Not all critics have accepted the thesis of 'Othello's mock-judicial mood'. Emphasis has been laid by some on Othello's loss of faith, or blindness to the truth of love, which leads him on to assume the role of 'an honourable murderer' executing justice on a living embodiment of infidelity. The imminence of the task before him restores his self-control and quenches his anger. He is no longer the husband maddened at betrayal, but the vindicator of justice, weeping with a heavenly sorrow, and slaying what he loves, doing "naught...in hate, but all in honour." He uses the language of the world, but not altogether in the world's way. Laertes fought Hamlet in 'honour' when 'satisfied in nature.' And Othello means his hearers to understand that he has only acted as the husband of a guilty wife is bound to act. However, as C.H. Herford points out, the force of honour in him is not derived from any code of gentle or military obligation. It is the persuasion of a great passionate veracious nature.

It does not really matter much whether we look upon Othello as a mocking interpreter of justice or as a vindicator of divine dispensation in a disinterested spirit. We are saddened by the intensity of Othello's suffering as a man who has finally recognized the futility of all his achievements. His love for Desdemona and his conviction that she must die, must co-exist. Yet, the private agony which their co-existence causes, momentarily undermines his self-control and elicits from him a reference to the cruelty of the general order of things, of heaven itself. McElroy in *Shakespeare's Mature Tragedies* tells us that, while delivering his final soliloquy, Othello summons the best that is in him and dedicates it to the commission of a ghastly crime, consecrating himself almost ceremoniously to error. The magnitude of his error is exceeded only by the terrible intensity with which he believes it and struggles with it. The problems which proceed from his initial mistake are, for him, very real problems—problems of faith, order, patience, beauty, masking evil and such others. The appalling discovery of his error throws him into a paroxysm of grief. For him no future remains. Death alone can atone for his crime and he inflicts the punishment with his own hand. In this terribly painful scene there is almost nothing to diminish the admiration and love which heighten pity. And pity itself vanishes and love and admiration remain in the majestic dignity and sovereign ascendancy of the close.

The knocking of Emilia (distantly paralleled by the knocking at the castle gate in *Macbeth*) preludes the discovery. Emilia stands like Kent and Horatio, a beacon of common sense in a dark and reeling universe. Her knocking brings the action of the play into the light of common day. It is the outside world looking in and demanding its accounts. Her splendid defiance, first of Othello, then of her husband, is a great feature of the scene and contributes largely towards mitigating the excess of tragic pain. She brings us the relief of joy and admiration—a joy that is not lessened by her death. In this last scene, when, fearless of heaven and men and devils, she stands up to champion her dead mistress' purity, she is a sublime figure, and her death at the hands of her villainous husband is almost as moving as Desdemona's own.

In this scene Desdemona leaves the final impression that she is the sweetest innocent that ever did lift up eye. She is the most pathetic heroine in Shakespeare's world. It is doubtful if Cordelia, falsely murdered, could have uttered the last words of Desdemona: "Nobody, I myself, farewell:/Commend me to my kind lord, O, farewell!" She loved Othello with a love which was her doom. Innocent she loved and lived, and innocent she died.

There are some minor inconsistencies and obscurities in this scene. Critics have remarked that it is glaringly absurd that Desdemona should speak after she had been smothered. The strangling operation proves to have been complete. But Furness quotes an illustration to show that such short and sudden revival of life is possible in a person apparently dead. Accordingly, he is inclined to think that Desdemona lay still in bed like one dead. She was dying but not actually dead. These words were the last flicker of the lamp before it was out. In this scene Othello refers to the handkerchief as a gift from his father to his mother. But in the fourth scene of the Third Act he says that an Egyptian gave it to his mother. The explanation of this supposed inconsistency is that in the earlier scene Othello invented the story of the handkerchief merely to charm and impress his wife. But even this slight deviation from truth works its own retribution. Had not Othello over-excited Desdemona's fears by his description of the handkerchief, she might not have been led to prevaricate and into falsehood. The device of the two letters in the pocket of slain Roderigo appears a bit clumsy. The plot was hatched only in the early part of the night and its execution followed almost immediately afterwards. It is difficult to conceive when Roderigo found time to write or receive these letters. This device may not be happy, but it helps in clearing up the mystery of Iago's dark plot.

6

Date of Composition

The exact year of the composition of a play of Shakespeare is always hard to decide as a certainty. But there is little doubt that *Othello* was written after 1601. The play belongs to the group of *Hamlet*, *King Lear* and *Macbeth*. *Hamlet* was written before *Othello*, and *King Lear* and *Macbeth* were written after it. The first edition of *Othello* was a quarto, published in 1622 with the title page: "The/Tragoedy of Othello./The Moor of Venice./*As it hath beene diuerse times acted at the/* Globe, and at the Blackfriers by/*his Maiesties Seruants./* Written by William Shakespeare,/Vignette/London,/Printed by N.O. for Thomas Walkley, and are to be sold at His/Shop, at the Eagle and Child in Brittans Burffe/1622."

In 1623 appeared the First Folio, containing *Othello*, among the *Tragedies*. An independent manuscript seems to have been used for the Folio Text. Apart from many improved readings, the Folio copy contained over one hundred and fifty verses omitted in the earlier edition, while, on the other hand, ten or fifteen lines in the Quarto did not appear in the Folio. The text of all modern editions of *Othello* is based on that of the First Folio. A notable difference between the Quarto and the Folio texts is that, in the Quarto text oaths and asseverations are retained while in the Folio version they are either omitted or toned down. It should be remembered that the 'Act against Swearing' was passed in 1606. The Quarto text contains oaths. There can be no doubt that the play was written earlier than 1606.

Malone, a great literary critic and Shakespearian scholar,

an authority in respect of the order in which Shakespeare's plays were written, says that he knew that *Othello* was acted in 1604. For twenty years scholars sought in vain to discover upon what evidence Malone 'knew' this important fact. At last about the year 1840 Peter Cunningham announced his discovery of certain *Accounts of the Revels at Court* containing the item, "*By the King*'s 'Hallamas Day, being the first of Nov., *Matis Plaiers*, A play at the Bankettinge House att. Whitehall, called the Moor of Venis (1604).'" This document was later proved to be a forgery, but it is curious that the information it gives is genuine. It is now believed that Malone had, in 1791, access to the *Accounts of the Revels at Court*, rescued from a damp dungeon and deposited in the new Audit Office in Somerset Place.

But a still earlier date has been put forward lately by H.C. Hart, the editor of "Arden Shakespeare" of *Othello*. Hart thinks that the date of 1602 may yet be established. A case has been made out for the year 1602 in a letter published in the *Times Literary Supplement* of 10th October 1935. The letter quotes from *The Honest Whore*, Part I, by Dekker and Middleton (printed in 1604), the lines:

Hip. Oh you ha kild her by your cruelty?

Du. Admit I had, thou killst her now againe; And art more savage than a barbarous Moore!

The allusion to "a barbarous Moore," it holds, must be read in close connection with the context of the date, and suggests that Dekker is referring to the murder of Desdemona by Othello enacted on the stage in Shakespeare's famous tragedy. It is known that Philip Henslowe paid Dekker and Middleton five pounds for writing this play at some date between January 1 and March 14, 1604. If so, the date of *Othello* must be put back at least a year. The London theatres had been closed during Elizabeth's illness and after her death on March 24, 1603, an outbreak of plague compelled the closing of the theatres before May 19, and they seem to have remained shut till April 9, 1604. Thus, if we accept this allusion the latest possible date of *Othello* is March 1603.

Certain lines and words in the First Quarto of *Hamlet* suggest that *Othello* had been on the acting list some time before July 26, 1602, the date on which James Roberts entered on the Stationers' Register "A booke called the Reveng of Hamlett Prince of Denmarke."

The third scene of the First Act of *Othello* contains the following passage:

Duke. Whoe'er he be, that in this foul proceeding
Hath thus beguil'd your daughter of herself,
And you of her, the bloody book of law
You shall yourself read, in the bitter letter,
After its own sense, (I.3.65-68)

Halliwell sees in the above a reference to the Twelfth Public Act, which was passed in the first Parliament of James, sometime between March 19 and July 7, 1604, and was levelled against conjuration, witchcraft and dealings with evil and wicked spirits. Halliwell holds that the Duke refers to such a law when he tells Brabantio that his accusation of the employment of witchcraft shall be impartially investigated. Thus, the date of composition of this tragedy may be positively assigned to the year 1604.

Judging by the test of verse and style, critics have placed *Hamlet*, *Othello*, *King Lear*, *Macbeth*, and *Measure for Measure* in the same period of Shakespeare's dramatic career, namely, 1604 to 1610. Dowden observes: "...year after year, one great tragedy succeeds another.... *Othello* (1604) is pursued by *Lear* (1605), *Lear* by *Macbeth* (1606), *Macbeth* by *Antony and Cleopatra* (1607), *Antony and Cleopatra* by *Coriolanus* (1608)."

All these evidences prove that *Othello* was written sometimes between 1601 and 1604. An analysis of the nature, thought, style and verse and use of words in the great tragedies of Shakespeare, which were written at or about the same time, points to 1604 as the probable year of the composition of *Othello*. In print, however, as stated in the beginning, it first appeared in Quarto of 1622 and later it was included with a number of additional passages, in the First Folio collection of 1623.

7

Sources of *Othello*

Shakespeare mainly derived the plot of *Othello* from a story in the *Hecatommithi*, or "A Hundred Tales," of Giovannibattista Giraldi Cinthio, an Italian novelist and professor of philosophy at Ferrara. The *Hecatommithi* is divided into ten groups or 'Decades' of tales. The source of *Othello* lies in the seventh tale of the third Decade, which has for its general theme, "the unfaithfulness of husbands and wives." Cinthio's *Hecatommithi* was published first at Monteregale, in Sicily, in 1565. No English translation of the novel existed in Shakespeare's time, but a French translation appeared in 1583, and through this medium the tale might have reached England. It cannot, however, be ascertained whether Shakespeare may have read Cinthio's story in the original language or read it in translation. Collier states: "Shakespeare may have read Cinthio's story in the original language; it is highly probable that he was sufficiently acquainted with Italian for the purpose."

Although Shakespeare was indebted to Cinthio for the outline plot of *Othello*, he did not closely follow the novel, the *Hecatommithi*. On the other hand, he handled the plot of the story freely enough. Cinthio's story offered to Shakespeare only the outline of an intrigue and a catastrophe, ingeniously managed, but without a hint of greatness. The Moor, in the novel, is merely gross and simple. The ensign meanly avenges himself for his rejection by his commandant's wife. He is at bottom a coward, and has to be encouraged by a bribe. His own wife is a feeble accomplice. Disdemona herself alone offers a suggestion of pathos. All the persons, save the heroine, are cast in a petty mould, and the story itself is an ordinary barrack-room scandal of the day, passably well told. The whole creative, transforming work remained for Shakespeare to do. The original story of Cinthio may be stated in brief now in order to understand the changes and improvement made by Shakespeare.

There lived in Venice a valiant Moor (no name given), held in great esteem for his military talent and services. Disdemona (spelling in the original story of Cinthio), attracted by his high virtues, fell in love with him and married him, in spite of the opposition of her kinsmen. They lived in great happiness at Venice until the Moor was chosen to the military command of Cyprus, whither his wife insisted on accompanying him.

The Moor took with him a favourite ensign (an infantry officer who carried the regimental colours; he became Iago in Shakespeare's play), a man of great personal beauty but of the most depraved heart, a boaster and coward. His wife, a young and virtuous lady, accompanies him, and becomes a friend of Disdemona.

The ensign falls passionately in love with Disdemona who, wrapped up in love of her husband, pays no regard to him. His love then turns to bitter hate, and he resolves to charge her with infidelity, and to fix the Moor's suspicions upon a favourite captain of his (Cassio in Shakespeare's play).

Soon after, the captain strikes and wounds a soldier on guard, for which the Moor cashiers him. Disdemona endeavours to reconcile her husband with the captain. The Moor is half persuaded by his wife's entreaties to restore the captain to his office. The ensign now sees his opportunity of arousing the Moor's jealousy. First, he merely hints to the Moor that his wife may have good reason to bring back the captain, and refuses to enlighten the Moor any further.

Next time when Disdemona pleads for the captain, the Moor gets angry. He begins to suspect her, and seeks further enlightenment from the ensign. The ensign tells the Moor that his wife loves the captain and hates him for his black complexion. The Moor demands positive proof. The ensign steals an embroidered handkerchief which Disdemona used to carry about with herself. He leaves it in the captain's bedchamber. The captain, knowing it to be Disdemona's handkerchief, takes it to Disdemona when the Moor is out. But as he knocks at the door, the Moor returns and the captain runs away without returning the handkerchief.

The Moor, who saw it all, now comes to his wife and demands the handkerchief which was his gift to his wife. She cannot produce it. This confirms the suspicion of the Moor about his wife's infidelity. The Moor resorts to the ensign for counsel. But he will not decide on any action until he actually sees the handkerchief in the captain's possession. Later the Moor has an opportunity to see the handkerchief in possession of the captain. In fact, the ensign points out to him the captain's wife sitting at the window and taking out the pattern of the handkerchief, which convinces the Moor of his wife's guilt beyond doubt.

The Moor and the ensign now plot to kill Disdemona and the captain. One night the ensign meets the captain on his way to visit a courtesan, and strikes a blow on his right thigh, cutting off the leg. The ensign mingles with the crowd that has gathered round the mangled captain and pretends great sympathy with the victim.

Disdemona is greatly affected by the news of the captain's misfortune, which further confirms her husband's suspicion. The Moor consults the ensign how to kill her. Acting on the ensign's plan the Moor allows the ensign to beat Disdemona to death with a stocking filled with sand, leaving no sign of violence on her body, and then both the Moor and the ensign pull down a portion of the ceiling on to her body after laying her in bed, to make it appear that she has been killed in an accident. Then the two villains raise a cry that the house is falling and the neighbours come round and find Disdemona lying dead.

After Disdemona's death the Moor becomes distracted with grief and turns upon the ensign whom he degrades and drives away from him. The ensign revenges himself by disclosing the murder to the captain who accuses the Moor in the senate of Venice, whereupon the Moor is arrested, tried, tortured and then banished. Later the Moor is killed by Disdemona's kinsmen. The ensign pursues his career of crime till he is arrested on a charge of murder and put to death with torture.

As there is a version of the story in the *Hecatommithi* that formed the plot of *Measure for Measure* and as that play was probably written soon after *Othello* was composed, it is likely that Shakespeare read Giraldi Cinthio's book in the first years of the seventeenth century. There was a French translation of Cinthio's book, yet from internal evidence it appears that Shakespeare read the original Italian version of the book. The probability that Shakespeare read the Italian text is reinforced by his use of the word "acerb" in "The food that to him now is as luscious as locusts, shall be to him shortly as acerb as the coloquintida. (I.3. 349-50)" The Folio substitutes the common word 'bitter.' Cinthio tells us that the love which this villain had borne Disdemona 'turned to bitterest hatred' (in acerbissimo odio). Indeed, the play seems to suggest that Shakespeare could read Italian with ease. Thus, Othello's account of the magical origin of the handkerchief given to Desdemona, not found in Cinthio who merely relates that it was finely 'embroidered in the Moorish fashion,' may well be derived from the description in Ariosto's *Orlando Furioso* of Hector's magical tent which his sister, the damsel Cassandra, inspired by 'prophetic fury' (a phrase used in *Othello*, III.4.70), had worked with her needle. Thus, it appears, that Shakespeare had the idea of magical handkerchief from Ariosto direct, not from Harrington's translation, because the English version has nothing corresponding to the words 'furor profectico,' which Shakespeare echoes. Shakespeare speaks of a "sibyl," Ariosto, of the 'damsel' Cassandra. But, Boiardo, in a similar connection which Ariosto obviously had in mind, also speaks of a sibyl. Had Shakespeare read Boiardo's *Orlando Innamorato* as well as its sequel *Orlando Furioso*, the possibility cannot be ruled out.

And if Shakespeare read Italian, it is more than likely that he was familiar with the *Discorso* in which Cinthio expounded his theory of tragedy. In his introduction to the *Hecatommithi*, Cinthio makes a group of men discuss the problem of success in married life. The secret of such success, the leader of the group insists, must be looked for in a spiritual union of the partners, though he suggests that this kind of union is difficult to maintain if husband and wife, owing to the circumstances of their birth or upbringing, have a different outlook on life or have been accustomed to different modes of living. The discussion may well have been before Shakespeare's mind when he set about the writing of this play. The theme of both *Othello* and Cinthio's tale is that of a marriage which begins as a spiritual union but is brought to disaster through differences of race and social tradition. Disdemona, Cinthio tells us, is attracted to the Moor not by physical desire but by his great and valorous spirit, while the Moor, on his side, falls in love with the beauty and nobility of her mind. And Disdemona points to the moral of the story when she declares to the ensign's wife that her fate is a warning to Italian girls not to marry a man divided from them by race, religion and manner of life.

Shakespeare would have seen other opportunities in Cinthio's story. The contrast between the apparent honesty and the actual villainy of the ensign provided an opportunity of exploring once again the nature of 'seeming,' fresh as Shakespeare was from Hamlet's discovery that one may smile and be a villain, and just before he created the character of Angelo in *Measure for Measure*. Above all, he must have been struck by the dramatic possibilities of making a noble hero kill the woman he loved.

Shakespeare made several alterations in the original story to raise the stature of his hero. Othello is introduced on the night of his elopement showing signs of his native self-command. The urgency of the summons on account of the Turkish attack, a situation invented by Shakespeare, displays Othello's value to the state. His nobility is manifested by his defence against the charge of witchcraft. For this Shakespeare went to Holland's translation of Pliny's *Natural History* where he found the story of C. Furius Cresinus, a former bondslave (cf. "Bond-slaves, and pagans, shall our statesmen be." *Othello*, I.2. 99) who was accused of acquiring great possessions 'by indirect means, as if he used sorcery and charms and witchcraft drawn into his own ground that increase fruits.' Cresinus' defence begins with the words, 'My Masters' (cf. My very noble and approv'd good masters:" *Othello*, I.3. 77) and pointing his plough and other implements he says: 'Behold these are the sorceries, charms, and all the enchantments that I use (cf. "what charms,/What conjuration, and what mighty magic," *Othello*, I.3. 91-92. "This only is the witchcraft I have us'd:" *Othello*, I.3. 169.). Other details of Othello's defence, "The Anthropophagi, and men whose heads/Do grow beneath their shoulders," (I.3. 144-45), may be derived from another chapter of Holland's translation (VII.ii). Shakespeare would have found in the same source an account of the "coloquintida" (I.3. 350), a kind of bitter apple, of the "mines of sulphur" (III.3. 334), of "mandragora" (III.3. 335), of "perfect chrysolite" (V.2. 146), and of the "Arabian trees" (V.2. 351). T.W. Baldwin, however, argues that Shakespeare read Pliny in the original Latin, probably using Dalecampinus' index to the work, and he states that he has found "nothing anywhere to indicate that Shakespeare did use Holland." He argues that the expression "Arabian trees" comes from Ovid (*Metamorphoses*, X), that the "antres vast" (I.3. 140) probably came from *The Aeneid* (I.52, III.617) and that "deserts idle" (I.3. 140) come from the Latin text, not from Holland.

There was a third source of Othello's defence—Sir Lewes Lewkenor's translation of Contareno's *The Commonwealth and Government of Venice* (1599). In his "Address to the Reader" Lewkenor speaks of his pleasure in conversing with travellers. He also contrasts 'soft beds' of those who stay at home with the hardships of travellers. Othello speaks of his hardships and contrasts the "flinty and steel couch of war" with the "thrice-driven bed of down" of civilians (I.3. 230-31). In the Epistle Dedicatory Lewkenor apologizes for 'the untuned harshness of my disjointed style' and speaks of 'the violence of my own fortune'. In the same way Othello apologizes for his rude speech (I.3. 81) and Desdemona in the same scene refers to her "downright violence, and scorn of fortunes" (I.3. 249). Lewkenor writes, 'a wise and well-speaking traveller, to whose tongue I would willingly endure to have mine ears inclined.' Othello speaks of Disdemona in Shakespeare's play that she would "seriously incline" (I.3. 146) to hear Othello's tales and "with a greedy ear" (I.3. 149) "Devour up my discourse" (I.3. 150).

The main source of Shakespeare is, however, Cinthio. But Shakespeare has not followed Cinthio's story in its totality. He has made certain changes. In the original story all characters except Disdemona are unnamed. But for the purpose of the drama Shakespeare has to give names to different characters. He has also changed the spelling of the name of the heroine. He has omitted many details and incidents of the original story as unnecessary and superfluous. In Shakespeare's play Othello goes to Cyprus alone and Disdemona follows him in another ship with Iago. In the original story the Moor and Disdemona go to Cyprus together on board the same ship. This change makes for proper dramatic effect.

For the purpose of meeting dramatic ends Shakespeare introduces some additional characters in the persons of Brabantio, Montano and Roderigo. Roderigo has been introduced for providing a motive for Cassio's brawl. Shakespeare took a hint from his own early play *Twelfth Night* (1601) where Sir Toby Belch uses Sir Andrew as his purse by promising to assist him in his wooing of Olivia, just as Iago has promised to help Roderigo in his wooing of Disdemona, in exchange of money. The creation of Roderigo makes the incident of the brawl a deliberate device to get Cassio dismissed, and not merely a lucky accident which the ensign makes use of for his own purposes.

The ensign of the original story loves Disdemona and believes that she loves the captain. So, as a disappointed lover he wreaks vengeance on both. In Shakespeare's play there is no such motive of Iago's disappointment in any attempt to win the love of Disdemona. Shakespeare has made the character of Iago more subtle and complex.

Shakespeare makes Cassio a more important character than the captain in the original story. Cassio's drunkenness is Shakespeare's invention. It is used to explain his lapse from duty without too much alienation of our sympathies. The main lines of the character are determined by his innocence with regard to Disdemona, by his appointment as Othello's lieutenant, by his love of Othello, and by the fact that he is wounded when returning from a courtesan's house. Shakespeare combines the copier of the handkerchief with the courtesan, Bianca. In the story it is the wife of the captain, who is seen at her window copying the embroidery of Disdemona's handkerchief. The handkerchief which in the story is picked up, rather stolen, by the ensign from Disdemona while she caresses his little daughter, is picked up, in the drama, by Emilia and given to Iago because of his importunity. Thus, the handkerchief episode in the original story differs from that in the play. In Cinthio's account we find: "And he [ensign] having a girl of three years old, which child was much beloved by Disdemona, one day that the hapless lady had gone to stay at the house of the villain, he took the little girl in his arms and gave her to the lady, who took her and gathered her to her breast. This deceiver, who was excellent at sleight of hand, reft the handkerchief from her girdle so cunningly that she was unaware of it and departed from her right joyful." According to Swinburne, the incident substituted by Shakespeare is less probable and less tragic. He comes to the conclusion that the sole reason for this change is that it is impossible to imagine Iago fathering a child. "In Shakespeare's world, as in nature's it is impossible that monsters should propagate: that Iago should beget, or that Goneril or Regan should bring forth," says Swinburne. However, this change may be taken up as an instance of the superiority of Shakespeare's version of the loss of handkerchief. There is, first, a purely theatrical reason for the change. Shakespeare's stage children are never as young as three, and a much older child would hardly have done in this scene. Shakespeare has also, perhaps, thought it artistically unwise to introduce a little girl only for the handkerchief episode, the girl having no part to play in furthering the tragedy. Moreover, the change is justified because whereas the ensign's wife in the story is a young and virtuous lady, Shakespeare makes Emilia of lower rank than Disdemona and of a much coarser fibre. Besides, the introduction of a child would have involved a passage of dialogue which would have lessened the intensity of the temptation scene, and to make Disdemona visit Emilia's house would have altered the relation between the two women. The immense superiority of the drama at the handkerchief episode is beyond question. Shakespeare allows Desdemona to forget her handkerchief in the only circumstances when her neglect of the love token is a proof of her love. She offers to bind Othello's forehead with it, and he brushes it aside as too small. To remember her handkerchief would be a blemish. For, it is a thing now that has failed in the only use of serving her beloved. Cassio does not, like the captain in Cinthio's tale, recognize the handkerchief as Desdemona's. He cannot, therefore, try to return it. And Bianca is far more likely than his wife to provoke Cassio to those fleers and gibes and notable scorns which Othello is to interpret as the signs of his triumph over Desdemona. Othello's character has also been considerably retouched. In the play he commands the reader's respect and sympathy.

In the story the ensign's wife knows of the plot against Disdemona, but she dares not reveal it. Emilia, on the other hand, is ignorant of Iago's devilish machinations. And as soon as she realizes the truth she sacrifices her life for the love of her mistress by revealing the truth in the presence of her husband, Othello and others. Thus, her character has been ennobled in the play.

The murder of Disdemona, in the play, is less brutal and shocking than it is in the original story. In the original story the ensign strikes Disdemona to the ground in the presence of the Moor by means of a stocking filled with sand, and it is he who also gives the blow by which the murder is completed. A portion of the ceiling is then pulled down by both the Moor and the ensign together to give the event the appearance of an accident. In the play Othello kills Desdemona himself on the bed by strangling, and the pulling of the ceiling is entirely excluded. Othello allows Disdemona to pray and makes no attempt to escape the responsibility for his deed. Cinthio's Moor apparently remains unaware of Disdemona's innocence and refuses to confess his guilt. The denouement of the story is completely transformed by the insertion of the willow-song scene, of Disdemona's forgiveness, of the immediate discovery of the murder, of Emilia's exposure of Iago, of the news of Brabantio's death, and of Othello's suicide. Shakespeare, moreover, brings Iago to justice for his present crimes, not, as in Cinthio, for another crime altogether. In the original story the Moor, after his murder of Disdemona, is "brought over to Venice for trial, is tortured for confession and on his not confessing, he is banished and is ultimately killed by his wife's relations. In the play Othello kills himself at Cyprus almost immediately after the murder of Desdemona. In Cinthio the ensign attempts other crimes and is tortured to death in the process of extorting confession from him. The fate of Shakespeare's Iago is left in the hands of Cassio.

The most significant departure from the original story is Shakespeare's compression of the time of action. In the original story the Moor and Disdemona, after their marriage, lived for a fairly long time in settled matrimonial happiness at Venice. In due course, and not on account of a sudden military demand, the Moor goes to command the military forces of Venice in Cyprus. He feels distressed when the call comes to him, for it means his separation from Disdemona. Time moves slowly and in normal course in the original story. But it moves very fast in the play. The voyage to Cyprus takes place on the very day of the marriage. The tragedy follows on what seems to be but the second day after Cyprus is reached. In the interval required for the sea voyage from Venice to Cyprus, Othello and Desdemona sail in different ships. By this compression of time the union of Othello and Desdemona is not permitted by Shakespeare to deepen into a close domestic bond. Besides, accident and coincidence contribute more largely to the catastrophe in the play than in the original story.

There is no historical background to the story of Cinthio. Shakespeare uses the attack of the Turks upon Cyprus in 1570 as the historic background of the action in *Othello*. Cinthio makes sensuality the main motive of the ensign's revenge. In Shakespeare the "motiveless malignity" has its foundation in pure egotism of Iago.

8

Othello: A Distinctive Shakespearian Tragedy

When Shakespeare was at work at *Othello*, he had before his mind certain ideals of tragic effect which he sought to achieve, of course, with varying diversity of details in different cases, but with a certain common artistic method. According to Bradley a Shakespearian tragedy is pre-eminently the story of one person in high life, leading up to and including the death of the hero. It is a tale of suffering and tragedy, leading to death. To the medieval mind tragedy meant a total reversal of fortune, falling unawares upon a happy man, as the effect of the operation of an unseen power. Shakespeare's idea of the tragic fact goes beyond this. The calamities do not simply happen; they proceed mainly from actions and those actions, from the character of men. Thus, the centre of the tragedy lies in action issuing from character. In all the tragedies it is possible to trace the tragedy to a certain error or weakness in the hero. Thus, the fault of Othello is his credulity and too simple a nature.

The focus of the tragic interest in a Shakespearian tragedy is always the character of the central figure, the hero. The hero is generally a man of lofty and almost superhuman disposition, thinking and doing great things in a sordid world which is opposed to him. He is one who has some inherent weakness. He is subjected to both external and internal conflicts which oppress his soul and madden him into what the world always calls folly. The situation and circumstances in which he is placed are such as are specially suited to work upon his peculiar weakness, bringing about his ultimate ruin. There is always a sinister, mysterious force, call it chance or accident or fate or destiny which seems bent upon undoing him and against which he is powerless. The fall of the tragic hero is calculated to excite pity, horror and fear, but pathos and sympathy of the audience are never lost by him. The moral order of the universe is rather justified than violated by the tragic end. The death of the hero and that of some others mark the close of the drama, but death is of little account in accounting for the tragic feeling because it is the defeat or ruin of the soul which precedes the death, that is the real culmination of the action issuing out of character.

According to Professor Allardyce Nicoll *Othello* is the best of Shakespeare's tragedies. Dr Johnson eloquently praises this play as he says: "The fiery openness of Othello, magnanimous, artless and credulous, boundless in his confidence, ardent in his affection, inflexible in his resolution, and obdurate in his revenge; the cool malignity of Iago, silent in his resentment, subtle in his designs, and studious at once of his interest and his vengeance; the soft simplicity of Desdemona, confident of merit, and conscious of innocence, her artless perseverance in her suit and her slowness to suspect that she can be suspected, are proofs of Shakespeare's skill in human nature, as I suppose it is in vain to seek in any modern writer." He continues: "The gradual progress which Iago makes in the Moor's conviction and the circumstances which he employs to inflame him, are so skilfully natural that, though it will perhaps not be said of Othello as he says of himself, that he is 'a man not easily jealous,' yet we cannot but pity him when at last we find him 'perplexed in the extreme.' The virtue of Emilia is such as we often find, worn loosely, but not cast off, easy to commit small crimes but quickened and alarmed at atrocious villainies." Hazlitt observes: "*Othello* excites our sympathy to an extraordinary degree. The moral it conveys has a close application to the concerns of human life than that of almost any other of Shakespeare's plays."

In *Othello* the tragedy involves the ruin of three characters—Othello, Desdemona and Iago, the former two giving rise to true tragic pathos, the latter only involving the ruin of evil by the force of evil itself. The central character of the hero, Othello, is as important as the character of Desdemona. It is doubtful if the latter is not more inherently tragic than the former. Othello is a noble-minded generous soldier, utterly ignorant of the world of wickedness and its mean designs. His naïve simplicity is irritating, his blind truthfulness is appalling; but far from being vexed at his simplicity or enraged at his blindness, we are numbed by the infinite pathos of his situation and the malice of chance which puts him in the hand of the one man in the world who could have the heart to ruin him. Desdemona is pure as a saint, innocent as a child, generous as the fruitful earth. She does not know even to defend herself in circumstances which irritate even the simplest lamb to rebel. The force of evil—causeless envy, cold intellectual malice, heartless delight in egoism—is made concrete in the person of Iago. He takes the meanest advantage of the noble trustfulness of Othello, abuses his simplicity, and out of the single weakness of his character forges the weapon which kills the souls of two of the noblest in imaginative creation. The noble Moor is subjected to an external conflict, but much more to the far more tremendous internal conflict between his love and his sense of honour. Chances array themselves against him and poor Desdemona; while not a single chance, that might at one stroke bring down the whole fabric of Iago's plot, favours him by timely occurrence. Othello discovers everything, but discovers a bit too late. It is as if fate had appointed the inexorable tragic catastrophe for him only to relent when it was sure that the discovery of his mistake would lead him to end his own life by violence.

Thus, in the tragedy of *Othello* Shakespeare has made his characters fight blindly in the dark, and ate has brought each to his or her desired end. ut the end of the tragedy raises us above despair. Desdemona's sincere love for her husband survived the ultimate trial. Othello perceived his own calamitous error, and he recogni ed Desdemona 's purity and loyalty. nd it was evil that suffered defeat. The villain Iago did not turn out to be victorious in the end. He was caught at last in his own toil and was led to his trial.

Othello is also distinctive as a Shakespearian tragedy as the principle of construction that is discernible in Shakespeare's other tragic dramas does not appear to have been strictly followed in it throughout. The drama can be divided into three parts. The first part or exposition is confined to the First Act. Roderigo and Iago first appear on the scene and bring us information of the secret marriage of Othello and Desdemona. Othello is talked about but the dramatist keeps him out of sight in the first scene. The appearance of Iago in the opening scene is calculated to give us at the very outset a strong impression of the force which is to prove fatal to the hero's happiness, so that, when we see the hero himself, the shadow of fate already rests upon him. The seed of the conflict of action is sown in the very first scene of the drama. Iago hates Othello for having appointed Cassio his lieutenant in supersession of his own claim, and Roderigo, being disappointed in his love for Desdemona, makes common cause with him. In the Second Act the seed of conflict germinates, and the crisis is reached in the first scene when Othello re-unites with Desdemona in Cyprus. Iago makes Roderigo believe that Desdemona is in love with Cassio. In pursuance of his instruction, Roderigo draws the drunken Cassio into a fight which results in the latter's dismissal. Iago requests Cassio to implore Desdemona to intercede and persuade Othello to reinstate him. The threads are thus laid out and the net is woven in this Act and the next two, for enmeshing not only the hero, but also Cassio and Desdemona. The actual conflict begins in the third scene of the Third Act. All the five Acts appear to surge undeviatingly towards the climax which is reserved, as it were, until almost the fall of the final curtain.

Although *Othello* is roughly divided, as indicated above, into three parts as a tragedy, its scheme of construction differs to some extent from that of the other tragedies of Shakespeare. In the first half of the play the main conflict is merely incubating. Then it bursts into life and goes storming without intermission or change of direction to its close. In consequence the second half of the tragedy has become exciting to a degree. The First Act is full of stir. The long first scene of the Second Act is occupied largely with mere conversations, artfully drawn out to a dimension which can scarcely be considered essential to the plot. The drama reaches its crisis too early in the reunion of Othello and Desdemona in Cyprus in this scene. The crisis is reached by conflict, but not with the force which is the cause of final destruction. The Third Act weaves the given threads into the net which Othello, in his vehemence, draws over his own head. It is easily seen that from this point everything runs on in a straight line, without digression, towards the single goal. It is only the second scene of the Third Act that seems to be a make-shift, which might well be dispensed with. But to make up for this, the conclusion of the same Act, as well as of the Fourth and Fifth Acts, are the more masterly in composition. The catastrophe spreads out over a considerable space. This unique method of construction adopted by Shakespeare in *Othello* by which the conflict is made to develop very slowly, presented certain difficulties, but Shakespeare has very skilfully surmounted them.

The main action of *Othello* consists in the agony of a simple and honest soul through the devilish intrigue of a wily villain, which turns the intense love of the hero for his wife into hideous jealousy and causes him to murder the innocent wife and lay violent hands on himself. Unlike his other tragedies Shakespeare tells this story in *Othello* in a very simple and direct manner. From the landing in Cyprus onward, no other interest is allowed to conflict even remotely with the absorbing dread, indignation and suspense excited by Iago's game. Cassio's dismissal moves our sympathy, but pity gives way to an acute anxiety when we realize that Desdemona's pleading for his reinstatement is to be the web which will fatally ensnare them both. Bianca and Roderigo count only as tools of Iago, and have no other value in the play. Even the public and military interest promised at the outset by the menace of the Turkish attack, is promptly eliminated when its purpose has been served, and the agents and victims of the tragedy have been assembled at its scene in Cyprus.

The beauty of composition in *Othello* is unique. It demands, above all things, harmony, clearness and design, that is, it demands that the final aim of the action, the point to which the dramatic development finally leads, should, from beginning to end, be perceptible through the separate scenes, and that the characters, the action, and the plot should be developed as rapidly as clearly. The beauty of this arrangement is exhibited in the highest perfection in *Othello*. The secret of the dramatic power of *Othello* is in its sustained unity of interest, in the fact that the central theme is before us from first to last. In *Othello* we are not asked to solve any problems, and our interest is never distracted from the trials of the hero and the heroine. The plot of Iago, its progress and success, occupies every atom of sympathy in the human breast. We sympathize with his victims and marvel at his malignity, and can think of no other issue in the play as being of the slightest importance. No minor character, though real and human, is allowed to interfere with the central theme of the drama. Thus, *Othello* is the most perfectly constructed of all the tragedies of Shakespeare and it has a distinctive position among the tragedies not only of Shakespeare but also of his contemporaries and predecessors.

9

Othello: A Tragedy of Intrigue

Bradley holds *King Lear* Shakespeare's greatest work but not his best play, and most readers will agree with him. Indeed, to most readers *Othello* is not the greatest work of Shakespeare, but none will deny that it is his best play. It has neither the variety nor the depth of *Hamlet*, none of the overwhelming power of *King Lear*, none of that 'atmosphere' which, in *Macbeth*, keeps us awfully hovering on the confines of a world outside that of our normal experience, none of the sweep and exultant power of *Antony and Cleopatra*, nor has it that range in time, which marks all the other four. But its grip upon the emotions of the audience is more relentless and sustained than that of the others. The plot is completely simple with no sub-plot and no distractions. To tell it in brief, it is about a man disappointed of promotion which he thought he had a right to expect, determines on revenge, and in part secures it. It can be stated a bit elaborately thus: "An ensign, expecting promotion to a vacant lieutenancy, is exasperated when his general appoints another man over his head. He determines to revenge himself on the general and secure the dismissal of his rival. By a series of adroit moves he persuades the general to believe in his wife's adultery with the lieutenant. As a result the general kills, first his wife and then, on realizing his mistake, himself. But the ensign fails in the second part of his design, since his plot is disclosed. The lieutenant receives yet further promotion and the ensign faces trial and torture." Nothing could be simpler. And when the story or the scheme is largely concerned with one of the strongest and most distressing of human emotions, the plot is likely to be a powerful one. According to M.R. Ridley, none of the other three great tragedies has much of a plot in this sense, and that *Antony and Cleopatra* has even less. *Hamlet* has the making of a first-rate plot in which we should watch move and counter-move with excitement, a plot in which the devising and execution of play-scene would be a well-forged link. But, as it is, owing to Hamlet's state of mind, the moves are all on one side, and the play-scene leads to nothing in action, only to intellectual confirmation. In *King Lear* the two sub-plots have a firm structure, with development and resolution, but the main action is not properly a plot at all; it is merely the progress through madness to recovered sanity and a new sense of reality of the great central figure. In *Macbeth* the only thing that can be called a plot is the murder of Duncan, and this comes so early, is so suddenly devised and hurriedly executed, that it does not seriously engage our interest and serves mainly as a starting point for the main action which is concerned with the deterioration and steady progress to downfall of the two main figures. *Antony and Cleopatra* is deliberately episodic. In all these four plays what grips our interest is, 'the characters.' We do not ask, 'What will the next move be?' or 'Will he see the danger before it is too late?' but rather, 'What kind of people are these?' or 'What kind of people are they going to be by the end of the play?' In none of them is there that implication followed by explication, which Aristotle thought one of the features of great tragedy, and of which Shakespeare himself was a master in another kind of play. *The Merchant of Venice*, *Much Ado About Nothing* and *Measure for Measure*, for example, have all theatrically effective plots. But, they are comedies and Shakespeare used this form only once in high tragedy, and this is where *Othello* differs in structure and in effect from others. It belongs to a different order of plays—that order of which, ever since it was written, *Oedipus Tyrannus* has been justly held the great exemplar.

Thus, *Othello* is pre-eminently a tragedy of intrigue, as the action and catastrophe of the drama depend largely on intrigue. Iago, having been superseded by Othello in his choice of his lieutenant, is enraged. He is determined to bring about Othello's ruin, and fortunately for himself he finds it not a very difficult task. Othello is noble in every respect, but there seems to be a joint in his armour loose. He extorts, as it were, from Iago the villain's vague innuendoes and readily suspects the fidelity of his beloved wife. Iago is emboldened. He pursues Othello like his evil spirit, and with his light, and therefore the more dangerous insinuations he leaves Othello no rest. A more artful villain than this Iago has never been portrayed. He spreads his net with a skill that nothing can escape.

For the purpose of carrying his hellish intrigue to a successful issue, Iago uses three characters in the play as his instruments. His first instrument is Roderigo. He uses Roderigo simply as a tool to further his own designs. He has another interest, too. He gets all the money he can out of Roderigo on the pretext of purchasing gifts for Desdemona in order to win her over to Roderigo. The second instrument is Cassio whom Iago suspects of undue familiarity with his wife, Emilia. Emilia is the third instrument employed for stealing the handkerchief of Desdemona to be used as ocular proof of Desdemona's adultery with Cassio.

Iago's intrigue begins by manipulating Othello's noble and unsuspecting character. He gradually turns it into the opposite of itself and finally makes Othello destroy his most beloved object. Othello does not know of Iago's hatred, of his revengeful spirit, of his wickedness and cunning. He does not see the cliffs upon which his life is to be wrecked. Hence he cannot order his purposes and actions in accordance with them. His mode of action, therefore, does not directly arise from his character. It is rather caused by an inconceivable imposition practised upon him by another person. Without this imposition, there is in Othello's whole being not even the smallest corner from which such monstrous deeds could burst forth. It is only this external influence which first breaks down his whole character, as it were. That he allows himself to be deceived arises, it is true, from his own individuality, but only partially. For, on the other hand, the deceit is so cunningly contrived, so favoured by circumstances, that even the most cautious and most circumspect person would have been deceived by it.

Thus, the main plot of *Othello* turns on intrigue. Iago dominates it from beginning to end. Iago tricks Roderigo out of his money, Cassio out of his honour and lieutenancy, Othello out of his love and Desdemona. To accomplish his designs he depends simply on manipulation of persons and circumstances. Roderigo is a ready tool of his. Through Roderigo he provokes Cassio into a brawl on the night of celebrations. But apart from that, he puts one person against another. After Cassio is cashiered, he sends Cassio to Desdemona with the object that each should compromise the other. At one stroke he succeeds in turning Othello against Desdemona and Cassio.

Moulton writes: "When we turn to analyse the Plot, this is found to be a network of Intrigue—the mode of action in which Jealousy most naturally finds vent; and the intrigues, however elaborate, are by the movement of the plot drawn to a simple culmination which remains for all literature the typical climax of tragic jealousy." Moulton distinguishes four intrigues in the play: (1) Iago's intrigue against Roderigo, (2) Iago's intrigue to gain Cassio's place, (3) Iago's intrigue to get rid of Cassio altogether, and (4) Iago's intrigue to destroy the happiness of Othello and Desdemona. Iago uses Roderigo simply as a tool to further his own designs. He has another interest, too. He gets all the money he can out of Roderigo. Against Cassio he has a double intrigue. He covets the post of Othello's lieutenant which Cassio has got undeservingly, according to him. Besides, he is jealous of the fortunes of Cassio. So, he involves both Cassio and Desdemona and plots to get rid of Cassio. Iago's intrigue against Othello is the result of his hatred of Othello and his suspicion that Othello has debauched his wife. His plot to get rid of Desdemona does not have any sound reason except marring the happiness of Othello. He may or may not have a plausible motive, but he plots all the same to ruin their happiness. And it is the plots and intrigues of the crafty villain Iago working upon the simple, believing minds of some of the characters in the play that bring about the tragedy. Hence, *Othello* is a tragedy of intrigue rather than a tragedy of character.

10

Othello: A Domestic Tragedy

In *Othello* Shakespeare comes nearest to writing a domestic tragedy, a type of drama popular on the Elizabethan stage. This kind of tragedy, however, cannot reach the same heights and has not the same motive force as a play where the characters are monarchs and leaders of men. Shakespeare seems to have perceived this and generally avoided the drama of private life. But, in *Othello* the figures are of lower rank, less removed from ordinary life than in other great tragedies of Shakespeare. In those others we have a king, a ghost of another king, lately dead, a queen, and a prince (*Hamlet*); a king, three princesses, and two dukes (*King Lear*); a king, soon murdered, a usurping king and queen, and two princes one of whom succeeds to the crown (*Macbeth*); a queen and the two great rivals for the rulership of the 'world' (*Antony and Cleopatra*). In *Othello* the figure in the highest station is the Duke of Venice, who is no more than a figure head, and apart from him we have a senator and his daughter, and three army officers, one belonging to the highest rank. This makes more difference in impression than we always realize. It is no doubt true, as Johnson said, that Shakespeare, though he deals with kings and queens, thinks only on men; but, nonetheless, very high rank does, if only subconsciously, diminish our feeling of intimacy and thereby makes the impact not less great but less stabbing. Further, in the other tragedies we are made aware that the fates of the characters, though they affect us by sympathy for them as individual men and women, affect also the destinies of kingdoms and peoples. It is noteworthy that all these other tragedies end with the re-establishment of the ordered government.

Othello is a tragedy different from the other tragedies of Shakespeare. It is no doubt an inconvenience for the Venetian state to be deprived of the services of its greatest general, but there is no more to it than that, and so we are left free to follow simply the disastrous fortunes of people like ourselves, and we are shocked to find one of them caught in the cruel grip of an emotion to which we are all liable. Marital jealousy was a common theme in the Elizabethan domestic drama, and still common in the comedies of London life, but the effect of the play of *Othello* on the minds of readers and audience is far different from the effect of say, for example, Thomas Heywood's *A Woman Killed with Kindness*. For, although Othello is a private man, Shakespeare has contrived to endow him with all the traditional dignity of a hero of a tragedy. The means by which such an end is achieved are by subtle references to his dignity and position. At the very beginning Othello tells Iago: "I fetch my life and being/From men of royal siege (I.2.21-22)." He is chosen commander-in-chief of the forces of a powerful and historic state. Throughout the play he is presented as a man out of the common, both in character and abilities, and he takes such deference as a natural right. He is invested, too, with something of the glamour and mystery of the orient. And finally, he is a great figure of romance. All this raises him up to stand as a shining example among men, and in proportion to the greatness of his position, his character, and his influence, is the greatness of the tragedy.

But in spite of his great stature as a tragic hero, Othello is treated in a different way in the tragedy. There are a few of us liable to be called upon to avenge the murder of a royal father, to be prompted by ambition to murder a king for his crown, to resign our crowns or to waste outstanding talents and sacrifice the rule of half the world for love of a queen, but we are all liable to blinding jealousy. In the other tragedies of Shakespeare we are spectators. The spectacle may be in the highest degree terrifying, soul-searching and in the end uplifting, but we do never feel that we want to participate in it, to speak to the characters, to advise them or to warn them. We simply watch the action, but in *Othello* we are involved in it.

At the beginning of the play we see Othello in the council chamber of the Senate of Venice. The consciousness of his high position never leaves him. At the end when he is determined to live no longer, he seems to be anxious, like Hamlet, not to be misjudged by the great world. But he is superseded in the government of Cyprus by Cassio before he dies. His deed and his death, therefore, have not that influence on the interests of a nation or an empire, which serves to idealize and to remove far from our own sphere the stories of Hamlet and Macbeth, of Coriolanus and Antony. *Othello* presents before us a tragedy of our own world. First, there is the external conflict in the family. The right of the daughter to choose a Moor for her husband is asserted against the will of the parent. Secondly, there is the internal conflict in the family between husband and wife. The married pair, though successful in their external struggle with the father, are now rent asunder.

The political and historical facts connected with the play are restricted to the earlier part of the drama, while almost the entire play deals with Iago's diabolical scheme to rouse suspicion in the mind of Othello about the faithlessness of his wife, Desdemona, in order to destroy the marital bliss and happiness of Othello. As Iago works upon the simple and credulous nature of Othello, we do not remember Othello's official rank and position; we become interested in Othello, the man. Shakespeare has most ably presented the great agony suffered by Othello as the latter finds his genuine love betrayed. The situations and the characters created by the dramatist have a universal appeal. Even in our present-day society we will meet with persons like Othello, Iago and Desdemona; only they have changed their names. Thus, as the play is based on family relationships and as the tragedy is a human tragedy caused by jealousy and apparent betrayal of love, it may be termed as a domestic tragedy.

11

The Plot-Structure

As a Shakespearian tragedy represents a conflict which terminates in a catastrophe, any such tragedy may roughly be divided into three parts. The first of these sets forth or expounds the situation, or state of affairs, out of which the conflict arises; and it may, therefore, be called the exposition. The second deals with definite beginning, the growth and vicissitudes of the conflict. It forms accordingly the bulk of the play, comprising the Second, Third and Fourth Acts and usually a part of the First and a part of the Fifth. The final section of the tragedy shows the issue of the conflict in a catastrophe.

The opening scene of *Othello* takes us right into the heart of the action. The conversation between Iago and Roderigo informs us of Desdemona's runaway marriage with Othello, which releases all the forces of action and reaction. It partly reveals Iago's motive and future action and also shows that he is going to use Roderigo as a mere tool. So much for the preliminaries of the action of the play. The second scene makes a still clearer presentment of Iago's motive and character. He has his own axe to grind, and cares but little for Othello or anybody else in the world. The third scene carries the private affair of Othello into the impersonal region of politics, to the imperative demand of which Brabantio's opposition bows. Brabantio's opposition later appears to be a minor crisis, which is almost forgotten in the subsequent developments.

The Second Act transfers the scene of action to Cyprus. The first scene, the exposition of the motive of the play being now partly over, seems to be preparatory to Iago's intrigue, upon which the whole action of the play hinges. Iago's soliloquy at the end of the first scene serves the further purpose of exposition. The second scene is but a connecting link. The third scene is packed with events. The drunken brawl into which Cassio is enticed, leads to his dismissal and this gives Iago the necessary opportunity to work his design upon Othello.

It is not until the third scene of the Third Act is reached that the tragic conflict arises. It is at first mere suspicion, sown by Iago, in Othello's mind. Iago never for a moment leaves Othello until it is nursed into active and pestilential growth by Iago's subtle insinuations. The conflict in its final form becomes both internal and external. It becomes a conflict between love and honour in Othello's own heart. The subtle force of Iago's insinuations is the external foe he has to contend with. But finally he succumbs to the evil suggestions of Iago. The tragic end is already in sight now.

It should be noted that accident helps Iago twice in the furthering of his design. First, Emilia picks up Desdemona's handkerchief which Iago craftily puts in Cassio's chamber. Cassio, attracted by the intricate design on the handkerchief, gives it to Bianca to copy the design. Secondly, at the most opportune moment Bianca appears with the handkerchief and returns it to Cassio, while Iago holds Cassio in conversation and Othello watching them unseen. Desdemona's inability to produce the handkerchief, when Othello demands it, partly confirms Othello's suspicion. Next Othello has "ocular proof" of her guilt when he finds it in the possession of Bianca who gives it to Cassio. We have now reached the first scene of the Fourth Act.

The catastrophe comes with Othello's resolve to smother Desdemona. A brief pause is allowed in the second scene of the Fourth Act, when Othello questions Desdemona about her infidelity. The shadow darkens in the third scene. In the first scene of the Fifth Act Cassio is wounded by Roderigo who is killed by Iago who has cut Cassio's leg in two, and thus Iago fulfils his part of the pact. In the second scene follows the murder of Desdemona, Othello's realization of the grievous mistake and his suicide. Thus the final end is reached.

Although some critics may think otherwise, *Othello* appears to observe the classical rules of construction to a great extent. According to the convention of the ancient Greek tragedies, a play must maintain the three unities of action, time and place. It means that the plot must centre round one single theme, the duration of time for the incidents to happen must not exceed twenty-four hours and all the incidents must happen at the same place. The unity of action or theme is maintained in *Othello* by the absence of any sub-plot and by all the incidents leading to the intense suffering and death of the tragic hero, Othello. The affairs of Roderigo and Cassio are all connected with the main story. The duration of the incidents in the play dramatically exceeds the classical limit of twenty-four hours by about twelve hours only. The main incidents of the play, namely, the rousing by Iago of Othello's suspicions about Desdemona and her murder by Othello occur at the same place—Cyprus.

Apart from the principle of three unities there is another principle of classical drama, which is embodied in Aristotle's *Poetics*, that a play must have a beginning, a middle and an end, with a reasonable proportion between these three parts. The beginning called 'the exposition' must not be too long. The middle must steadily proceed to the climax which should come at such a stage as would have space for the final catastrophe at the end. In these concluding parts space must be found for the hero's recognition of the justice of his own fate. In *Othello* these three parts are properly balanced. The First and a part of the Second Act serve as the exposition. The Third Act serves to bring about the crisis. The Fourth and the Fifth Acts present the catastrophe. The Third Act being the longest of all the Acts serves as the key-stone to the Arch.

Besides observing these classical rules of architectural design, the classical tragedy has to emphasize the sway of fate. This is served in *Othello* by the accident of the dropping of Desdemona's handkerchief and picking it up by Emilia, which serves as the starting point of the crisis. By this chance happening Othello's doom takes on a definitely fateful complexion. This would not have been the case if Othello were merely a victim of another man's villainy. Emilia's fond desire to please her wayward husband Iago by securing the handkerchief for him also emphasizes the sway of fate. She innocently helps, led on by an invisible power of destruction, in the ruin of her mistress, and indirectly also in her own undoing as well.

Othello, thus, conforms to the principles and conventions of the classical drama. It also fulfils the general requirement of dramatic structure consisting in a skilled intermixture of suspense and irony. Shakespeare nowhere exploits too much the crude device of suspense and surprise. And in *Othello*, too, he has not done it. As Stopford A. Brooke observes: "In Shakespeare...expectation is everywhere, surprise nowhere." Shakespeare rouses pity and fear in respect of Othello by withholding from him important information, which he freely communicates to his audience. Throughout the play Shakespeare keeps his audience fully acquainted with the villainy of Iago. That tragic irony through which the audience understands while the characters on the stage do not, is employed in respect of almost all the characters. We find this tragic irony at work in Cassio's unwilling consent to drink, Desdemona's pleading on behalf of Cassio and Emilia's handing over to her husband the fatal handkerchief. Suspense and surprise, however, are employed at the catastrophe. Most unexpectedly Cassio is not killed while Roderigo is. Most surprisingly Iago is betrayed by his own wife. Surprise reaches its climax in Othello's killing himself at the end of a long speech that never suggested the possibilities of such an act.

It has been suggested by some critics that the plot of *Othello* is absurd. They hold that it is impossible that a person like Othello would act upon such allegations as are made by Iago without putting them to a severe test. They point out that it is a play purely of accident and its apt title would be "The tragedy of the handkerchief." They say that Iago is unnaturally villainous and Othello is unnaturally gullible. The entire action of the play is lacking in adequate motive.

Against this charge of unnaturalness and absurdity of *Othello's* plot it should be remembered that it is an Elizabethan play and not a modern drama or a contemporary psychological novel. In Shakespeare's time nobody asked of a novelist or a dramatist as to how the mind of a criminal presented by him worked. Iago is only a representative, although on a magnified scale, of the conventional stage villain of the time. Just as in the case of the Devil of the medieval Mystery play, there was no necessity to trace Iago's villainy to a natural or sufficient motive. He embodies the spirit of mischief-making for its own sake. Equally conventional is the gullibility of Othello. As it is the traditional business of the villain Iago to deceive, the appointed role of Othello, the hero, is to be deceived. The Elizabethan audience never felt the central situation of the play to be in the least absurd. They accepted the postulate that Iago was there in the play to display his wickedness and Othello was a man who could be easily befooled by that villain.

It is enough for Shakespeare to make his otherwise absurd situation plausible. In this he succeeds very well. He stresses Othello's simplicity and his total ignorance of the ways of the women and the society. He emphasizes Iago's profound wisdom in the ways of the world. To make Othello's deception by Iago look less unnatural or absurd Shakespeare brings in other victims of Iago's irresistible fraud. Cassio and Roderigo are easily deceived by Iago as Othello is. Shakespeare has endowed Iago with a subtlety, resourcefulness and presence of mind of an extraordinary kind. He thus makes perfectly plausible at the moment every trick practised by Iago. Othello is endowed with an extraordinary measure of goodness and simplicity to match the extraordinary villainy of Iago. By a skilled portraiture of the principal characters, Shakespeare overcomes the absurdity that inheres in the plot. Iago and Othello are so drawn that they quite fit in with the plot. Desdemona also is depicted in such a way that her extreme gentleness and delicacy make a suitable contribution towards the effectiveness of Iago's villainy. Her nature is infinitely sweet and bashful. She cannot even utter the shameful word which her husband hurls at her.

Thus, the plot of Iago thrives so well because he is Iago and because his victims are Othello and Desdemona. The motiveless malignity of Iago, the generous credulity of Othello and the angelic delicacy of Desdemona combine to produce the tragic result and make the tragic event look natural and plausible. Professor G.P. Baker in his book *Dramatic Technique* aptly remarks: "*Othello* is a masterpiece because Shakespeare knew Othello, Iago and Desdemona so intimately that by their interplay of character upon character they shape every scene perfectly." It is indeed Shakespeare's credit that he has transformed a crude story of an Italian novella by his superb power of imagination and unmatched structural skill, into a soul-stirring tragedy, that makes us forget all inconsistencies and improbabilities in the story and leaves in us a sense of profound waste and pathos.

12

Art of Characterization

The supreme excellence of Shakespeare as a dramatist lies in his power of characterization. It is neither in diction and versification, nor in construction and the aids to construction, that the progress of the English drama incurred its deepest debt to Shakespeare. That which has given the greatest and most enduring potency to his influence upon English drama and in ever-widening circles upon the modern Western drama in general, is his own supreme gift as a dramatist, the gift of the power of characterization. In the drawing of characters ranging over almost every type of humanity, in which the experience of succeeding generations has recognized a fit subject for the art of either the tragic or the comic dramatist, he has infinitely surpassed all his predecessors and remains absolutely without a peer. Hazlitt, who was among those who recognized Shakespeare's power of characterization as his greatest excellence as a dramatic artist, observed in his book, *The Characters of Shakespeare*: "Each of his characters is as much as itself, and as absolutely independent of the rest, as well as of the author, as if they were living persons, not fictions of the mind. The poet may be said, for the time, to identify himself with the character he wishes to represent, and to pass from one to another, like the same soul successively animating different bodies." In fact, Shakespeare's plays are properly expressions of the passions, not descriptions of them. His characters are real beings of flesh and blood. They speak like men, and not like the mouthpieces of the author.

When Shakespeare conceived a character, whether real or

imaginary, he not only entered into all its thoughts and feelings, but seemed instantly, as if by touching a secret spring, to be surrounded with all the same objects, the same local, outward and unforeseen accidents which would occur in reality. In this he seems to be different from his contemporaries. Comparing Shakespeare's characters with those of Marlowe and Ben Jonson, M.M. Reese has observed: "Shakespeare was not interested in the man in whom the balance was entirely overthrown. Jonson was the chief among the dramatists who liked to examine the character who pursues a course of rational calculation, the man whose defects do not spring from an excess of passion but from an excess of reason. Iago was such a man. In them the will is strong, and it allows them to subdue the passions which might distract them from their chosen purpose; but the reason is warped, and the goal—usually acquisition of some kind or other—becomes so insistently important that all impulses are killed which do not lead to it." Marlowe created some high-aspiring creatures of passion, in whom reason was inadequate either to restrain the upward drive of will or to teach them what to do with their conquests when they had achieved them. Shakespeare regarded these ungoverned passions as calamitous. Nature always seeks a balance, and the admirable man is he in whom blood and judgment are finely commingled; not the calculating, passionless man, nor he whose obsessive desires betray him to unkindness, but the man who is open and free, temperate, brave and loving. Such men are rare, and the best of them may fall to their ruin if they are perplexed in the extreme. The pathos of Shakespeare's tragedy does not come from the downfall of wicked men whose fate is seldom interesting, but from the suffering of man betrayed to evil by that in them which is potentially noble. Othello is such a character. He is noble, magnanimous and believing, unaware of the wickedness of the world and is forcibly drawn to his ruin by a powerful evil personified in Iago.

In presenting his characters Shakespeare is highly tolerant. He does not take sides and pronounces no judgment. In the quality of tolerance he excels all other authors. He never winks at anything. But as he understands everything, so, without exactly pardoning it, he invariably adopts a strictly impartial attitude towards everything and everybody. He is never hard on any of his characters—not merely in the case of Lady Macbeth and Cleopatra, where there is no difficulty, but in those of Iago and Edmund, of Richard and of John, where there is. The difficulty does not exist for him. And yet he has no sneaking kindness for the bad and evil character. The devil Iago has his due at the end.

Different critics have tried to interpret the characters of Shakespeare in their own way, but the interpretations are not determined solely by the genius of or the authority of particular interpreters; they reflect the general intellectual tendencies of the time. From Coleridge to Dowden this interpretation was dominated by the intellectual bias which found meaning and significance everywhere and, in particular, discovered in the speech, demeanour and fortune of every Shakespeare's character, the working out of a single and coherent dramatic intention. Bradley has also, to a great extent, followed the same method. But in 1900 a pronounced reaction against this type of interpretation became apparent. Bergson gave up intelligence as the master faculty in man in favour of the instinctive intuition. The prevailing psychology from James and Wundt and McDougall, was preoccupied with those aspects of the mind, which depend most closely upon the sense-stimuli, upon the half-unconscious and involuntary activities of instinct and habit. Modern psychology, by its disclosure of the phenomena of dual and multiple personality, has eased the path of those who find real inconsistency in any part of Shakespeare's characters. On the other hand, the modern realist of the more mechanical type lays hand upon every appearance of inconsistency in the character as a sign of incongruity or incoherence in the art. Professor E.E. Stoll and Schucking are the leaders of such type of critics. "What is to be made of this heap of contradictions!" exclaims Professor Stoll after a summary of the demeanour of Othello.

But it is impossible to interpret Shakespeare's characters by any definite method, because they are the product of the poetic exploration of the hidden springs of human conduct. Shakespeare is particularly happy in drawing female characters. His women act not on thought, but on instinct which, once it is accepted, admits of no argument. Desdemona's acceptance of Othello as her husband and her pleading for Cassio are purely instinctive. Desdemona, Ophelia and Cordelia do not belong to a type. Each is, in a sense, born of the situation, and inspired by it. The loyal wife, the deserted maiden, the daughter who becomes her father's protector—none of them has a thought or a feeling that forgets the situation and her own part in it, so that all of them win the love of the reader by their very simplicity and intensity. On the theatre, as in life, character is made by opportunity, and welded to endurance by the blows of Fate. The most beautiful characters of Shakespeare depend for their beauty on their impulsive response to the need of the moment. Through the whole of the dialogue appropriated to Desdemona there is not one general observation. Words are with her the vehicle of sentiment, and never of reflection. It may well be doubted whether Shakespeare was fully conscious of this. He worked from the heart downwards and his instinct fastened on to the right words. The comparative simplicity of character which distinguishes Shakespeare's women from his men is maintained throughout his plays. Love and service are as natural to them as breathing. They are the sunlight of the plays, obscured at times by clouds and storms of melancholy and misdoing, but never subdued or defeated. In the tragedies they are the only warrant and token of ultimate salvation, the last refuge and sanctuary of faith. And although this is true of the female protagonists in his plays, his other female characters also leave a distinct stamp of their individuality as we find in Emilia and Bianca.

13

Character—Sketches

MAJOR CHARACTERS

Othello

Othello is essentially a soldier. Since he was seven years of age, he had been a soldier. This was his occupation before he married Desdemona and it continues to be his passion even after his marriage. On the very day of his marriage he receives the Senate's commission that he should proceed at once to Cyprus to be in command of the army that would fight against the Turks. Without a moment's hesitation and with no sense of regret for his leaving his newly married wife, he rushes to his charge. Yet we see that he most eloquently defends his wooing of Desdemona before the senate. He may not be elegant and accomplished like a courtier. He is at best a soldier and he speaks in the rugged and manly accents of a soldier. His greatness as a soldier is not only acknowledged by the senate, but also by his enemy, Iago. The Duke pays him a glowing tribute. Though Othello may be an alien and stranger, yet the safety of the Venetian republic lies on his shoulder. Again, it is by relating to Desdemona his heroic deeds and adventures in the battlefield that he captured her imagination. Desdemona was drawn to Othello not by the usual charms of youth or beauty that attracts a maiden's heart. She found in him the hero of her dreams—a valiant warrior.

Othello must not be conceived as a Negro, but as a high and chivalrous Moorish chief. He tells Iago: "I fetch my life and being / From men of royal siege." In consonance with his royal birth he is characterized by a lofty dignity and self-possession. By mere words he stops the fight between his followers and those of Brabantio: "Keep up your bright swords, for the dew will rust 'em;/Good signior, you shall more command with years/Than with your weapons." Lodovico also recalls his self-possession, when, wrought by jealousy, Othello has totally lost it, violent passion usurping its place:

> Is this the noble Moor, whom our full senate
> Call all in all sufficient? This the noble nature,
> Whom passion could not shake? whose solid virtue
> The shot of accident, nor dart of chance,
> Could neither graze, nor pierce?
>
> (IV.1.260-64)

Othello is totally ignorant of the ways of the world and so may easily be worked upon by a villain. He completely trusts everyone, including the wicked Iago whom he believes to be absolutely honest. It is his great misfortune that a villain in human form like Iago should enter into his life. Merely out of his own devilish nature Iago resolves to deceive Othello by the stupendous lie that his wife Desdemona is on adulteress. Iago stirs up in Othello a deep jealousy and fiery wrath against Desdemona and her alleged lover Cassio. Othello has never learnt to probe into human motives or to seek for the inner truth beneath the outer appearances. Iago takes full advantage of this ignorance of Othello who becomes a passive tool in Iago's hand and kills his innocent wife without pausing for a moment to test the truth of what Iago said.

Othello makes on us the impression that he is a great man with a noble soul, thrust by Fate into the clutches of a demi-devil and succumbing to his machinations because of the excess of his noble virtues. Iago works successfully on Othello not because he was a credulous fool, or a person over-jealous by temperament, but because he was an idealist, great and noble in his mind and spirit, but a misfit in the world of a scheming villainy. Othello's tragedy is, therefore, the result of an interaction of his own character and the circumstance in which he is placed.

Othello describes himself as "one not easily jealous, but being wrought,/Perplex'd in the extreme; (V.2.346-47)." This self-estimate has an essential truth in it. There are two classes of critics, who are inclined to view that Othello was easily jealous. Of them some look upon Othello as a noble barbarian who has become a Christian. They think that beneath the surface Othello retains the savage passions of his Moorish blood and suspiciousness regarding female chastity common among oriental peoples. Others are misled by the preconceived notion that *Othello* is a tragedy of jealousy and hence they hold that jealousy must be the fatal flaw in Othello's character.

Such views about Othello's character are based on the wrong understanding of the play. Granville-Barker, in his *Prefaces to Shakespeare*, has observed: "Of vanity, envy, self-seeking and distrust, which are the seeds of jealousy in general, Othello, it is insisted from the beginning, is notably free, so free that he will not readily remark them in others—in Iago, for instance, in whom they so richly abound." A few striking facts in his social and private life will show his unsuspecting nature. Desdemona herself says (III.3.) that Othello, while wooing her, often employed Cassio as a go-between. No lover jealous by temperament would even seek the services of such an intermediary. At the Council Chamber Desdemona seeks the Duke's permission to follow her husband to Cyprus. Othello adds his request to the Duke to grant her prayer. He states as his reason that he wants her "to be free and bounteous to her mind." No jealous husband is so generously liberal to his wife's wishes. Othello entrusts Iago the responsible task of conveying Desdemona to Cyprus. A newly married husband of a jealous disposition is never likely to act in this trustful manner. Social virtues of a young and beautiful wife generally provoke suspicion in the mind of a fairly aged and jealous husband. But Othello appreciates and extols them. He tells Iago when the latter indirectly tries to make him jealous:

'tis not to make me jealous,
To say my wife is fair, feeds well, loves company,

Is free of speech, sings, plays, and dances well;
Where virtue is, these are more virtuous:
(III.3.187-90)

Iago's insight into human nature is remarkable. He is bent on undoing Othello and is not expected to praise the Moor extravagantly. His soliloquies that express his inmost feelings refer to the "free and open nature" (I.3.397) and "constant, noble, loving nature" (II.1.284) of the Moor. These virtues mentioned by this shrewd observer of human nature are quite incompatible with jealousy. Even Desdemona, in reply to Emilia's query, "Is he not jealous?" says, "Who, he? I think the sun where he was born/Drew all such humours from him" (III.4.25-27). Thus jealousy is not the leading feature of Othello's character, but it is forced upon him by the almost superhuman art of Iago. Othello's character is of a noble and loving type and Iago knows that to destroy Othello's love is an immensely formidable task. Iago therefore begins to practise upon his unsuspecting friendship at first by broken hints and dark insinuations.

In the third scene of the Third Act Othello, accompanied by Iago, comes upon Desdemona just as Cassio is leaving her. As if to himself Iago utters: "Ha, I like not that." At once Othello supposes that the dismissed lieutenant has made improper advances to her. Then comes from Desdemona an inopportune pleading for Cassio's reinstatement and her persistency deepens the mist in Othello's mind—the mist of suspicion that has already been raised by Iago. As soon as Desdemona parts from Othello and as he watches her withdraw, his passion of love asserts itself. In his ecstasy of love for her he says: "Excellent wretch, perdition catch my soul,/But I do love thee, and when I love thee not,/Chaos is come again." (III.3.91-93) This is meant to imply that though he begins to be disturbed about Cassio, he does not entertain any doubt about Desdemona's fidelity.

Just at this point Iago again insinuates with the subtle question: "Did Michael Cassio, when you woo'd my lady, / Know of your love?" (III.3.95-96). The question stealthily creates the impression that there is some darker mystery behind, some monster in his thought too hideous to be shown. Then he proceeds to set the scheme of mischief at work. He now manages to be heard, and still to seem overheard. Thus he may not be held responsible for his words. And there is a dark frightful significance in his manner, which puts the hearer in an agony of curiosity. The more Iago refuses to tell his thoughts, the more he sharpens the desire of knowing them. When questioned, he so states his reasons for not speaking, as, in effect, to compel the Moor to extort the secret from him. Thus, he kindles Othello's intensest craving to know what the horrible truth is. Then Iago directly warns the Moor to guard against the torments of a jealous husband: "O, beware jealousy; /It is the green-ey'd monster, which doth mock/That meat it feeds on" (III.3.170-71). Then he subtly uses the word 'cuckold' to hint obliquely that the alternatives before Othello may not be between his wife's guilt and innocence, but between his knowledge and the mere suspicion of it.

As yet Othello does not see the plain drift of Iago's remark, but understands that Iago believes Desdemona to be faithless. So, he protests:

No, Iago,
I'll see before I doubt, when I doubt, prove,
And on the proof, there is no more but this:
Away at once with love or jealousy!
(III.3.193-96)

Feeling that Othello is on the verge of believing, Iago proceeds to pour into Othello's mind the confirming circumstances. He asks Othello to look to his wife and "observe her well with Cassio." Then he points out that Desdemona is a Venetian lady and, "In Venice they do let God see the pranks/ They dare not show their husbands:" (III.3.206-7). But, though a Venetian lady Desdemona may not be guilty of deceitfulness. So, Iago insinuates that she is an adept in the art of dissimulation citing the instance that she has deceived her own father to marry Othello. As Othello listens to him in horror, "for a moment at least the past is revealed to him in a new and dreadful light and the ground seems to sink under his feet" (A.C. Bradley). In his confusion Othello says, "I do not think but Desdemona's honest" (III.3.229). To this Iago sneeringly replies, "Long live she so, and long live you to think so!" This is followed by a tentative but a hideous and humiliating suggestion that there was something unnatural in the love which Desdemona has given to a black alien after refusing the "many proposed matches,/Of her own clime, complexion, and degree" (III.3.233-34). Othello's confidence at this point is shaken. He dismisses Iago saying: "if more/Thou dost perceive, let me know more" (III.3.242-43).

Iago's work is now almost complete, but he has to make another artful suggestion. Upto the dismissal of Iago, according to Bradley, Othello does not show any sign of jealousy. His confidence is shaken; he is confused and deeply troubled, but he is not jealous in the proper sense of the word. In his soliloquy beginning with, "This fellow's of exceeding honesty" (III.3.262), the rousing of this passion may be traced. In this soliloquy the thought of another man's possessing the woman he loves is intolerable to him, and the impulse of revenge takes hold of his mind, but still the feeling of love has got a mastery of it. He declares: "If she be false, O, then heaven mocks itself, /I'll not believe it" (III.3. 282-83).

When Othello meets Iago again, he is on the rack. His torment has driven into a fiercer mood—now abusing Iago for opening his eyes, now furiously demanding ocular proof. Iago urges that strong presumptive circumstances should give Othello satisfaction. He first relates the tale of Cassio's dream. Next he proceeds to adduce another piece of evidence. He has seen Cassio wipe his beard with that handkerchief which Othello admits to have given Desdemona as his first gift. These are enough to raise the full passion of revenge in Othello. Othello's purpose is at once fixed. He makes up his mind to tear Desdemona to pieces and orders Cassio's death and appoints Iago his lieutenant. Othello thus bids farewell to love and welcomes in place of love, revenge, jealousy and hate, When Iago hints that he may change his purpose, Othello vows the eternity of his hate in language of a superb and terrible beauty:

Never, Iago. Like to the Pontic sea,
Whose icy current, and compulsive course,
Ne'er feels retiring ebb, but keeps due on
To the Propontic, and the Hellespont:
Even so my bloody thoughts, with violent pace
Shall ne'er look back, ne'er ebb to humble love,
Till that a capable and wide revenge
Swallow them up.

(III.3.460-67)

Commenting on Othello's conduct in murdering Desdemona, Stopford A. Brooke says, "It is jealousy that slays, jealousy which has conquered the infinite sorrow, love, and pity which has filled his soul before the deed." Frank Harris, too, is of the opinion that *Othello* "is a far finer and more complete study of jealousy and revenge than *Hamlet*" and that "Othello's jealousy of Desdemona is inevitable." These critics maintain that the passion of jealousy is rooted in Othello, and his very nature is prepared to receive the insinuations of Iago. Even when they admit that Othello is not of jealous temper, they think that he is "easily jealous."

But, a study of the text does not, however, confirm Othello's aptitude for such a passion. Coleridge is very bold and clear in the Moor's defence. "Othello", says he, "does not kill Desdemona in jealousy, but in conviction forced upon him by the superhuman art of Iago." He notes that when Othello enters Desdemona's bedchamber with the words, "It is the cause, it is the cause, my soul," the struggle in him is not between love and jealousy, but between love and honour. He is no longer the husband maddened at betrayal, but the vindicator of justice, weeping with a heavenly sorrow, and slaying what he loves. The deed he is going to perform is no murder, but a sacrifice. But the force of honour in him is not derived from any code of gentle or military obligation. It is the persuasion of a great, passionate nature that falseness, though so lovely that the sense aches at it, must be blotted out. So, when Desdemona meets his direct charge with words which can only reconvince him of her guilt, his feelings of disinterested judgment and patience give way to righteous indignation. And when Othello expresses such indignation as to speak to Desdemona, "O strumpet,...weepest thou for him to my face? (V.2.78)," we are inclined to feel that a feeling of personal animus again gets possession of Othello's mind, and when he stifles her with the words, "'Tis too late," we understand that he has only acted as the husband of a guilty wife was bound to act.

Thus, Othello kills Desdemona because his abstract sense of righteousness, purity and loyalty is outraged and because he cannot bear to think that, that which could destroy those qualities which he has worshipped, should exist for a moment longer than he can help upon the earth, although he conceives the task as the solemn act of disinterested justice and not as the ignoble vengeance of a jealous man. This is not to say, of course, that Othello does not feel some natural jealousy of a husband of a guilty wife. He would not be a man if he did not. But it is not the feeling uppermost in his mind when he goes about her death calmly and religiously. The remarks of Dr Brandes on this point are illuminating. He says: "This is not a representation of spontaneous but artificially induced jealousy; in other words, of credulity poisoned by malignity. Hence the moral which Shakespeare, through the mouth of Iago, bids the audience take home with them, 'thus credulous fools are caught,/And many worthy and chaste dames, even thus/All guiltless, meet reproach' (IV.1.45-47). It is not Othello's jealousy, but his credulity that is the prime cause of the disaster; and even so must Desdemona's noble simplicity bear its share in the blame."

In his last speech Othello says, "then must you speak/Of one that lov'd not wisely, but too well:" (V.2.344-45) Indeed, Othello loved Desdemona too well. He loved her absolutely. His love of Desdemona was warm and sincere. He gave up his nomadic habits, which had been so very dear to him, by marrying this lady. He gave vent to his real feelings for Desdemona when he tells Iago:

> But that I love the gentle Desdemona,
> I would not my unhoused free condition

Put into circumscription and confine
For the sea's worth.

(I.2.25-28)

And the reason of this heart-felt love Othello himself assigns to the fact that Desdemona pitied the dangers through which he had passed in his chequered life of a soldier. This apparition of exquisite womanhood enchanted him the more because its loveliness had the rarity and strangeness of romance. Her beauty ravished him with a poignancy which no mere acuteness of the senses could produce. There is a ring of unmistakable sincerity in his address to his wife on the sea-port of Cyprus:

O my soul's joy,
If after every tempest come such calmness,
May the winds blow, till they have waken'd death,
And let the labouring bark climb hills of seas,
Olympus-high, and duck again as low
As hell's from heaven. If it were now to die,
'Twere now to be most happy, for I fear
My soul hath her content so absolute,
That not another comfort, like to this
Succeeds in unknown fate.

(II.1.184-93)

In this rapturous meeting as well as many other passages of the drama Othello expresses the spiritual exaltation of love with an intensity nowhere surpassed in literature. Indeed, his extreme fondness of Desdemona permeates his whole being. Iago fully realizes the intensity of Othello's love for Desdemona. Hence he makes the malignant observation: "O, you are well tun'd now,/But I'll set down the pegs that make this music." (II.1.199-200) When he has thrown out his base insinuation and Othello's mind is slightly perturbed, Othello cries within himself: "Excellent wretch, perdition catch my soul,/But I do love thee, and when I love thee not,/Chaos is come again." (III.3.91-93) Othello does not readily believe Iago. It is because he loves Desdemona dearly. So, he cries out: "If she be false, O, then heaven mocks itself,/I'll not believe it." (III.3.282-83) Othello loves Desdemona with such vehement intensity that when he has what he believes to be the ocular proof of

Desdemona's infidelity, he feels he cannot outlive the love of his beloved:

> But there, where I have garner'd up my heart,
> Where either I must live, or bear no life,
> The fountain, from the which my current runs,
> Or else dries up, to be discarded thence,
> (IV.2.58-61)

Even in the bedchamber scene where Othello has made up his mind to slay Desdemona—not indeed as a husband maddened at betrayal, but as a vindicator of justice—his deep love does still stir his heart, and he weeps with a heavenly sorrow because justice compels him to slay the object of his love. He says: "I must weep,/But they are cruel tears; this sorrow's heavenly,/It strikes when it does love:" (V.2.20-22). He kisses her over and over again and at one moment is afraid that his passionate love of Desdemona may "almost persuade/Justice herself to break her sword:" (V.2.16-17). We thus see that Othello is perfectly right in affirming in his self-analysis that he "lov'd not wisely, but too well:"

With regard to the other point in his self-analysis that he loved not wisely, it may be said that this is also true, at least to some extent. In the first place his lack of wisdom lay in his choice of a wife. Being a foreign adventurer and a Moor and a man of middle age, he should not have chosen as his wife the beautiful daughter of a great Venetian Magnifico, who is only in her prime. A critic commented on this match: "We see before us a perfect womanhood in the most graceful shape, and perfect manhood in a form most repulsive; and it is as if day and night came together; the two cannot unite!" (Bodenstedt). And Othello himself feels this when Iago has contrived to inject suspicion into his mind:

> Haply, for I am black,
> And have not those soft parts of conversation
> That chamberers have, or for I am declin'd
> Into the vale of years,—yet that's not much—
> She's gone, I am abus'd,
> (III.3.267-71)

Othello feels in contrast with her, his colour and his race, and his soul is forced to feel this by the accusation of Brabantio that he must have practised by drugs on Desdemona, otherwise she could not have loved him.

Again, Othello's unwisdom lay in the fact of his having placed implicit trust in a young man of twenty-eight (Iago) whom, in spite of interest made for him, he has superseded by appointing Cassio his lieutenant. At the first insinuation of Iago against the loyalty of his wife, Othello should have suspected him of malice. Before suspecting the person he so dearly loved, he should have made searching inquiries personally. In the matter of the lost handkerchief he should have questioned Emilia. He ought to have questioned Cassio and Desdemona herself in a matter which touched his vital point. Instead of doing all this he let himself be foolishly entrapped in the toils of a villain and victimized by a miscreant. Iago's suggestion that Desdemona is false, comes upon Othello as a thunderbolt. Othello knows and believes Iago to be honest and he believes every word of Iago as absolute truth. So, he is stunned and his mind accepts the specious reasonings of Iago passively and without examination.

So much then for Othello's apparent unwisdom in being too easily convinced of Desdemona's guilt. It must, however, be borne in mind that the diabolical intrigue of Iago was planned with such consummate skill that it is very doubtful whether an honest and righteous husband, far less obtuse than Othello would not have been similarly led to suspect the chastity of his beloved wife. The truth is, as the editor of the Warwick edition of the drama has it, that Othello's love has all the traits of a deep and noble passion save one—insight into the soul of the woman he loves. What Othello is blind to, or only insecurely sees, is not her faults, but her childlike purity of nature. Had he seen it and realized it, he could not have been persuaded that it was not there. In this he was unwise and it is this that led to the tragic consequences.

Othello is the protagonist of the play. The conception of the tragic protagonist in Shakespeare is a mixture of the concept in a Greek drama and that of Shakespeare's own. The

Greek concept of a tragic hero is of a great and noble character suffering disaster for no fault of his own but from 'a blast of the envy of God.' This divine punishment of the Greek tragedy has been replaced by Shakespeare with an ever present sense of destiny. But, at the same time the tragic catastrophe in a Shakespearian tragedy is also due to a flaw in the character. The hero, at some early stage, has the choice and must take a decision. Othello has the choice of trusting his wife or listening to the villainous tempter. A broad-minded or discerning man would never have listened to the breath of slander, but Othello's mind is, in that sphere, like that of an untutored tribesman. He rushes wildly on a wrong course of action. It is the special characteristic of Shakespeare's tragic heroes that each is lacking in the particular quality or gift which is required to deal with the special problem he has to face.

Othello is a direct and soldierly character, to some extent, a one-track man, for he has lived and acted in the atmosphere of arms. He is a child of nature, a man of primitive race, guided by the impulse of the heart rather than by reason. He is of a passionate and rather jealous nature, although he thinks that he is not, and soon he is thirsting for vengeance against his wife on grounds that would never have been accepted as evidence by a sensible mind.

Othello fulfils the conditions and requirements of a tragic hero. He is a person of high degree and no mere private person. He is the General of the Republic of Venice and he is always conscious of his high position. Even just before the moment he lays violent hands on himself, he shows anxiety not to be misjudged by the great world. The actions and sufferings of Othello are of an unusual kind and lead to exceptional calamity and culminate in his death. His nature is also exceptional and it raises him above the average level of humanity. He has in him a great tragic trait. It lies in placing implicit faith in Iago whom he firmly believes to be honest, and this error brings about his ruin. In his latest hour Othello exhibits, as a tragic hero should, all the grandeur and all the nobility and sweetness of his nature, and leaves behind a triumphant scorn for the fetters of the flesh and the littleness of all the lives that must survive him.

The tragedy of Othello lies in this—that his whole nature was indisposed to jealousy, and it was such that he was unusually open to deception, and, if once, wrought to passion, he is likely to act with little reflection, with no delay, and in the most decisive manner conceivable. This is because of his soldierly nature. The sources of danger in this character are revealed but too clearly by the story itself. First, Othello's mind, for all its poetry, is very simple. He is not observant. His nature tends outward. He is quite free from introspection and is not given to reflection. Emotion excites his imagination, but it confuses and dulls his intellect. On this side he is the very opposite of Hamlet. He has also little experience of the corrupt products of civilized life and is ignorant of European women. Secondly, for all his dignity and massive calm, he is by nature full of the most vehement passion. Finally, Othello's nature is all of one piece. His trust, where he trusts, is absolute. Hesitation is almost impossible to him. He is extremely self-reliant and decides and acts instantaneously. If stirred to indignation, as "in Aleppo once," he answers with one lightning stroke. Love, if he loves, must be to him heaven where either he must live or bear no life. If such a passion as jealousy seizes him, it will swell into a well-nigh uncontrollable flood. He will press for immediate conviction or immediate relief. Convinced, he will act with the authority of a judge and the swiftness of a man in mortal pain. Undeceived, he will do like execution on himself.

The character of Othello is so noble, his feelings and actions follow so inevitably from it and from the forces brought to bear on it, and his sufferings are so heart-rending that he stirs a passion of mingled love and pity in the hearts of most readers. Othello puts his entire confidence in the honesty of Iago who has not only been his companion in arms, but, as he believes, has just proved his faithfulness in the matter of the marriage. The confidence is misplaced, but it is no sign of stupidity in Othello. For, his opinion of Iago is the opinion of practically everyone who knows him and that opinion is that

Iago is, before all things, 'honest'. Besides, he does not know Desdemona for long. Hence, Iago's subtle insinuations have a tremendous effect on his mind. His confidence is shaken. He is confused and deeply troubled. He feels even horror. But he is not jealous in the proper sense of the word. No doubt, the thought of another man's possessing the woman he loves is intolerable to him. No doubt, the sense of insult and the impulse of revenge are at times most violent. And these may be, in a sense, the feelings of jealousy proper. Yet these are not the chief or the deepest source of Othello's suffering. It is the wreck of his faith and his love. He is 'on the rack,' in an agony so unbearable that he cannot endure the sight of Iago. Anticipating the probability that Iago has spared him the whole truth, he feels that in that case his life is over and his "occupation gone" with all its glories. But he has not abandoned hope. The bare possibility that his friend is deliberately deceiving him—though such a deception would be a thing so monstrously wicked that he can hardly conceive it credible—is a kind of hope. He furiously demands proof, ocular proof. He forces it from the unwilling witness, and hears the maddening tale of Cassio's dream. It is enough. And if it were not enough, has not Iago seen a handkerchief spotted with strawberries with which Cassio has wiped his beard? The madness of revenge is in the blood of Othello and hesitation is a thing he has never known. He passes judgment and controls himself only to make his sentence a solemn vow.

Towards the close of the 'temptation scene' Othello becomes terrible, but his grandeur remains almost undiminished. Even in the following scene (III.4.) where he goes to test Desdemona in the matter of the handkerchief, and receives a fatal confirmation of her guilt, our sympathy with him is hardly touched by any feeling of humiliation. Iago deals Othello blow on blow and never allows him to recover from the confusion of the first shock. Othello is physically exhausted. His mind is dazed. He sees everything blurred through a mist of blood and tears. He has actually forgotten the incident of the handkerchief and has to be reminded of it. When Iago perceives that he can now risk almost any lie, he tells Othello that Cassio has confessed his guilt. Othello now trembles all over. He mutters disjointed words. A blackness suddenly intervenes between his eyes and the world. When he recovers, it is to watch Cassio, as he imagines, laughing over his shame. The sight only adds to the confusion of intellect. The madness of rage, and a ravenous thirst for revenge conquer him. The delay till nightfall is torture to him. His self-control has wholly deserted him, and he strikes his wife in the presence of the Venetian envoy, Lodovico. He is so lost to all sense of reality, that he never asks himself what will follow the deaths of Cassio and his wife. But before the end there is again a change. The supposed death of Cassio satiates the thirst for vengeance. The Othello who enters the bedchamber with the words, "It is the cause, it is the cause, my soul," is not the man of the Fourth Act bubbling for revenge. The deed he is now bound to do is no murder, but a sacrifice. He is to save Desdemona from herself, not in hate, but in honour, and also in love. His anger has passed, a boundless sorrow has taken its place. And this sorrow is heavenly. Terribly painful as the scene of murder is, there is almost nothing there to diminish the admiration and love which heighten pity for the hero. And, as Bradley observes, pity itself vanishes, and love and admiration alone remain, in the majestic dignity and sovereign ascendancy of the close. Chaos has come and gone and the Othello of the Council Chamber and the quay of Cyprus has returned, a greater and nobler Othello still. As he speaks at the end of the glory and the agony of his life, we find before us a man with a triumphant scorn for the fetters of the flesh and the littleness of all the lives that must survive him and when he dies upon a kiss, the most painful of all tragedies leaves us for the moment free from pain, exulting in the power of love and man's unconquerable mind. Indeed, Othello leaves at the end the impression of a mighty tragic hero.

Iago

Iago is a born villain. He has been endowed by Nature with a restless malignity that is constantly impelled to injure and destroy all that is good and beautiful. A noble soul like Othello, a charming and spotless young lady like Desdemona, a good and innocent man like Cassio are all a provocation to Iago's own vicious and ugly mind. He alone is the root of all the mischiefs and mischances in the play. The only motive that urges him to work wholesale havoc is his perverse and malicious glee at the sufferings of others. He is also prompted by an intellectual pride in his superior cleverness in outwitting others, especially those whom fortune has placed above him in rank and position. A character like this that waits for no provocation from without and is goaded on by his own wicked impulse to cause grave and fatal troubles to all is a terrible danger to the community to which he belongs. A single person like him is enough to create an all-round confusion and ruin. Iago is such an instrument of tragedy in *Othello*.

The wickedness of Iago is rooted in his nature. Evil is ingrained in him and must always seek to destroy good. Although he is only twenty-eight years of age, he is a perfect cynic. He hates Cassio, despises Othello and holds women in contempt. He is unable to recognize or believe in goodness in human nature. 'Virtue,' to him, is a 'fig' and, 'love,' 'a lust of the blood, and a permission of the will', while 'reputation,' 'an idle and most false imposition', whose loss is a trifle compared with a bodily wound. He believes all men to be vicious and all women to be wanton. Evil in him is free from scruple and is never disturbed by any 'compunctious visitings of nature'. Down to the last the evil in him remains intact. We find no repentance in him even after the terrible tragedies wrought by himself. He maintains a devilish consistency in his villainy from the beginning to the end. He is an incarnation of evil, as it were.

Iago is not merely a born villain but is also an artist in villainy. He not merely practises villainy but loves to practise it. He takes a keen intellectual pleasure in outwitting others. His half-truths, insinuations, poses and postures are cleverly designed and indicate a great skill in playing on people's feelings. He seems to be actuated by a desire to assert his power over his fellow creatures. No ordinary human motive explains Iago's crimes. When Othello appeals to Cassio: "Will you, I pray, demand that demi-devil / Why he hath thus ensnar'd my soul and body? (V.2.302-3), Iago refuses to answer and says: "Demand me nothing, what you know, you know,/From this time forth I never will speak word." (V.2.304-5) Dr Bradley remarks that Iago does not answer because he could not have answered it. It is, therefore, more difficult to come at, more difficult thoroughly to understand the real moving forces that have led Iago to act as he has done.

Iago makes various statements to Roderigo and he has several soliloquies. These tell us something about the secret springs of his action. He gives two reasons for his hatred of Othello. Othello has made Cassio lieutenant ignoring his claim for the post. Besides, he suspects that, "'twixt my sheets/He's (Othello) done my office" (I.3.385-86); with Emilia. Iago also has a mind to ruin Cassio. For, Cassio "has a daily beauty in his life,/That makes me ugly" (V.I.19-20). Iago also suspects Cassio of a criminal intimacy with his wife Emilia, as he says: "I fear Cassio with my night-cap too" (II.1.302.). He, therefore resolves to "Abuse him to the Moor, in the rank garb" (II.1.301). In addition to these he wants Cassio's place.

Dr Bradley is not inclined to accept Iago's account of the causes of action as true. A man moved by simple passions due to simple causes does not stand fingering his feelings, industriously enumerating their sources, and groping about for new ones. But this is what Iago does. And this is not all. These motives appear and disappear in the most extraordinary manner. Resentment at Cassio's appointment is expressed in the first conversation with Roderigo and from that moment is never once mentioned in the whole play. Hatred of Othello is expressed in the First Act alone (I.1.154). Desire to get Cassio's place scarcely appears after the first soliloquy and when it is gratified, Iago does not refer to it by a single word. The suspicion of Cassio's intrigue with Emilia emerges suddenly as an after-thought, not in the first soliloquy, but in the second, and then disappears for ever. Strangely enough that during Othello's sufferings he never shows a sign of the idea that he is now paying his rival in his own coin. His final reason for ill-will to Cassio never appears till the Fifth Act (V.l.19-20.).

Coleridge holds that Iago himself cannot assign any motive to his action. In his soliloquies Iago is only hunting for motives. So, Coleridge is awe-struck at "the motive-hunting of a motiveless malignity." Lytton Strachey also holds the same view and argues that inasmuch as Shakespeare deviated from Cinthio's story wherein to Iago is attributed a motive, namely, he is Disdemona's lover, it was the dramatist's intention to paint the villain by wholly divesting him of any motive for his diabolical action. Coleridge, however, does not use the phrase "motiveless malignity" in the sense of absolute malignity, that is, love of evil for evil's sake. What he really means is that Iago's malignity does not spring from the causes to which Iago himself refers in his speeches. And as every human action must have some actuating motive, Iago's villainous action must have one such motive. Iago, we know, is suffering from a great misfortune, by his vanity being wounded. He shies at the unpalatable thought that Cassio who, in his own estimate, is inferior to him in every respect, is so much in the world's eye and is happier and nobler than he is for the very gifts for which he envies him. And it is Othello who has undervalued him by preferring his rival to him. His thwarted sense of superiority, therefore, wants satisfaction, and this is the strongest force that drives him from inactivity to action. His original intention has been to punish Othello by putting him "into a jealousy so strong,/That judgment cannot cure; (II.1.296-97), to get Cassio cashiered and himself raised to Othello's favour. In this way he wants to wreak his vengeance on those whom he despises and the devilish humour of it will gratify his cruel vanity. With characteristic egotism (Iago-tism?) he has looked for no more tragic conclusion to his scheme than this. But his pawns, Othello, Desdemona, Cassio, Roderigo and Emilia prove other than what he has expected, and taking their games into their own hands, force Iago to play out as tragedy what he has begun as a comedy of self-gratification. So, we may conclude that pride in self, contempt for others, cynicism and delight in irresponsible power are the main motives of Iago's action.

About Iago's motives Herford remarks that Iago is too

profoundly immoral to feel the sting of wounded honour, and too conscious of his power to be gravely concerned about office and rank. Iago is a cynic to the core. He sees humanity from the wrong side. Courtesy to a lady to him is a "prologue to the history of lust and foul thoughts" (II.1.254-55). He tells Desdemona that a deserving woman is but fit "To suckle fools and chronicle small beer" (II.1.160). In reply to Roderigo's reverential remark about Desdemona that "she's full of most blest condition", Iago scornfully says that it is "Blest fig's-end!" (II.1.247-49) or utter nonsense. Iago is nothing if not critical. Spying into abuses is one important concern of his life. A person so cynical in his attitude towards men and things, is not likely to be moved to action by the sting of wounded honour and the disgrace of supersession. Hence the normal human motives are not likely to operate in such a man. Desire of advancement and resentment about the lieutenancy are factors in the cause of his action, but they do not constitute the 'real' factors. The moving forces behind his action are to be found in his character. The salient traits of his character are a keen sense of superiority, a contempt for others, a sensitiveness to everything that wounds his feelings and a general cynical and unreservedly coarse view regarding human relations. Othello is to him only a "credulous fool," Cassio, "an honest knave," Roderigo, a mere snipe and the virtues of Desdemona a "Blest fig's-end." He knows his price, but he is forced by circumstances to be his Moor's ancient. His sense of superiority meets with an affront. His thwarted sense of superiority, therefore, wants retribution. So, he proposes to make up his will "A double knavery" to heighten his sense of power or superiority. This, according to Dr Bradley, seems to be the unconscious motive of many acts of cruelty by Iago.

It is by analysing the soliloquies of Iago that we may have some idea of Iago's mind and nature. Hence a study of Iago's soliloquies is of much interest. It is a device that Shakespeare has used more powerfully in *Othello* perhaps than elsewhere. Iago's soliloquies serve a double purpose. They explain and analyse Iago's motives and throw light on his character. They also distinctly advance the action of the play. The most important function, however, of these soliloquies, is that they are a sort of running commentary on the action of the play, almost like the chorus in an ancient Greek tragedy. Much would have remained obscure and unintelligible, but for these soliloquies. Iago is a subtle, baffling personality. It is necessary, therefore, that he should take the audience into confidence in his soliloquies, although, however, he makes a mess of himself in trying to dissect and scrutinize his own motives.

There are as many as seven soliloquies given to Iago and each seems to mark an important development in the action of the play. These soliloquies are in I.1.144-159, I.3.381-402, II.1.167-178, 281-307, II.3.327-353, III.3.326-338 and V.1.11-22. In his first soliloquy he examines his feelings towards Othello. "I do hate him, as I do hell's pains," says he and feels that it will not be discreet to break with Othello openly. It is the first hint of his enmity towards Othello—enmity working underground. This soliloquy helps us receive at the very outset a strong impression of the force which is to prove fatal to the hero's happiness, so that when we see the hero himself, the shadow of fate already rests upon him.

Iago's second soliloquy is rather a piece of casuistry, or what we may say motive-grinding. When Roderigo has agreed to fill his purse according to Iago's advice and departed, Iago chuckles over the idea of having befooled his friend. In his eyes Roderigo is a downright idiot. So he muses within himself that a man of his intellect cannot afford to waste his time in the company of a fool like Roderigo, unless it were for the sake of fun or for the purpose of exacting money from him. He starts his soliloquy with "Thus do I ever make my fool my purse," and then he proceeds to analyse the grounds of his grudge against Othello. He says that he hates the Moor as he suspects an improper relationship between the Moor and his own wife, Emilia. Iago, however, is not sure of it, but he will act as if the suspicion were a fact. Iago finds that though he hates Othello, Othello holds him in high esteem. So, there is every chance of his plot against the Moor coming out successful. He then thinks of Cassio and plans to use the handsome Cassio as a means of rousing suspicion in Othello's mind in respect of Desdemona. He knows that the Moor is of "a free and open nature," "And will as tenderly be led by the nose.../As asses are." He will execute the "double knavery," a knavery against both Cassio and Othello, drawing his supply of money from the stupid Roderigo. His plot is hatched. Some time he will tell Othello that Cassio is too familiar with Desdemona. Cassio's looks and deportment will easily arouse Othello's suspicion and as Othello is frank and generous and has known Iago as an honest man, although it is a mask of honesty that he wears, Othello will allow himself to be led by the nose as asses are. Iago muses that he has got the outline of the plan in his mind and he has only to put this monstrous piece of villainy into execution by stealthy means. Immediately before this soliloquy comes an utterance of Iago, which may be treated as a soliloquy, although it is made in the presence of Roderigo. He there says that virtue is a meaningless thing. "Virtue? a fig! 'tis in ourselves, that we are thus, or thus: our bodies are gardens, to the which our wills are gardeners." According to Iago there is no such thing as virtue or man's natural mental disposition. It entirely rests with man as to what should be grown or weeded out of this garden (the body). Love is nothing but lust and it is lust of the blood that can be controlled by the will. This utterance of Iago reveals the sordidness of his mind and his low conception of love as a mere physical craving, in striking contrast to Othello's notion of love as a holy spiritual bond.

The next soliloquy of Iago attempts to analyse the motives that lead him to his course of action. He says in it that he believes that Cassio loves Desdemona and it is likely and believable, although he is not sure that Desdemona loves Cassio. Iago hates Othello, yet he admits that Othello is constant and magnanimous and will make an affectionate husband. It occurs to Iago that he himself loves Desdemona. But his love is not prompted by lust alone. Othello has debauched Emilia and Iago would therefore debauch Desdemona in retaliation. In case he does not succeed, he must excite in Othello's mind an unquenchable fire of jealousy. To enable him to do this, it is essentially necessary that his dupe Roderigo should carry out his instruction to the very letters. If

Roderigo proves reliable, Iago will be able to bring about Cassio's downfall, and he will pour into Othello's ears the fullest calumny against Cassio. At this stage Iago remembers that Cassio also has been in illicit love with Emilia. Iago's plot, therefore, will be so artfully laid that not Cassio alone will be ruined thereby, but also Othello himself. For, the slanders about Cassio will make Othello suffer unutterable pain, and he will at the same time be thankful to Iago for warning him. The details of the hellish scheme have not been clearly worked out in his brain. But Iago trusts that he will be able to hit upon suitable plans as the action progresses. A little before this soliloquy Iago speaks in an aside, which can be taken as a soliloquy, and it is Iago's running commentary on the little side show that is enacted between Cassio and Desdemona. To the wicked eyes of Iago their innocent courtesy is illicit love-making. Cassio may go on smiling in company of Desdemona, but Iago will fetter him in this act of courtesy. The plot is taking shape in Iago's brain. Coleridge calls attention, in this speech, to the importance given to trifles and made fertile by the villainy of the observer. With Shakespeare soliloquy generally gives information regarding the secret springs as well as the outward course of the plot, and, moreover, it is a curious point of technique with him that the soliloquies of his villains sometimes read almost like explanations offered to the audience. In the present soliloquy Iago appears to be inventing reasons for the malicious action he is about to take against Cassio and Othello. He seems to seek justification for himself. This may make us ponder that perhaps he is not totally devoid of moral sense. This soliloquy reveals the horrible and appalling nature of Iago's character, namely, a pride of intellect or lust of the brain, which exults above all things in being able to make himself and others pass for just the reverse of what they are. And this soliloquy is Shakespeare's supreme instance of psychological subtlety and insight. It is Iago's most striking disclosure of his real spring of action. For, it is not that Iago really believes or suggests that either Cassio or Othello has wronged him in the way he intimates; he is merely seeking to appease certain qualms of conscience by a sort of extemporized make-believe in that kind. In this soliloquy there appears to be a clear indication that Iago did not foresee at the outset the tragic consequences of his intrigue. He aimed only at befooling Cassio and Othello.

In his next soliloquy occurring in the middle of the third scene of the Second Act, Iago chuckles at his triumph over Cassio who is now dismissed. Iago has sent Cassio to Desdemona. This marks the second step in his plot involving Desdemona's honour. Iago now gloats over the idea that in view of the frank, honest and reasonable advice he has given to Cassio, nobody can accuse Iago of villainy. Desdemona can be easily induced to give her support to an honest cause and Othello, who is simply infatuated with his wife, cannot withhold consent to any request she makes. The course of action that he has advised Cassio to take will therefore admirably further his own designs. For, when Cassio will request Desdemona to repair his fortune and she will plead strongly for him with Othello, out of her natural tenderness, Iago will persuade the general to believe that his wife wishes to see Cassio recalled in order that she may have her passions gratified by him. The more earnestly Desdemona takes up Cassio's cause, the more suspicious will Othello become. Iago will, thus, make use of Desdemona's virtue to make her appear a shameful thing, and her goodness itself will provide the material of the snare by which Iago will entrap all of them. This soliloquy is a rhapsody of self-appreciation, according to Moulton. Iago is exultant over the treacherous advice he has given to Cassio with the exterior air of love and honesty. The inner workings of the arch-villain's mind are nowhere more clearly disclosed than in this soliloquy. Now, for the first time the whole sweep of his plot is revealed to himself as he thinks over the complications to which Desdemona's honest mediation can be made to lead, and he sees that his net will be big enough to enmesh all his victims at once.

The next soliloquy in the middle of the third scene of the Third Act marks the culmination of his plot. Iago has got Desdemona's handkerchief and is going to place it in Cassio's bedchamber. He has already injected the poison of suspicion into Othello's mind and the poison is already working. Now he is going to add the lethal dose to completely destroy his victim. For, he believes that, "trifles light as air/Are to the jealous, confirmations strong/As proofs of holy writ." Then as he finds Othello approach him, he speaks out in total self-satisfaction:

> not poppy, nor mandragora,
> Nor all the drowsy syrups of the world,
> Shall ever medicine thee to that sweet sleep
> Which thou owedst yesterday.

In the final soliloquy at the beginning of the Fifth Act Iago is reflecting on the consequences of the murderous deeds he has caused to be enacted. He has incited Roderigo to murder Cassio. Now he muses that whether Roderigo kills Cassio or Cassio kills him or each is killed by the other, he is the gainer everyway. For, if Roderigo lives he is sure to demand of Iago a return, to a large extent, of the gold and jewels that Iago has cheated out of him on the plea of passing them to Desdemona as Roderigo's gifts to her. So, Roderigo must die. If Cassio lives, he will make Iago look ugly by contrast with the constant beauty and grace of his life, and, besides, the Moor may expose Iago to him and that will put Iago to great danger. So, Cassio also must die. Thus, Iago seems to give some logical explanation for the heinous deeds he is causing to happen. Bradby quotes this passage to show that Iago is better than his creed. Iago's egoism is not absolute. His very irritation at goodness is a sign that his faith in his creed is not entirely firm. In this curiously naïve avowal Iago provides a fresh and startlingly novel explanation of his jealousy of Cassio. Whether he means he is made ugly to others or to himself, he cannot, then, in the one case be said to be an absolute egoist. At the same time it must be confessed that he chooses a curious moment to air his moral sense, and to kill Cassio on account of the irritation aroused by his superior virtue seems to make Iago a more complete, though more perverted, villain still. Indeed, such a motive seems worthier of a religious maniac than of Iago, even if it could be shown to have any force or grounding in the play itself. It is safer, perhaps, not to press such utterances as this too strongly, or to take every word of a soliloquy as being strictly in character. Iago's soliloquies on different occasions show clearly an uneasy conscience and an unconscious desire to persuade himself that he has some excuse for the villainy he contemplates. His momentary doubt towards the end whether Roderigo and Cassio must be killed, is another symptom of the obscure working of conscience or humanity. He does not show any pleasure in Othello's misery. When Desdemona kneels at his feet and implores his help to regain her husband's affection, his words seem to betoken some embarrassment and he makes haste to end the interview saying, "I pray you, be content, 'tis but his humour, / The business of the state does him offence, ... Go in, and weep not, all things shall be well" (IV.2. 167-68, 173). Thus, Iago is not an absolute infidel. He professes the creed that absolute egoism is the only proper attitude, and that loyalty and affection are mere stupidity or want of spirit. He tries to live up to this creed he professes, but does not succeed. His very irritation at goodness is a sign that his faith in his creed is not entirely firm. And if he does not really possess any moral sense, we should never have heard those soliloquies which so clearly betray his uneasiness and his unconscious desire to persuade himself that he has some excuse for the villainy he contemplates. These seem to be indubitable proofs that Iago is not an absolute infidel, and that, against his will, he is a little better than his creed, as Bradley observes.

In a Shakespearian tragedy the main source of the convulsion which produces suffering and death, lies in a villainous character. Shakespeare has handled all his villains with consummate skill, and the utmost dexterity is shown in his delineation of Iago. Critics are at a loss in probing the wicked depth of this consummate villain. There seems to be, indeed, two Iagos in the play—such is the surpassing excellence of Shakespeare's portrayal of the character. One is the 'honest' Iago as he is called by many including Othello. This is Iago masked. The word 'honest' is applied to him some fifteen times in the play, not to mention some half a dozen times where he employs the term, in derision, to himself. When the drunken Cassio fights Montano, Othello, who has hurried to the scene, exclaims: "Honest Iago, that looks dead with grieving,/Speak, who began this?" And it is with great difficulty that the General succeeds in making Iago speak the 'truth' against Cassio. Soon afterwards Iago comforts the lieutenant and advises him to approach Desdemona for intercession. He feigns so much concern on Cassio's account that even Emilia is persuaded to tell her mistress: "I know it grieves my husband/ As if the case were his." So complete is the villain's dissimulation that Desdemona believes too much in his honesty and bids Emilia, in her hour of sore trouble: "call thy husband hither." Even Emilia, his own wife, in spite of her living with this fiendish husband for some time, does not know his real character. The mask that Iago has chosen to wear is the most impenetrable. It is the mask of rough outspokenness, the straightforward, honest bluntness of the soldier who does not care what others think or say of him.

Iago's bond of friendship with Roderigo is the latter's purse. He engages Roderigo in a criminal quest of Desdemona and tells him, "Put money in thy purse" and repeats the advice several times. The crowning performance of this knavish villain is his foul trick on Othello. Outwardly he is very friendly to the Moor. He tells Othello that hearing Roderigo calumniating the great General, he has thought nine or ten times "to have yerk'd him here, under the ribs" (I.2.5.), but "with the little godliness I have,/I did full hard forbear him" (I.2.9-10). But we know that it is Iago who incited Roderigo to proclaim Othello as a public offender in the streets and to call aloud "with like timorous accent, and dire yell,/As when, by night and negligence, the fire / Is spied in populous cities" (I.1.75-77).

The love of Othello and Desdemona is gall and wormwood to this villain. At the sight of their sweet embrace he says within himself: "O, you are well tun'd now,/But I'll set down the pegs that make this music,/As honest as I am" (I.199-201). And he proceeds presently to his infernal task. "Ha, I like not that" (III.3.35), says he, as if in a half aside in Othello's presence, when both have seen Cassio leaving Desdemona in the garden of the castle. Othello asks him what he is saying and he looks reluctant to give out what is there in his mind, and compels Othello to extort from him the admission that he suspects something wrong between Cassio and Desdemona. Then he goes on poisoning the mind of Othello very cautiously, feeling his ground all the while. Once he is sure of success, he ventures to state about Desdemona:

> Not to affect many proposed matches,
> Of her own clime, complexion, and degree,
> Whereto we see in all things nature tends;
> Fie, we may smell in such a will most rank,
> Foul disproportion; thoughts unnatural.
> (III.3.233-37)

Then he persuades Emilia to steal Desdemona's handkerchief and when he receives it from her, he leaves it in Cassio's lodging stealthily. Later he tells Othello: "such a handkerchief—/I am sure it was your wife's—did I to-day/See Cassio wipe his beard with" (III.3.444-46). He next contrives by a cunning ruse to make Othello seemingly overhear a conversation between Cassio and himself about Bianca, and hoaxes his victim into believing that Cassio is boasting of his conquest of Desdemona. Thus, Othello is made to believe absolutely in his wife's infidelity. He thinks now that here he has had an almost ocular proof of her guilt, such has been the clever trap laid out by the villainous Iago.

The real and unmasked Iago is sometimes revealed in his monologues and occasionally in his confidences imparted to Roderigo. To Roderigo he says:

> For when my outward action does demonstrate
> The native act, and figure of my heart,
> In complement extern, 'tis not long after,
> But I will wear my heart upon my sleeve,
> For doves to peck at: I am not what I am.
> (I.1.61-65)

When Iago is fattening himself on Roderigo's money, he indulges in the boastful soliloquy:

Thus do I ever make my fool my purse:
For I mine own gain'd knowledge should profane,
If I would time expend with such a snipe,
But for my sport and profit:
(I.3.381-84)

Elated with the success of having sown the seed of jealousy in Othello's heart, Iago says to himself: "not poppy, nor mandragora,/Not all the drowsy syrups of the world,/Shall ever medicine thee to that sweet sleep/Which thou owedst yesterday" (III.3.335-38).

Thus, Shakespeare has handled the villain in *Othello* with so supreme an art that endless discussion has gathered round the question of the motives underlying Iago's actions. Hudson confesses that he cannot sound the depth of Iago's cunning. He says: "...in attempting to thread his intricacies my mind gets bewildered." In point of artistic effect Iago surpasses both Richard and Edmund, two of the Shakespearian villains. It is a nemesis at last that works the villain's ruin. Coleridge's estimate of this character is worth noting. He says: "The character, with all its inscrutable depravity, neither revolts nor seduces the mind: the interest of his part amounts almost to fascination, yet there is not the slightest moral taint or infection about it."

Cassio

Cassio is a well-bred refined Florentine young man. He has been appointed lieutenant by Othello. He is an innocent victim of Iago's dark intrigue. Iago's picture of Cassio is prejudiced and should not mislead us. Othello, an experienced and honest General, has thought Cassio fit for his lieutenancy, and later the Venetian Council appoints him the Governor of Cyprus in place of Othello. Cassio is no weakling and stands with a strong nerve Iago's cowardly attack on him in which he narrowly escapes, adding his name to the list of Iago's victims.

Cassio is a young man with a high sense of honour. When he finds himself disgraced by having been involved in a drunken brawl, he exclaims most pathetically: "Reputation, reputation, I ha' lost my reputation! I ha' lost the immortal part, sir, of myself, and what remains is bestial; my reputation,

Iago, my reputation!" (II.3.254-57). He bitterly hates the vicious habit of drinking and cries out: "O thou invisible spirit of wine, if thou hast no name to be known by, let us call thee devil!" (II.3.273-75).

The fact that he was the trusted go-between in Othello's courtship of Desdemona also shows that he was a young man with a high sense of honour. It is because he has an innocent mind, that he approaches Desdemona to plead for him with Othello. He has not the faintest idea that this might lend itself to a suspicion about his relationship with Desdemona. He has, to the same extent as Othello, a simple-mindedness and trustful nature that believes everybody to be innocent. His faith in the honesty of Iago is unshakable, and it is this that brings him to grief. But Cassio is no puritan. He has a young man's natural weaknesses, as is indicated by his connection with Bianca, a woman of ill fame.

Cassio is good-natured and good-looking. Iago admits his personal charm and says: "He has a person and a smooth dispose,/To be suspected, fram'd to make women false" (I.3.395-96). In fact, women run after Cassio on account of his good looks and the strumpet Bianca "dotes on Cassio" (IV.1.96). "He has a daily beauty in his life" (V.1.19), confesses Iago to himself, and this has made him a popular figure in Venice and Cyprus. Cassio honours and respects Desdemona as his General's beloved wife, and his own friend. He is rapturous when Desdemona lands in Cyprus: "O, behold,/The riches of the ship is come ashore!" (II.1.82-83). And Desdemona reciprocates his friendship by calling him "valiant Cassio" (II.1.87). Cassio's sentiments towards Desdemona amount to a sort of religion. No impure thought or image is allowed to mingle in his contemplation of her. The reverent admiration, the purity and warmth of enthusiasm with which he thinks and speaks of her, are all but angelic. In short, his whole mind stands dressed towards her in the very ideal of human respect.

Cassio is light-hearted and takes life gaily. Even though he knows he has "very poor and unhappy brains for drinking" (II.3.30-31) and has already taken one cup of wine, he cannot decline Iago's offer and presently gets ludicrously drunk. In consequence he lets himself be entangled in a drunken brawl with Roderigo and Othello cashiers him.

It is Cassio's unsuspecting and trustful nature that leads him to put his foot in Iago's trap. His loyalty and affection for Othello are not shaken by his dismissal, and his hope of success at the intercession of his charming friend, Desdemona, is not at all ill-founded. But he is totally unaware that the devil has been at work all the while and the attempt of Desdemona to create interest in his behalf is destined to encompass both of them in ruin. He has not given Iago the slightest offence. His only offence consists in this, that Othello has passed over Iago and appointed him his lieutenant! When he is wounded by Iago in the dark of the night and carried off in a chair, his pitiful condition, his distress and utter confusion are too deep for words. Amazed at hearing Othello admit that he and Iago "consent in Cassio's death," he meekly falters out: "Dear general, I did never give you cause" (V.2.300). His soldierly qualities have been appreciated by the Republic of Venice, and he is appointed Governor of Cyprus to supplant Othello.

Cassio, all radiant as he is of truth and honour, makes a superb contrast to Iago. His nature is the finest-grained and most delicately organized of all Shakespeare's men. He is full-souled, frank-hearted, open, unsuspecting and free. When he has been cashiered by Othello through the hidden instrumentality of Iago, he bewails to Iago the loss of his reputation and Iago, to make the case worse for Cassio, advises him with seeming friendliness to seek Desdemona's intercession.

To Cassio's credit it has to be noted that he is the only man in the whole play, who sees Desdemona as she truly is; and Cassio supplies the means by which we may measure the grandeur of Othello on the one hand, and the depravity of Iago on the other.

Desdemona

Desdemona "tends to become to us predominantly pathetic, the sweetest and most pathetic of Shakespeare's women, as innocent as Miranda and as loving as Viola, yet suffering more deeply than Cordelia or Imogen," observes Bradley, and he further adds: "Evidently, we are to understand innocence, gentleness, sweetness, lovingness were the salient and, in a sense, the principal traits in Desdemona's character."

There is an innate goodness and generosity towards all in Desdemona's heart. Like Othello, she, too, trusts everyone and has no notion of the world's wicked ways of thought and action. She is a coy and blushing girl who turns away from the addresses of the well-groomed Venetian gallants, listens in rapt attention to the romantic stories of Othello's life, and while her maidenly imagination is set aglow by the pictures of unknown lands of men whose heads do grow beneath their shoulders, her heart quivers with a strange pity for this man of many woes and in her artless simplicity she makes the offer of her heart to him. His father has rightly judged her as he says before the Duke: "A maiden never bold of spirit,/So still and quiet, that her motion/Blush'd at her self" (I.3.94-96). Yet she braves her father's displeasure in marrying Othello. For, it is not on the spur of the moment or out of a fascination of the eye that Desdemona falls in love with Othello. There is deep mental affinity between her and Othello centring round a passion for military prowess and valour, and it is this spiritual magnetism rather than any physical or material attraction that draws the two together. Desdemona is not an imbecile or perverted girl attracted by a wild adventurer. She is not a spoilt, rich man's daughter, longing for an abnormal and startling sensation. She is a sober girl who attaches greater value to mental and moral qualities than to the charms of youth and beauty. She feels a deep admiration for Othello's perilous exploits and heroic deeds in the battle-field, and this admiration for Othello's noble qualities outweighs any prejudice of colour or any regard for custom or convention. She declares: "I saw Othello's visage in his mind" (I.3.252). In her attraction for Othello there is the essential quality of true love, which is sympathy. As Othello says: "She lov'd me for the dangers I had pass'd,/And I lov'd her that she did pity them" (I.3.167-68). There is an innate goodness and generosity towards all in

Desdemona's heart. She takes up the cause of Cassio merely because she feels sympathy for him in his distress.

The most distinctive aspect of Desdemona's character is her grace and dignity. Desdemona arrives in Cyprus before her husband, and while anxiously awaiting Othello's ship, she maintains her poise as befits a well-educated daughter of a Venetian senator. Easily adapting herself to her strange environment, she indulges Iago's jibes at the female sex with the same good manners and pleasant humour as she is subsequently to display towards Othello's Clown. But when confronted by a real crisis of happiness or misery, Desdemona is more at a loss for words. When she is re-united with Othello at Cyprus, her restrained greetings are in strong contrast to Othello's fond eloquence. Much later, when quite unexpectedly Othello strikes her in public, she retains her dignity and her quiet reply to this great insult and injury is simply this: "I have not deserv'd this" (IV.1.236). When Othello calls her a strumpet, she merely says: "By heaven, you do me wrong" (IV.2.83). She has such a refined and delicate taste that when she speaks to Iago about the hateful name given to her by Othello, she cannot utter the word and asks, "Am I that name, Iago?" (IV.2.120). As Iago does not understand what name Desdemona is speaking about, Emilia explains: "He call'd her whore" (IV.2.122). Desdemona tends to suffer in silence and seldom finds words to express her deepest feelings. On the other hand, when she is pleading Cassio's cause with her husband, she becomes most talkative, which is a clear indication that her actions in this respect are motivated only by sympathy and kindness and that she is not deeply involved emotionally. By contrast, for Othello's foul epithets she has no reproaches. Her mind seems to be numbed. Yet, in her innocence, a measure of her innate dignity and composure returns when she is called upon to serve as hostess at the banquet for the Venetian dignitaries. Later, alone again with Emilia, she does not bewail her altered fortunes or try to defend her slandered innocence; instead, she recounts the tale of the maid Barbary, sings the "Willow" song, and expresses virtuous incredulity when Emilia defends those wives who abuse their husband's trust.

"The deepest source of all the woes and guilt of the play lay in Desdemona's extraordinary innocence of the word. topford . roo e Too innocent to suspect that she is suspected she cannot for a long time understand the motives of thello 's harshness. t is her innocence that brings death upon her and her faith in her " ind lord is not obliterated even when she is dying. n her suffering she appears passive and defenceless and in her death we find the infinite endurance and forgiveness of a love that nows not how to resist or resent. he is in fact the most lovable of ha espeare's women. n her character and sufferings there is a nameless something that haunts the reader's mind.

Desdemona is tactless. er tactlessness is the cause of her ruin. nd this tactlessness springs from her innocence and purity. f she has imbibed the worldly maxims which Emilia dispenses in the third scene of the ourth ct she might have averted the disaster. he ma es a capital blunder in engaging herself to solicit for assio. he has not the remotest idea that her action might be misinterpreted. he does not recoil even at the visible displeasure of her lord. woman of the world would have ta en the hint and pressed no more assio 's suit. ago in spite of himself meant but the simple truth when he said "she is so free so ind so apt so blessed a disposition that she holds it a vice in her goodness not to do more than she is re uested . . . ot till the last moment does the truth brea into her mind that she has compromised herself by pleading for assio.

Desdemona appears to be one of the simplest in the range of ha espeare 's women characters. There seems to be no problem attached to her as there is to ordelia in the instance of her stubborn refusal to gratify the vanity of an aged father. Desdemona seems to us more sinned against than sinning and to be a personality of simple virtue falling a victim to the machinations of ago as a dove does to a haw . ut a careful examination of the scheme of all ha espeare 's dramas shows that his characteri ation is never so simple as this and that external circumstances alone are not the cause of the tragedy which ensues to any character. There is some weakness in the character, which is partly responsible for his or her ruin. In Cordelia's case there is a stubbornness akin to that of Lear himself, which made her tactless and unnecessarily frank. In Ophelia there is a want of intellect, and an inability to see the situation for herself and make a bold choice accordingly. The result is that she fails Hamlet in his hour of need and does not play the part which she might have done in averting the tragedy. Similarly, though we grant and admire the beautiful character of Desdemona, with its virginal purity and confidence in the good of the world, it cannot be denied that she is not perfect. There is the deception of her father, in the first place, for she has evidently been allowing the courtship of the Moor for some time before he carries her off. There is also a tendency to tell innocent lies, rather than speak with full candour, as she does in the case of the handkerchief. These are trifles, of course, and do not for one moment supply an explanation of the cruel fate that overtakes her. But they are trifles which serve once more to illustrate that, "character is destiny," for, they are the very faults which are most deadly in her particular circumstances. Cordelia, frank and outspoken by nature, would have made light of the problem of explaining to Othello about the handkerchief. The fact is that, at heart Desdemona is a little afraid of her overpowering husband when he shows signs of anger. Desdemona is more feminine and yielding than Cordelia, and so less qualified to hit back.

Desdemona's weakness lies in her lack of worldly wisdom. She is almost too innocent. Before sallying forth into the world, man or woman needs a certain equipment of knowledge. It is only by teaching the youthful person something of the nature of evil that he or she is equipped to avoid it. Desdemona simply does not believe that it exists, and cannot think that there are such women as will play the wanton although they are married. In the midst of a society with such predatory characters as Iago, she is like a dove in a colony of hawks. The greatest protection against sin is knowledge, and Desdemona does not have it. Despite the beauty and purity of her character, she cannot protect herself against the attack of calumny, for something more dynamic is then required. Her lack of worldly wisdom and experience contributes to the tragic catastrophe.

Bradley holds that Desdemona has a frank, childlike boldness and persistency, which are full of charm, but are unhappily united with a certain want of perception. These graces and this deficiency appear to be inextricably intertwined, and in the circumstances conspire tragically against her. They, with her innocence, hinder her from understanding Othello's state of mind, and lead her to the most unlucky acts and words. And unkindness and anger subdue her so completely that she becomes passive and seems to drift helplessly towards the cataract in front of her.

In Desdemona's incapacity to resist, there is also, in addition to her perfect love, something which is very characteristic. She is, in a sense, a child of nature. That deep inward division which leads to clear and conscious oppositions of right and wrong, duty and inclination, justice and injustice, is alien to her beautiful soul. She seems to know evil only by name, and her inclinations being good, she acts on inclination. This trait with its results may be seen if we compare her, at the crises of the story, with Cordelia. In Desdemona's place, Cordelia, however frightened at Othello's anger about the lost handkerchief, would not have denied its loss. Painful experience had produced in Cordelia a conscious principle of rectitude and a proud hatred of falseness, which would have made a lie, even one wholly innocent in spirit, impossible to her; and the clear sense of justice and right would have led her, instead, to require an explanation of Othello's agitation, which would have broken Iago's plot to pieces. In the same way, at the final crisis, no instinctive terror of death would have compelled Cordelia suddenly to relinquish her demand for justice and to plead for life. But these moments are fatal to Desdemona who acts precisely as if she were guilty.

It is her innocence and unwisdom that lead Desdemona to blunder in the handkerchief episode. She feels secure in Othello's love. So, she instinctively considers a lost handkerchief of small account and she is incapable of suspecting that a great deal depends on her reply. This lack of wisdom and want of thought lead her to take Cassio's defence so eagerly that she maddens her husband. And she does this twice at the most unlucky times, even at the hour of her death. Thus, apart from the machination of chance and villainous Iago, Desdemona herself cannot be absolved from the responsibility of bringing about her own ruin.

Emilia

Emilia is Iago's wife and the confidant and foil to Desdemona. Her character is drawn with a skill which is not generally noticeable in Shakespeare's other female characters of secondary importance. Shakespeare has presented Emilia as a woman of lower birth so that she is no more than a waiting maid to Desdemona. Emilia is a woman of the world and of coarser texture than her mistress. She is frank in her expression of the moral weakness of men and women. She is devoted to her husband in a blind and unquestioning way. She has no idea of Iago's wicked thoughts and plans. In perfect innocence she secures for him Desdemona's handkerchief. She thinks that by doing so she is only gratifying her husband's whim. Her faith in her husband's innocence and honesty continues all through the play until the end. Of course her silence, when Desdemona shows obvious distress at the loss of the handkerchief, is a grievous fault on her part. But she does not wish to betray her husband in what she considers to be a trifling matter. When in the last scene Othello tells her that it is her husband who has told him of Cassio's intrigue with Desdemona, she thrice repeats her cry of wonder and disbelief, "My husband?" But if her loyalty to her husband is what a wife's feeling should be, her loyalty to her mistress, Desdemona, is far above the average. In the last scene she gives her husband away to vindicate Desdemona's innocence in which she has an absolute faith. She risks her all and gives her life to maintain the honour of her mistress.

There is some coarseness and vulgarity about her. While Othello asks her to wait at the door, while he tortures himself as well as Desdemona by vile accusations, she has been listening at the door. Later in the presence of her husband she repeats again and again the filthy word 'whore' which gentle Desdemona cannot even bring herself to pronounce. And while Desdemona's heart is heavy with anguish at the loss of her husband's love, Emilia can only think of "so many noble matches" Desdemona has forsaken. It seems, Emilia is not very scrupulous in matters of virtue. She has a better knowledge of married life—of the neglect and ill-treatment of husbands and of the infidelities of wives—than Desdemona. She will not easily give away her virtue, but if the prize were great, she would not have any scruples in doing so.

Emilia becomes serious and energetic when great demands are made of her. She, however, becomes an unconscious accomplice of Iago in the procurement of the handkerchief, as she does not have any suspicion of the magnitude of her guilt. That is why when the mystery of the handkerchief is revealed to her after Desdemona's murder, she exclaims in an outburst of surprise and disbelief, "My husband?" thrice.

There are several contradictions and inconsistencies in Emilia's behaviour in course of the play. These are to be accounted for by the necessity of the plot. Besides, Emilia is not a girl with a subtle or penetrating mind, and is unable to look through outer appearances into inner motives or purposes. Had she told the truth about the handkerchief in time, had she scolded Othello in proper time for his suspicion about Desdemona, as she does at the end of the play, the tragedy would not have taken place.

Emilia serves an important purpose by stealthily collecting Desdemona's handkerchief and giving it to her husband, Iago. Thus she unconsciously helps Iago's scheme. It is this handkerchief which Iago uses as the ocular proof of Desdemona's infidelity, which finally leads Othello to destroy his wife whom he loves so much. Again, Emilia acts as an instrument of divine justice by unravelling at the end the villainy of her husband and establishing the purity and innocence of her mistress, Desdemona. Thus, the major course of action in the play is guided by Emilia.

In drawing the portrait of Emilia, Shakespeare has departed materially from the original in Cinthio, and made her a vulgar woman with no breeding or gentility about her. According to Iago she bestows on him too much of her tongue and, "She puts her tongue a little in her heart,/And chides with thinking" (II.1.106-7). She is unscrupulous in trifles and sadly lacks imagination. She is a woman of low cunning, and apparently well-informed of the ways of the work-a-day world, but she has not a bad heart. She is unutterably vulgar in her categorical reply to Desdemona's inquiry whether she would ever think of deceiving her husband. She openly says:

And have not we affections?
Desires for sport? and frailty, as men have?
Then let them use us well: else let them know,
The ills we do, their ills instruct us so.
(IV.3.100-103)

Yet all her defects disappear into nothingness when she discovers Desdemona murdered by Othello. It is at this moment that she shows herself possessed of a high degree of spirit and of energetic feeling. She turns like a tigress on Othello and reviles him for his guilt and folly in having "kill'd the sweetest innocent/That e'er did lift up eye" (V.2. 200-1). In this last scene when, fearless of heaven and men and devils, she stands up to champion her dead mistress' purity, she is a sublime figure, and her death at the hands of her villainous husband is almost as moving as Desdemona's own. From the moment of her appearance after Desdemona's murder to the moment of her own death, Emilia is transfigured and yet she remains perfectly true to herself. She is the only person who utters for us the violent common emotions which we feel, together with those more tragic emotions which she does not comprehend. She brings us too the relief of joy and admiration—a joy that is not lessened by her death. The feelings that Emilia evokes in the closing scene of the play, contribute largely towards mitigating the excess of tragic pain. "She stands, like Kent and Horatio, a beacon of common sense in a dark and reeling universe." (Guy Boas)

MINOR CHARACTERS

Brabantio

Brabantio is a senator of Venice and Desdemona's hoodwinked father. He is an influential person with powerful friends whose support he can command at need. He is also held in high esteem by the Duke. He is a man of rank and wealth in Venice. Iago says that Brabantio "hath in his effect a voice potential/As double as the Duke's" (I.2.13-14).

Brabantio loves his daughter dearly. He is also very much conscious of his high position. So, his daughter's elopement with "a lascivious Moor" gives him a great shock. He exclaims: "This accident is not unlike my dream" (I.1.142). Brabantio has brought up his daughter in an atmosphere of strict discipline. So, when Desdemona appears before the Senate to give her opinion to Othello's reply to the charges of using magical charm to win over Desdemona to him, Brabantio tells her: "Do you perceive in all this noble company,/Where most you owe obedience?" (I.3.179-80). In credulous tone he accuses Othello before the Duke of having won his daughter "By spells and medicines, bought of mountebanks" (I.3.61). He, however, grudgingly accepts Desdemona's own version of the affair. The Duke tries to console him by some encouraging platitudes:

> When remedies are past, the griefs are ended,
> By seeing the worst, which late on hopes depended.
> To mourn a mischief that is past and gone,
> Is the next way to draw more mischief on.
> What cannot be preserv'd when fortune takes,
> Patience her injury a mockery makes.
>
> (I.3.202-7)

Brabantio tops it by his dignified irony:

> He bears the sentence well, that nothing bears
> But the free comfort which from thence he hears:
> But he bears both the sentence and the sorrow,
> That, to pay grief, must of poor patience borrow.
>
> (I.3.212-15)

We pity the old and lonely Brabantio. While leaving his daughter for good, he warns Othello: "Look to her, Moor, have a quick eye to see:/She has deceiv'd her father, may do thee" (I.3.292-93). Shakespeare has made a fine picture of a father's grief in the opening scenes, and the bare sketch of Brabantio is striking proof of what Shakespeare could do in a few strokes. Brabantio is a character full of dignity and personality, and not a mere lay figure. His passion is similar to that of Shylock when robbed of his daughter by a 'Christian'. He parts from the Moor in offended dignity, but we are made to feel that he has taken away a wound in his heart. The shock and strain of Desdemona's desertion finally breaks him and when his death from "pure grief" is reported by Gratiano (V.2.205-7) we are not at all surprised.

Brabantio appears only in the First Act after which we hear nothing of him till in the last scene when his death is reported by Gratiano. Yet, he is a fully rounded figure whom Shakespeare shows swinging from one extreme to the other, offering Othello hospitality and showing high regard for the Moor and then roundly abusing him for marrying his daughter, frantically raising his household to find Desdemona, and then revealing quiet resignation when confronted with an accomplished fact. His parting warning to Othello is, of course, to be subsequently re-echoed by Iago ("She did deceive her father, marrying you;" III.3.210) with great dramatic impact.

Roderigo

Roderigo is a young Venetian gentleman with plenty of worldly riches. He has been paying court to Desdemona but receives encouragement neither from her nor from her father. He is a very contemptible character in the play. He loves Desdemona with a carnal, lustful heart and has been charged by Brabantio not to haunt about his doors (I.1.96). Roderigo's main fault is his incorrigible stupidity coupled with a feeble moral sense. Iago has undertaken to further Roderigo's suit for the hand of Desdemona, and Roderigo, as appears from his speech with which the play opens, has bribed Iago lavishly for the purpose. Desdemona has, in the meantime, eloped with Othello and Roderigo laments in jealousy and disappointment:

"What a full fortune does the thicklips owe, / If he can carry't thus!" (I.1.66-67). Roderigo cannot now win Desdemona as a wife but hopes to make her his mistress, and to this end sells all his land and uproots himself. Iago makes a tool of him by inflaming his passion and persuading him of the frailty of all women. His only motive is to rob Roderigo of his money as he says, "Thus do I ever make my fool my purse" (I.3.381).

In the first scene of the First Act Roderigo helps Iago in raising a hue and cry and rousing Brabantio and loudly calumniating Othello in the foulest of terms. When it appears that Othello and Desdemona are already married, Roderigo loses heart and proposes to drown himself. Iago then persuades Roderigo to believe that Desdemona is in love with Cassio, and that with the removal of Cassio he will have the fairest chance of gaining Desdemona. That is why Roderigo lends his hand at Iago's plot to disgrace Cassio. Iago tells Roderigo to "find some occasion to anger Cassio" so that he may "haply with his truncheon may strike at you," and thus Cassio may be cashiered and Roderigo will "have a shorter journey to your desires." And the fool, Roderigo says, "I will do this" (II.1.277). Iago contrives to make Cassio drunk and Roderigo fastens a quarrel on him. Iago manages to see that Othello is roused, and the result is that Cassio is dismissed. Iago's plot is laid to remove Cassio because the latter has been appointed lieutenant in preference to himself, and he uses Roderigo to serve his own end. But, Roderigo is of too obtuse an intellect to perceive this.

In the play Roderigo serves a mirror to reflect Iago's mind. It is to him that Iago reveals himself freely. He tells Roderigo: "I am not what I am" (I.1.65). He tells Roderigo the truth unhesitatingly. If we piece together Iago's observations in his talks with Roderigo, we will find a clue to Iago's character. Roderigo provides a medium between Iago and the audience and so helps to avoid too much soliloquy on the part of Iago. Before Roderigo alone Iago takes off his disguise and presents his own real self. For Iago does not have any regard for Roderigo's understanding.

Iago has made Othello believe that Desdemona is in illicit love with Cassio. It has been arranged that Othello will strangle Desdemona in her bed, and Iago will be Cassio's undertaker (IV.1.). Roderigo is at hand. He complains that Iago has been putting him off with false hopes. He tells Iago pointblank: "I have wasted myself out of means: the jewels you have had from me, to deliver to Desdemona, would half have corrupted a votarist: you have told me she has receiv'd 'em, and return'd me expectation, and comforts, of sudden respect, and acquittance, but I find none" (IV.2.187-92). He threatens Iago by saying: "I will make myself known to Desdemona" (IV.2.198-99). Iago humours Roderigo and tells him that, "there is especial command come from Venice, to depute Cassio in Othello's place" (IV.2.220-21), and so to prolong the stay of Desdemona in Cyprus, Cassio is to be made "uncapable of Othello's place, knocking out his brains." (IV.2.229-30), when he returns in the night from supping "with a harlot." Roderigo believes in Iago and attacks Cassio on the way, but unfortunately he himself is wounded. Iago, finding his plot foiled, wounds Cassio from behind and, pretending Roderigo as Cassio's assailant, kills him. Thus, Justice, for once in the play, shows her face. Like Emilia, Roderigo is Iago's tool, and like her, he, too, dies at the hands of Iago.

Lodovico

Lodovico is a kinsman of Brabantio, a senator of Venice, and a noble Venetian. He is sent to Cyprus by the Venetian Senate to recall Othello. He is a good example of the Venetian envoy or civil servant. He is entirely Shakespeare's own invention. There is no corresponding figure in Cinthio's tale.

Lodovico is well-bred and courteous. He is energetic in speech and action. When Othello strikes his wife in his presence, his protest goes to the utmost of what is possible within the forms of good breeding towards an officer in Othello's authoritative position. He says: "My lord, this would not be believ'd in Venice,/Though I should swear I saw it" (IV.1.237-38). Later he tells Iago:

> Is this the noble Moor, whom our full senate
> Call all in all sufficient? This the noble nature,
> Whom passion could not shake? whose solid virtue
> The shot of accident, nor dart of chance,
> Could neither graze, nor pierce?
> (IV.1.260-64)

Lodovico is shocked at the behaviour of Othello, yet his reaction to the incident only betrays his noble bearing, high culture and respect for the General.

Lodovico is young and good-looking. Desdemona tells Emilia about him: "This Lodovico is a proper man" (IV.3.35), and that "He speaks well" (IV.3.37). Emilia admits this and says that Lodovico is "A very handsome man" (IV.3.36), and adds: "I know a lady in Venice would have walk'd barefoot to Palestine for a touch of his nether lip" (IV.3.38-39).

It is Lodovico who finds Cassio lying wounded, and is close at hand when Iago fatally stabs Roderigo. He produces letters, found in the pocket of dead Roderigo, which reveal Iago's villainy. After this he announces that Cassio is to replace Othello as governor of Cyprus and that the Moor is to be placed under arrest for the murder of Desdemona. And when Othello kills himself, he calls Iago a "Spartan dog" and gives instructions for the hellish villain to be put to torture. Lodovico is a dutiful and loyal officer of the Venetian court. He performs his duty well and helps in bringing the play to its inevitable end.

Gratiano

Gratiano is brother of Brabantio and a noble Venetian. He is an elderly, rather infirm senator. He is introduced only in the final Act. He has accompanied Lodovico on the official mission to Cyprus. It is he who along with his kinsman, Lodovico, finds out Cassio lying wounded after he has been attacked by Roderigo and surreptitiously wounded by Iago. With Lodovico he serves an important purpose of officiating for the state of Venice in the capture of and meting out of proper justice to Iago. After Desdemona's murder he informs that her father has meanwhile died of grief over the circumstances surrounding her marriage with Othello. It is he who prevents Othello leaving the bedchamber and who subsequently declares that torture will open Iago's lips. "Torments will ope your lips" (V.2.306), says he when Iago says, "From this time forth I never will speak word" (V.2.305). After witnessing the Moor's self-inflicted death, he is instructed by Lodovico to take possession of Othello's property. Gratiano appears for a little while and speaks but little. But whatever he has said presents him as a dignified senator. While guarding Othello he can tell him even: "If thou attempt it [escape], it will cost thee dear" (V.2.256). Thus, Shakespeare has individualized him though he is a minor character.

Montano

Montano is the Governor of Cyprus, whom Othello is sent to replace. He is a young and wise officer who has previously served under Othello's command. He admires and honours Othello. He says of Othello, "'tis a worthy governor" (II.1.30), and that "the man commands/Like a full soldier" (II.1.35-36). He is glad of Othello's appointment as Governor of Cyprus and is as anxious as Cassio for his safe coming.

The Venetian Senate receives a despatch from him concerning the imminent Turkish invasion of Cyprus, and he is referred to as their "trust and most valiant servitor" (I.3.40). Although he does not have Cassio's mercurial ardour, he is considered in Venice a grave and sagacious person. He is dutiful and honest. When he encounters Cassio who is tipsy and who insults him and wounds him when he tries to intervene between Cassio and Roderigo, he thinks that Othello should be informed of Cassio's behaviour. Subsequently, he gives his version of the incident to Othello and Cassio is cashiered. Thus, Montano has a keen sense of duty and he is fearless in the presence of danger. He joins in the pursuit of Iago when Iago escapes after murdering his wife. He becomes the master of the situation. He asks Gratiano to "guard the door without, let him not pass,/But kill him rather; I'll after that same villain" (V.2.242-43). Thus, he proves himself a true soldier who can take a decision instantly and has the personality to command.

Duke of Venice

The Duke of Venice appears only in the third scene of the First Act of the play. There he presides over a meeting of the Senate discussing about the anticipated attack of the Turks. The Duke is calm and dignified and has a keen concern for the affairs of the state. He summons up a council at dead of night. When danger is imminent he makes immediate arrangements for the defence of Cyprus and sends for the valiant general, Othello. Just then Brabantio appears before him demanding justice, accusing Othello of seducing his daughter, Desdemona.

The Duke is open-minded and recognizes the fairness of the match between Othello and Desdemona as he listens to what both Othello and Desdemona have to say. He is above the prejudices of race or nationality. He tells Brabantio: "Your son-in-law is far more fair than black" (I.3.290). He recognizes and honours merit wherever it may be found. Although Iago tells Othello that Brabantio has "in his effect a voice potential /As double as the Duke's" (I.2.13-14), it is proved to be a mere false assumption, as the Duke is able to make Brabantio see reason about his daughter's elopement with the Moor and prevail upon him to accept the inevitable. The Duke is wise and sympathetic with Brabantio. He tries to console the aggrieved father with platitudes with, however, little effect. He then orders Othello to proceed that very night to Cyprus, giving Desdemona permission to follow her husband there, should she wish to, when Desdemona refuses to stay with her father during Othello's absence and Brabantio is determined not to take his daughter back. Thus, in his brief appearance the Duke of Venice leaves an impression of a noble, sagacious and dutiful ruler.

Bianca

Bianca is a mistress to Cassio. In some ways she serves as a dramatic foil to Desdemona. Her sudden appearance in the fourth scene of the Third Act helps to contrast Cassio's behaviour of gentle aspect and chivalrous dignity towards Desdemona with his more natural responses towards the flaunting courtesan of Cyprus, who makes no bones about his attractions for her.

Bianca is a common courtesan. Iago has nothing but hatred for her. He tells Roderigo about Cassio: "he sups to-night with a harlot" (IV.2.232-33). Bianca chases Cassio about the streets, makes a public spectacle of her infatuation for him, flies into a raging temper and accuses him of double-dealing. But she is also shrewd and witty. She does not allow herself to be bullied by Iago, when he tries to implicate her in the midnight ambush. When Iago tells her: "I charge you go with me," and Emilia exclaims, "Fie, fie upon thee, strumpet!" Bianca boldly protests: "I am no strumpet, but of life as honest/As you, that thus abuse me" (V.I.119-22).

The basic purpose of introducing Bianca is to enable Othello to be properly duped. Cassio's mocking and lewd remarks about Bianca in the supposed hearing of the eavesdropping Moor are just the sort of comments which the Moor has already steeled himself to hear about Desdemona. And right at this moment Bianca comes across Cassio and angrily returns Desdemona's handkerchief to him, refusing to copy the design on it as asked by Cassio. This is the most crucial moment in the play as it confirms Othello's suspicion about Desdemona's infidelity, as Othello takes it to be an ocular proof of Desdemona's secret intimacy with Cassio. Thus, Bianca plays a very important role in the development of the plot, although she appears for a short while only in three scenes of the play.

14

Role of Chance and Accident

Most of the events of the drama, *Othello*, from its very conception to the catastrophe, appear to have been brought into being by chance or unreason. Stopford A. Brooke writes in this connection: "Fate dominates *Macbeth*, but here in *Othello* chance or unreason, blind and deaf, is at the centre of human life.... The conception of the play, the movement of it, the events in it, the bringing about of the catastrophe are all apparently in the realm of chance." This statement of Brooke is amply borne out by a study of the tragedy of *Othello*. In the first place it is chance that Desdemona's love for the Moor has its origin. It appears to be almost unnatural that Desdemona, brought up amidst the refinements and ceremonies of Venetian life, should be fascinated by Othello, a stranger with tawny skin and fierce traditions in his blood. Emilia, the wife of Iago, who had already lived with the villain for some years, thought her husband to be only wayward and a bit impatient. It was due to accident that she had not known him better. It was the greatest of malignant accidents that gave Othello such a man as Iago for his ensign, the one man who would and could plan such an intrigue. Othello himself, a distinguished soldier and a grave and noble character, as Shakespeare depicts him in the first two Acts of the play, falls a prey to the evil machinations of Iago, a young man of twenty-eight. It never occurs to him that he may have angered Iago by preferring Cassio to him. He should have stuck Iago at the first innuendoes. Instead, he is all attention. "At a dozen points in the story," points out Sir Walter Raleigh, "a slip or an accident would have brought Iago's fabric about his ears." But, such an event does not occur. And all this is due to chance and unreason.

It is true that Iago has marvellous, and almost devilish ingenuity. Yet chance or accident seems to have favoured him greatly. He gets hold of Desdemona's handkerchief by a lucky chance. He has often begged Emilia to steal it. Desdemona drops it by inadvertence. Emilia picks it up and gives it to Iago. Iago places it in Cassio's bedchamber. Cassio gives it to Bianca to copy out its design. It is a most strange coincidence that with that very handkerchief Bianca should arrive at the moment when Iago holds Cassio in a tell-tale conversation and Othello watches unseen.

Bradley writes: "This influence of accident is keenly felt in *King Lear* only once, and at the very end of the play. In *Othello* after the temptation has begun, it is incessant and terrible. The skill of Iago was extraordinary, and so was his good fortune. Again and again, a chance word from Desdemona, a chance meeting of Othello and Cassio, a question which starts to our lips and which any one but Othello would have asked, would have destroyed Iago's plot and ended his life. In their stead, Desdemona drops her handkerchief at the moment most favourable to him, Cassio blunders into the presence of Othello only to find him in a swoon, Bianca arrives precisely when she is wanted to complete Othello's deception and incense his anger into fury. All this and much more seems to us quite natural, so potent is the art of the dramatist." But it confounds us with a feeling that, for these star-crossed mortals there is no escape from fate. Indeed, the accidents and chance happenings remind us strangely of the words: "There's a divinity that shapes our ends." But in the construction of the drama chance seems to have no part to play. The master-artist has drawn everything with a wizard's brush, and all improbabilities are depicted with so creative and formative an imagination that the whole play seems eminently probable.

When Shakespeare was writing his great tragedies of *Hamlet*, *Macbeth*, *King Lear* and *Othello*, his outlook on life was entirely different from what it was when he had been working on the comedies and the English historical plays. Somehow a relation between his soul and the dark and terrible forces of the world was established and to escape from a thorough investigation and sounding of the depths of life was no longer possible. The contemporary writings of Ben Jonson, Marston and other authors displayed a general feeling of revulsion that the world was rotten and love was loathsome. But, Shakespeare took up dreadful subjects to write upon and treated them unrelentingly. And he was not the impersonal artist in these tragedies. His belief in a divine justice is shaken in *Hamlet*, is almost mocked at in *Measure for Measure*, is really absent from *Macbeth*, is replaced by a belief in chance as at the root of the universe in *Othello*, and in *King Lear* it is altogether gone. That is why it appears to us that the tragedy in *Othello* is more the working of chance happenings than the outcome of the follies of characters.

15

Double-Time in *Othello*

The question of the duration of the action of the play, *Othello*, presents an interesting problem. The arrangements of Acts and scenes in the play suggest that we have, excluding the voyage to Cyprus, part of a day at Venice and about thirty-six hours at Cyprus. Thus, the action of the play seems to cover only three days at most. The First Act takes but a day. Then there is an interval for the voyage from Venice to Cyprus. The Second Act takes another day. The incidents of the Third, Fourth and Fifth Acts occur on one and the same day. But there are evidences in the play, which suggest that the action of the play took a considerably long period to happen.

In the second scene of the Fourth Act Roderigo's speech beginning with, "I have wasted myself out of means," implies that a sufficiently long time has elapsed since his arrival at Cyprus, so that his money and his patience are both nearly exhausted. In the third scene of the Third Act Emilia, as she picks up Desdemona's handkerchief, says: "My wayward husband hath a hundred times/Woo'd me to steal it." It implies a prolonged period of time in the action. In the same scene Iago says he lay with Cassio "lately" and heard him murmur of Desdemona in his sleep. The word "lately" implies that they have been some time in Cyprus and Cassio's supposed dream points to a long period of intimacy between him and Desdemona. In the fourth scene of the Third Act Bianca reproaches Cassio with having kept away from her "seven days and nights." In the first scene of the Fourth Act Iago tells Othello that he will make Cassio narrate, "Where, how, how oft, how long ago, and when / He has and is again to cope your wife." In the same scene Lodovico comes with letters from the Venetian senate recalling Othello and deputing Cassio in his place. Now, here we must presume a sufficient interval of time to have elapsed before the senate could hear of the state of affairs at Cyprus and send orders for substituting Cassio in the place of Othello. The cross-examination of Emilia by Othello in the second scene of the Fourth Act gives us the impression of their having been at Cyprus for a considerable period of time. In the same scene Roderigo complains of being too long fed on mere hopes of meeting Desdemona, and of being put off every day with some pretext, while his money has almost all been used up.

The main action of the play moves fast with the exception of one interval which is irrelevant to its movement. The First Act represents a period of time very little longer than that occupied on the stage. It will be noticed that the second scene of this Act can follow the first scene with no supposed interval, that the first fifty-six lines of it serve to cover the interval during which Brabantio is seeking Othello, and that the movement of the whole party to the Council Chamber is covered by the forty-seven lines of discussion between the Duke and the senators. The only point at which the stage time is unduly brief is while Iago is going to the Sagittary and conducting Desdemona back again. But this is covered by the forty odd lines of Othello's speech. Indeed, it is worth noticing how skilfully the whole thing is covered. The speech lasts for no more than two minutes. But it ranges widely both in time and in space, so that any normal audience, measuring it by impression, and not by a stop watch, feels that it has lasted longer than it actually has. The rapid movement of the First Act, seeing that it is separated from the Second by a considerable interval, is important only thus far, that it sets the tempo for the rest of the play.

Between the First Act and the Second Act there is an interval of any length we may choose. All we know about it from the text is that it is some days longer than the "se'nnight" of II.1.77, though we can, if we care to, work out from a map how long it would take a sailing ship to complete a tempestuous voyage from Venice to Cyprus. But the supposed deviation is quite unimportant because of the distribution of the main characters during the voyage. Othello sails in one ship, Cassio in a second, Desdemona, Iago and Emilia in a third.

All of them meet again for the first time, and within half an hour of one another, in Cyprus. The represented time from then to the end of the play is some thirty-three hours. They land somewhere about four o'clock on Saturday (II.2.9-10) as a proclaiming gentleman announces, "this present hour of five." The scene of the cashiering of Cassio begins just before ten o'clock (II.3.13) and lasts till early on Sunday morning (II.3.365). Cassio makes up his mind to petition Desdemona "betimes in the morning" (II.3.320). He does so and there follows the temptation scene (III.3.). It is then just possible to assume some interval, but it will be rather awkward because the lines 15, 16, 19 and 30 of the fourth scene of the Third Act seem to indicate continuity. Desdemona has become immediately aware of the loss of the handkerchief and Othello's "O hardness to dissemble," comes naturally only straight after the temptation scene.

Between the Third and the Fourth Acts an interval may be creditably inserted. But it seems that the 'feeling' both of the audience in the theatre and of the reader in the study is against it. When once Iago has Othello on the rack, it would be undramatic to allow a respite. And from the beginning of the Fourth Act there is no possibility of an interval. The messengers from Venice arrive and are invited to supper "to-night" (IV.1.257). This supper ends at the beginning of the third scene of the Fourth Act. Later, at night ("between twelve and one" IV.2.236), Cassio is attacked and Roderigo killed, and very soon after this Othello kills Desdemona.

This rapid continuity of movement is not only, from the point of view of dramatic tension, desirable, but also, from the point of view of credibility, imperative. If Iago's plot does not work fast, it will not work at all. If Othello meets Cassio and asks him the question which he asks too late, in the last scene ("How came you, Cassio, by a handkerchief,/That was my wife's? V.2.320-21), the plot of Iago will be frustrated. And Iago is actually aware of this. He says: "The Moor / May unfold me to him; there stand I in peril" (V.1.20-21). And not all Iago's adroitness can avert the likelihood of such a meeting for more than a short time. He is, indeed, only saved by Othello's fit (IV.1.50) when Cassio enters and has to be got rid of.

But this rapidity of movement, from one point of view, is inevitable while from another point of view it makes nonsense of the whole business. After the arrival in Cyprus, there is no point of time at which the supposed adultery could have taken place, and even Othello's credulity cannot be supposed to accept blank impossibilities. Nor has there been any opportunity before the arrival, since Othello sails on the day after his marriage. It should be observed that the whole of Iago's suggestions and Othello's reactions to them depend on the supposition of 'adultery,' that is, extra-marital relationship, and not promiscuity or a liaison preceding the marriage. Othello's poisoned fear is that he has been made a cuckold, nor that he has been merely anticipated.

Something therefore has to be done to make the whole progress of the plot credible. And Shakespeare does it by a number of indications of so-called long-time. The theory of the so-called 'double time scheme' was first propounded by Wilson in three brilliant articles in *Blackwood's Magazine* (November 1849, April and May 1850). The theory may be briefly stated as follows: As we read the play we come across two sets of time-note, both equally definite and self-consistent. According to one set of time-note, the action of the play, after Othello's arrival at Cyprus, seems to comprise itself into a period of something less than two days, while the other set of time-note points unmistakably to a longer interval of time before the catastrophe. One is short time, the other is long time. The long time is the true historic time while the short time is the dramatic time whereby days, weeks and months may be contracted to the utmost. The short time produces the impression of haste and vehemence, the long time produces the impression of probability.

We learn that on the very night of his marriage Othello is ordered to start for Cyprus. The time required for the voyage is kept out of count and in the following Act we hear of Cassio's arrival at Cyprus first, being separated from Othello by a storm. Next comes Desdemona under the escort of Iago and finally comes Othello. All these arrivals occur on the same day (Saturday, as we learn later). On the same night a general festivity is proclaimed in view of the providential destruction of the Turkish fleet and the celebration of Othello's marriage. It is followed by the brawl in which Cassio, under the influence of wine, strikes Roderigo, and Cassio is sacked.

On the morning following the night of the brawl, Cassio, acting under the advice of Iago, goes to request Desdemona to intercede for him with Othello (III.1.33-38). In the third scene of the same Act while Cassio is pleading with Desdemona for his restoration, Othello enters accompanied by Iago. Desdemona at once starts urging Othello to restore Cassio to his office, and, from her speech beginning with, "Why then to-morrow night, or Tuesday morn" (III.3.61), it appears that it was Sunday morning when the conversation took place. Hence, the party must have arrived at Cyprus on Saturday.

In the same scene Iago begins to poison Othello's mind with suspicion of his wife's virtue. The handkerchief is dropped by Desdemona and it is later picked up by Emilia who gives it to her husband. Then, as Othello enters again, Iago, with the fatal handkerchief still on his person, tells Othello that he has seen Cassio wipe his beard with a handkerchief very like the one given by Othello to Desdemona. The scene ends with Iago undertaking to kill Cassio.

In the next scene Cassio is sent for by Desdemona. Othello enters and tests Desdemona about the handkerchief and leaves in a rage. Next Cassio meets Bianca and requests her to copy the pattern in the handkerchief, which, he says, he has found in his bedchamber.

In the first scene of the Fourth Act Othello keeps himself concealed in a place from where he can watch the interview between Iago and Cassio, in the course of which Cassio is made to talk of Bianca, and his gestures and movements are all misinterpreted by Othello, who notices all this from his hiding place, because of previous instruction by Iago. Now, Bianca appears on the scene and reproaches Cassio about the handkerchief he has given to her, returns it to him and departs inviting him to sup with her "to-night." Next enters Lodovico who is invited by Othello to sup with him "to-night." In the second scene of the Fourth Act Iago persuades Roderigo to undertake the "removing of Cassio" "this night" "between twelve and one" as Cassio returns from Bianca.

In the next scene Lodovico takes his leave after the supper, and Desdemona is asked to go to bed immediately and dismiss her attendant, while Othello goes out for a short walk promising to return "forthwith." In the first scene of the Fifth Act Cassio is set on in the dark and wounded surreptitiously by Iago who kills Roderigo declaring him as the assailant of Cassio. In the last scene Othello strangles Desdemona as she lies on her bed. Then attracted by the loud cries of "murder" raised by Emilia, Montano, Gratiano, Iago and others enter. Othello kills himself, but not before he has been disabused about his wife's faithlessness. All this takes place on the same night.

The party arrives at Cyprus on Saturday. On the night of Saturday Cassio is dismissed on breach of discipline. On the next morning Cassio seeks an interview with Desdemona. On the same day Iago sets to work and succeeds in poisoning Othello's mind, and Desdemona loses her handkerchief and Othello tests her about it, followed by Iago's plan of murdering Cassio, which is executed on Sunday night, as well as the strangling of Desdemona, which takes place immediately afterwards. Thus, so many events with their tragic issues are packed into a day and a half.

The difficulties as to the space of time covered by the events of the play are numerous. In the first place, we learn that Iago and Roderigo have been long acquainted and that Iago has been borrowing money from Roderigo apparently on the strength of pretending to support his courtship of

Desdemona. This implies that the acquaintance and friendship between Emilia and Desdemona must have existed before the latter's marriage to Othello. But considering their respective social positions such relation between the two does not appear very probable. Again, there must be an interval between the First and the Second Acts, but there can be none, except of a few hours, between the next Acts, as the incidents are evidently continuous and cannot have occupied more than forty-eight hours. Yet we find Roderigo complaining both at the end of the third scene of the Second Act and again in the second scene of the Fourth Act that he has teen put off by Iago with same excuse or other and has spent nearly all his money. Again, in the fourth scene of the Third Act we have Bianca reproaching Cassio with keeping a week away from her. "What, keep a week away? seven days and nights?/Eight score eight hours" (III.4.171-72). Yet, according to the drama, Cassio cannot be on the island for more than two days. This variation of time can only be explained by supposing that Bianca was Cassio's mistress in Venice and had followed or accompanied him to Cyprus. Still greater is the difficulty as to the recall of Othello from Cyprus. For, the letters of recall must have been sent before the senate could have known that Othello had reached the island. There are also allusions, which will be easily recognized by the reader, implying a longer period of married life of Othello and Desdemona, than is possible consistently with the text of the play.

Cinthio's Moor had evidently been resident long in Venice before the expedition to Cyprus. Shakespeare's Othello tells us that he had never been in Venice until nine months before the opening of the play, having spent his life until then in the field. Iago's later hints that Othello is completely ignorant of the ways of Italian women are therefore well grounded. Cinthio, again, relates that the Moor and Desdemona had lived in perfect harmony together in Venice for an unspecified period, during which, one might suppose, persons so deeply in love would have had plenty of opportunity of getting to know each other and of resolving such temperamental discords as their differences of race and upbringing might give rise to.

Shakespeare's couple have no married life together at all. He deliberately leaves the sequence of events in his opening scene vague. We are evidently intended to assume that the marriage knot has only just been tied by some priest at the Sagittary when Iago arrives to warn the bridegroom that Brabantio has been informed and is about to cause trouble. Now, as they are talking Cassio arrives with a summons from the Duke. Before leaving for Cyprus Othello says to Desdemona: "I have but an hour/Of love, of worldly matters, and direction,/To spend with thee; we must obey the time" (I.3.298-300). In a word, they obey Shakespeare's time to such purpose that their first night at Cyprus is their wedding night and even that is disturbed by Cassio's brawl. Thus, they have no intimacy of any kind, and Iago's trump card is his reminder that Othello actually knows very little either about Italian women in general or of the true character of Desdemona in particular. Thus, by discarding Cinthio's plot of the married life in Venice, Shakespeare at once tightened it up and greatly increased the dramatic cogency of the plot.

Yet, this change gave rise to further difficulties which might well have seemed insuperable to any ordinary dramatist. For, if Othello and Desdemona consummate their marriage during the first night at Cyprus, when could she have committed adultery that Iago charges her with? An accusation of pre-marital incontinence would not have served either his purpose or Shakespeare's, since adultery was required to make Othello a cuckold, and it is the dishonourable stigma of cuckoldry that maddens Othello, once his confidence is gone. From this dilemma Shakespeare escaped by means of the contrivance of "double time."

During the last four Acts Shakespeare kept the two clocks going, one registering short time or dramatic time, the other registering long or historical time. Short time concerns the sequence of events on the stage, which follow each other without pause or any suggestion of intervening interval. Shakespeare was obliged to do this because Othello must be left no time for reflection or the questioning of any one but Iago. Otherwise, the whole flimsy fraud that is practised on him would probably collapse. When, however, critics begin to compute the length of this short time and reckon it as twenty-four hours from the first night at Cyprus, when the marriage is consummated, to the murder of Desdemona, they are emphasizing something which Shakespeare was equally at pains to keep carefully out of sight. Indeed, what his short-time clock registers is never duration but speed, the rush of events rather than the flight of hours. There is but one reference to this last, and it occurs when the short-time clock has only just got going. "Pleasure, and action, make the hours seem short" (II.3.369), says Iago to Roderigo, and thus prepares the spectators for the speed at which subsequent events will move.

Shakespeare adopted "double time" for the same reason that he adopted short time, because he was compelled to do so. He used short time to prevent the audience realizing that Othello's acceptance of Iago's tissue of falsehood was in reality absurd. He used long time to persuade the audience that the adultery, which was rendered impossible by cutting out the period of married life, as indicated in Cinthio, had nevertheless taken place. Long time, therefore, consists, in effect, of a series of references to the duration of time during which the married life could have occurred. Where it had been spent, Shakespeare was not careful to say. Sometimes, he seemed to suggest that Desdemona might have begun her intrigue with Cassio in Venice, at others, we are given the impression that weeks or more may have elapsed since their arrival at Cyprus. He was, of course, careful, too, that the hints of long time should never clash in any obvious way with those of short time. He only began to introduce plain hints of long time when the excitement of the jealousy scene was reaching its height.

Shakespeare was not essentially concerned with time and the calendar at all. The play's essential action lies in the processes of thought and feeling by which the characters are moved and the story is forwarded. And the deeper the springs of these, the less do time, place and circumstance affect them. His imagination was now concerned with fundamental passions, and their swift working demanded uncumbered expression. He might falsify calendar for his convenience, but we shall find neither trickery nor anomaly in the fighting of the intellectual battle for Othello's soul. And in the light of the truth of this the rest will pass unnoticed.

16

Images and Symbols in *Othello*

The distinctive feature of the plays of Shakespeare is the profusion of images found in them. To Shakespeare anything, whether concrete or abstract, an object or an idea, immediately calls up an image. This is a characteristic of the Elizabethan writers and Shakespeare freely indulges in it. M. Taine lays most stress upon the copiousness of Shakespeare's imagery. He says that it is a series of paintings, which is unfolded in his mind. Shakespeare does not seek them, they come of themselves; they crowd within him, covering his arguments. George Rylands, referring to Shakespeare's fondness of the exuberant use of image observes that, this passion for either spinning out an image or accumulating diverse images to illustrate a single idea is very dominant in Shakespeare's early work. Shakespeare is in the habit of using recurrent or dominating images in his plays. They play a part in raising, developing, sustaining and repeating emotion in his plays, which is somewhat analogous to the action of a recurrent theme or motif in a musical composition.

In *Othello* there is a very close connection between the imagery of the dialogue and the development of character. We often find that the imagery is used to indicate a spiritual change in the character. In the speeches of Othello poetic images arise almost naturally. Othello has a rich poetic imagination and so it is a part of his very nature to use imagery. Iago, on the other hand, does not possess a highly imaginative mind as Othello does. His outlook is speculative, scientific and rational. Hence, we will find few images even in his soliloquies. And when he uses images, he does it deliberately to influence others. There is a difference between Othello and Iago in their use of images. The prosaic brevity of Iago's images stands in direct contrast to the poetic force and grandeur of those used by Othello. Thus, Iago says of Cassio in a soliloquy:

> If I can fasten but one cup upon him,
> With that which he hath drank to-night already,
> He'll be as full of quarrel and offence
> As my young mistress' dog:
>
> (II.3.44-47)

Again, to Roderigo, Iago says: "our bodies are gardens, to the which our wills are gardeners" (I.3.320-21). This is characteristic of Iago who speaks often in prose. Othello, when he is stirred to emotion, speaks in eloquent poetry. When he meets his dear Desdemona again, safe at Cyprus, he speaks out:

> O my soul's joy,
> If after every tempest come such calmness,
> May the winds blow, till they have waken'd death,
> And let the labouring bark climb hills of seas,
> Olympus-high, and duck again as low
> As hell's from heaven.
>
> (II.1.184-89)

At the end distracted with grief, knowing that Desdemona was innocent, and he has committed a heinous crime in murdering her, he cries out: "Blow me about in winds, roast me in sulphur,/Wash me in steep-down gulfs of liquid fire!" (V.2.280-81). Iago will never be able to use such imagery, just as Othello can never utter the cold, cynical and almost unemotional words of Iago. Thus, in *Othello* the imagery has the prime function of helping to contrast the emotional states of the important characters. Shakespeare has also used skilful images with a view to presenting a colourful picture of Othello's background and experience. Othello speaks before the Senate of "deserts idle,/Rough quarries, rocks and hills, whose heads touch heaven," of "Cannibals, that each other eat;/The Anthropophagi, and men whose heads/Do grow beneath their shoulders" (I.3.140-41, 143-44), and later he refers to "the Pontic sea," "the Propontic" and "the Hellespont" (III.3.460, 463). Reference to this rough Nature indicates the rough and sturdy nature of Othello. Iago speaks of Othello that "The Moor a free and open nature too" (I.3.397), and it is precisely his open nature that is revealed in his use of language and images. Othello speaks what is in his heart without measuring its impact on others, while Iago speaks what is expedient and uses his language as a means of influencing others.

It is also to be noticed that there are very few really pleasant images in *Othello*. Most of the images are connected with unpleasant or repulsive themes. Iago often refers grossly to the more carnal aspects of sexual life, to disease, infections and plagues, and such themes infiltrate into the language of Othello, too, as he falls more and more under the influence of Iago. Thus, being sufficiently poisoned in mind against Desdemona by Iago, Othello speaks in a soliloquy:

> I had rather be a toad,
> And live upon the vapour in a dungeon,
> Than keep a corner in a thing I love,
> For others' uses: yet 'tis the plague of great ones,
> (III.3.274-77)

The image of the 'toad' recurs when Othello charges Desdemona with falsehood:

> But there, where I have garner'd up my heart,
> Where either I must live, or bear no life,
> The fountain, from the which my current runs,
> Or else dries up, to be discarded thence,
> Or keep it as a cistern, for foul toads
> To knot and gender in!
> (IV.2.58-63)

The main image of *Othello* is that of animals in action, preying upon one another, mischievous, lascivious, cruel, or suffering, and through these the general sense of pain and unpleasantness is much increased and kept constantly before us. More than half the animal images in the play are Iago's, and all these are contemptuous and repellent—a plague of flies, a quarrelsome dog, the recurrent image of bird-snaring, leading asses by the nose, a spider catching a fly, beating an offenceless dog, wild cats, wolves, goats, and monkeys. To these Othello adds his pictures of foul toads breeding in a cistern, summer flies in the shambles, the ill-boding raven over the infected house, to toad in a dungeon, the monster too hideous to be shown, bird-snaring, again, aspics' tongues, crocodiles' tears and his reiteration of goats and monkeys.

In *Othello* we see a low type of life, insects and reptiles swarming and preying on each other, not out of any special ferocity, but just in accordance with their natural instincts; mischievous and irresponsible wild cats, goats, monkeys or harmless innocent animals trapped or beaten. This reflects and repeats the spectacle of the wanton torture of one human being by another, which we witness in the tragedy.

If animals in action symbolize the main motive in *Othello*, there is another recurrent image which gives the atmosphere and background. As is fitting, with a setting of two famous sea-ports, the sea, its images and language, play an important part throughout. Iago uses sea-imagery easily. When complaining that Othello had passed him over for Cassio, he describes himself as "lee'd, and calm'd," (I.1.30). Iago knows that the state has not another of Othello's "fathom" (I.1.152) and so he "must show out a flag, and sign of love" (I.1.156). He coarsely describes his general's marriage in terms of a pirate taking a prize galleon. When he sees his plots shaping well, he murmurs with satisfaction: "My boat sails freely, both with wind and stream" (II.3.59). Caroline Spurgeon suggests that the sea-imagery is often used by Shakespeare to recapture the sea-faring atmosphere of the Venetian environment.

Othello's use of sea-images is noteworthy as they come naturally. On each occasion these images mark a moment of intense emotion. The first, at the height of his happiness, when he rejoins Desdemona at Cyprus, is an exclamation which is one of the most poignant and moving in the play. The next is at the height of his torture, when, having been shown the handkerchief, suspicion becomes certainty and he vows vengeance. There he affirms to Iago the unalterable quality of his resolve by comparing it to the "icy current, and compulsive course" of the ebbless "Pontic sea." And at the end, when he has carried out his resolve, and has suffered and realized all, again it is in sea language that he expresses his equally set determination to follow Desdemona: "Here is my journey's end, here is my butt, / And very sea-mark of my utmost sail" (V.2.268-69).

Shakespeare has clearly a very acute sense of smell, and he is peculiarly sensitive to bad smells. It is above all in *Othello* that we are made conscious of the foul and horrible smell of evil. The evil smell of sin is, in *Othello*, as constantly kept before us as are its foulness and dirt. When Iago tentatively suggests to Othello that, in choosing to marry him—a black man—Desdemona has already shown a perverted and unnatural taste, he exclaims: "Fie, we may smell in such a will most rank,/Foul disproportion; thoughts unnatural" (III.3.236-37). Emilia, when she realizes what Iago has done, cries: "Villainy, villainy, villainy!/I think upon't: I think I smell't: O villainy!" (V.2. 191-92). Again the horror of the contrast between the fair looks of Desdemona and what he believes her deeds, is made vivid by Othello entirely by means of smell. He laments: "O thou, black weed, why art so lovely fair?/Thou smell'st so sweet, that the sense aches at thee" (IV.2.69-70). And in answer to her piteous query, "Alas, what ignorant sin have I committed?" Othello gives her ample description of its character in his agonised cry: "What committed!/Heaven stops the nose at it" (IV.2. 72, 78-79).

Shakespeare's keen sense of colour contrast is often connected with a dominant emotion or theme and runs throughout a play; as the thought of the befouling of the purity of Desdemona and the opposition of her colour and that of the Moor expresses itself in black and white all through *Othello*. It is kept before us in Iago's contemptuous use of "black ram" and "white ewe" (I.1.88-89) and in his witty dialogue with Desdemona: "If she be black, and thereto have a wit,/She'll find a white, that shall her blackness hit." (II.1.132-33). It is found in the Duke's summary of Othello's character: "If virtue no delighted beauty lack,/Your son-in-law is far more fair than black" (I.3.289-90). Othello's call upon "black vengeance" (III.3.454) or his agonized ejaculation," my name, that was as fresh/As Dian's visage, is now begrim'd, and black/As mine own face" (III.3.392-94) or in his emphasis on the purity and fairness of Desdemona, "that whiter skin of hers than snow,/And smooth, as monumental alabaster;" (V.2.4-5) or in his lament "O ill starr'd wench,/Pale as thy smock, when we shall meet at count" (V.2.273-74), or in Emilia's cry, "O, the more angel she,/And you the blacker devil!" (V.2.131-32) the imagery of colour contrast is to be noticed.

With *Othello*, Shakespeare is at pains to make language and character fit with great precision and the Moor's images can be regarded as pieces of genuine self-revelation. Iago, too, betrays his nature in his language, but chiefly by the way he adapts himself to his partner in conversation. A study of Shakespeare's imagery also helps us to realize a little more fully and accurately one of the many ways by which he so magically stirs our emotions and excites our imagination, and it sometimes even throws a fresh ray of light on the significance of the play.

17

Shakespeare's Use of Prose and Verse

A tragedy is a serious play and it has been the custom since ancient times to use verse as the medium of expression. But the Elizabethan dramatists did not follow the practice rigidly. It has been found that verse and prose are mixed in the same play, in the same scene and sometimes in the same speech. The same character speaks verse at one time and prose at another. Although no hard and fast rule can be laid down as to when a dramatist should use prose and when he should use verse, yet certain general observations can be made about the method in Shakespeare's use of verse and prose. Verse is used usually by Shakespeare to indicate strong feeling or emotion. Characters of high rank and position speak in verse which sounds dignified. Again, a servant or a low-class character who usually speaks in prose, is often made to speak in verse as a mark of respect, when speaking to his master or superior. Such a character also speaks in verse when he or she is moved by strong passion. On the other hand, a person belonging to a high rank or position speaks in prose when he speaks to his servant or to a subordinate person.

The above observations about Shakespeare's use of prose and verse in his drama may be illustrated from *Othello*. Othello and Desdemona, the protagonists of the play, are persons of high rank. Othello is the General of the Venetian army. Desdemona is the daughter of a senator. So, they normally speak in verse. But when Othello is in a state of mental chaos (IV.1.35-43, 177-81), he speaks in prose. For, in Shakespeare prose is used for incoherent language of madness frenzy and mental paralysis. Othello's prose speech of directions to his wife (IV.3.7-9), is intended to emphasize the rigid formality of the words. Desdemona turns to prose when she talks in a playful mood with Iago (II.1.138-40, 143-47, 161-64). But she uses verse in her pleading colloquy with Iago (IV.2.113-16, 150-66).

Iago, the villain, who is but an ensign of Othello, speaks naturally and normally in prose. But, we should remember that he is playing an important role throughout the entire play. So, there is a distinct purpose in every change in his speeches. Prose and verse coincide with and expose the subtle changes in his mood. When Iago is jocular, simple and "honest Iago," he speaks in quick prose. But when he is feigning honest indignation or expressing real hatred, he is an emotional being and hence, all his soliloquies are in verse. In his soliloquies he hatches the successive steps or exalts in their success. At his first entry in the beginning of the play, he is seething with anger because Othello has ejected him and chosen Cassio as his lieutenant. This seems to be the real Iago speaking from the heart. His hatred of Cassio jets out in spasms of indignant rhetoric (I.1.8-33). Verse can only be the medium of such an expression. It is not until Brabantio also loses his temper that Iago regains his self-control. Then outwardly once again he is the mocker speaking prose (I.1.108-13). Next he appears in company with Othello. He is now feigning indignation, and verse is the proper medium for his speech now (I.2.1-5, 6-17). At the end of the Council Chamber scene he is left alone with Roderigo. Again, the mask is on and he speaks a flippant supple prose (I.3.319-33, 335-62, 364-72), until Roderigo leaves him. Then once more he is left alone, and his real emotion breaks out in powerful passionate verse (I.3.381-402), as the idea of his plot begins to grow. With Othello and Desdemona he habitually speaks verse. It is the language of conscious superiority to his credulous victims. But, when in the Fourth Act Othello uses the prose of frenzy, Iago also adopts with him prose. With superior persons he uses verse. When he addresses Montano in the brawl scene he uses verse (II.3.113-21). In the same scene he talks prose in familiar talk with

Cassio (II.3.26-29). He looks upon Roderigo as a snipe and almost throughout with Roderigo he talks prose of contempt. It is in the opening scene, however, he uses with Roderigo the ceremonial language of verse. Again, in the opening speech of the first scene of the Fifth Act addressed to Roderigo, he speaks in verse, as it makes the excitement of the critical moment.

Cassio is a lyrical character and hence he speaks verse habitually. But, in familiar talk with Iago in the drinking bout in the third scene of the Second Act, and in the contemptuous talk about Bianca in the first scene of the Fourth Act, he drops to prose. The prose-character of Iago inspires Cassio'a anguished prose colloquy with Iago in the third scene of the Second Act, where he laments about his lost reputation.

Emilia is seen in company with her mistress, Desdemona, her master, Othello, and her husband, Iago. She is on deferential terms with them all. Hence she uses verse. She falls into prose only once, in the cynical confession of her last confidential talk with Desdemona (IV.3.70-76).

The Clown is a comic character and so he speaks in prose. The herald announcing the proclamation in the second scene of the Second Act uses prose. The sailor in the presence of the Venetian senate uses the ceremonial language of verse in deference (I.3.14-16). Bianca is a low-class woman and uses prose normally. But in her wishful pleading with Cassio (III.4.170-74) she passes to verse.

The Duke and the senators are noble men and they use verse regularly. Of course, there is one exception. When the Duke turns from the affair of Othello's marriage to the urgent business of the state, he slips into prose (I.3.221-28). Thus, the matter-of-fact dry realistic situation induces the adoption of prose.

Shakespeare, thus, has followed a definite method in using prose and verse for the speeches of different characters in his play. The use of prose or verse depends sometimes on the rank and position of the characters, sometimes on the emotions expressed by them and sometimes on the situations in which the utterances are made.

18

Othello: A Work of Art

"The beauties of this play [*Othello*] impress themselves so strongly upon the attention of the reader," observes Dr Johnson, "that they can draw no aid from critical illustrations." In the opinion of Malone, this tragedy is "perhaps the most perfect" of all Shakespeare's works. Coleridge considers that *Othello* displays "the whole mature powers of the author's mind in admirable equilibrium." Macaulay states that, "*Othello* is perhaps the greatest work in the world."

Critics have noticed a great deal of change in Shakespeare's power of art, when, on the completion of his great comedies, he betook himself to tragedies. Shakespearian scholars are divided in opinion as to whether any change had come upon the temper of the dramatist when he took in hand the composition of tragedies. There are some who hold that it was only for art's sake that the great dramatist made use of his knowledge of the darker side of human life; while there are others who opine that the great tragedies arose out of a soul in trouble and that Shakespeare was not, in his tragedies, an impersonal artist. Nevertheless all critics agree in acknowledging that when he was writing *Othello* Shakespeare was already a master craftsman and that his executive power had improved in capacity and it was working almost of its own accord.

Othello is a drama in which chance or unreason predominates everywhere. According to Stopford A. Brooke, "The conception of the play, the movement of it, the events in it, the bringing out of the carastrophe, are all apparently in the realm of chance." Notwithstanding this aspect of unexpectedness, the master-artist has wonderfully built up the whole drama by means of scenes which follow one another in the most orderly and rational manner.

Othello begins with a wonderful rush into the main subject. Sir Walter Raleigh points out, "the subdued voices, talking earnestly in the street, of money, and preferment, and ancient grudges, are the muttering of the storm which breaks with tropical violence in the sudden night-alarm, and is lulled into quiet again in the Council chamber of the Duke. But this cloud is only the vanguard of the darkness that is to follow, and of the winds that are to blow till they have wakened death." The dramatic advantage of the play lies in the fact that Othello moves to his doom before us for fourteen and a half out of the fifteen scenes of this play, and if we are witness for the first time, we do not know till twelve lines from the end the ultimate piteousness of his fate.

In the first scene which is indeed a mêlée of passion and noise, the dramatist represents Othello as calm and dignified, and it is piteous to think of him, as he is a few days later, racked and torn with agony, all his quiet lost, all his dignity departed. In the second scene the hero's deportment before the Senate is self-confident and child-like in its innocence, and Desdemona is frank and full of the boldness of innocence. When Othello, trusting completely in the integrity of Iago, leaves Desdemona in his charge, his words, "My life upon her faith: honest Iago,/My Desdemona must I leave to thee" (I.3.294-95), seem pregnant with foreboding. Iago is hypocritical to the core and before the First Act has come to a close, he is already weaving the net for enmeshing the Moor, Desdemona and Cassio. It is indeed in the First Act that the foundation of the whole play is laid.

The Second Act opens with a great storm at sea. "The wind-shak'd surge, with high and monstrous main," has its prototype in the inner souls of the human beings who are brought on the stage. Shakespeare very artfully makes Iago arrange and spread out the details of his impending attack on Othello. In the Third Act Othello's soul is on the rack. The outward storm and the quarrels depicted in the former Acts are there no more. They have been replaced by the spiritual tempest in the breast of Othello. With a wonderful low and cunning stratagem Iago is made to devise ruin for the magnanimous Othello and the guileless Desdemona. William Hazlitt remarks that the Third Act of *Othello* is the author's "finest display, not of knowledge or passion separately, but of the two combined, of the knowledge of character with the expression of passion, of consummate art in the keeping up of appearance with the profound workings of nature, and the convulsive movements of uncontrollable agony, of the power of inflicting torture and of suffering it." In the fourth and the last scene of this Act, Othello tests Desdemona in the matter of the handkerchief, and although he has shown himself as most terrible before this, when in the company of Iago, his grandeur, thanks to the dramatic skill of Shakespeare, remains almost undiminished. But, the Othello of the Fourth Act is Othello in his fall. "His fall is never complete, but he is much changed," observes Bradley.

Desdemona, the pure and innocent Desdemona, is a woman wanting in intellectual power, and too full of perfect artlessness. Had one symptom of an angry spirit appeared in that lovely martyr, our sympathy with her would have been endangered, but Shakespeare knew better how to portray such a character. She dies a martyr to her love uncomplaining, unprotesting.

Shakespeare's art is at its highest when he invents Iago. For Othello we have the highest admiration and with Desdemona we are in complete sympathy. To compass their ruin was needed a monster in human shape. Shakespeare has, therefore, to make a heroic effort to bring into being a character like Iago. According to Hazlitt, "The character of Iago is one of the supererogations of Shakespeare's genius." The purpose of the dramatist might possibly have been served by an ordinary rogue. But, Shakespeare was always inclined towards a glorious excess. Event follows event quite naturally and rationally until a net is woven to take Othello in its toils. Left to himself, even when the toils are closing in upon him, Othello would have rent them asunder, and shaken them off. When he grows impatient and seems likely to break free, Iago is at hand, to keep him still and compel him to think as a muddled man does.

Othello is finally lashed into the extremity of jealousy. The great soldier in him is at last dead and the incomparable hero bids farewell to "the plumed troop, and the big wars, / That makes ambition virtue" (III.3.355-56). The erstwhile happy lover takes a vow before heaven to take the life of the devoted wife who has been represented to him as unchaste. In the second scene of the Fifth Act Othello stifles Desdemona, but before he perpetrates this cruel act he has kissed his sleeping wife. And when Iago's villainy is revealed by the letters found in the pocket of dead Roderigo and by the disclosures made by Emilia, and Desdemona's innocence is established, Othello stabs himself to "die upon a kiss." Thus, Othello's genuine love for Desdemona is established and he does not lose our sympathy for the murderous deed he has done.

At the first sight Iago would appear to have triumphed. But we find that evil does not prevail in the end. So the devil has his due at the end. Iago is imprisoned and is tortured. But Othello and Desdemona do not deserve their suffering, and their death was a mistake. We feel in our hearts the deepest pity for both of them. Shakespeare has delineated the story with so much perfection of detail that it could have come to no other conclusion but the one it has in the tragedy. His art of handling the story makes it natural, convincing, yet breath-taking.

Othello is a finished piece of dramatic art. Here the progress towards the climax of the tragedy is executed with absolute mastery. The passion rises with a positively musical effect. Iago's devilish plan is realized step by step with consummate certainty. All details are knit together into one firm and well-nigh inextricable knot. And the utter carelessness with which Shakespeare has treated the necessary lapse of time between the different stages of the action, has, by compressing the events of months and years into a few days, heightened the effect of strict and firm cohesion which the play produces effortlessly.

19

Universal Appeal of *Othello*

Of all the tragedies of Shakespeare, Othello has a special universal appeal because of its theme. It deals with people who are to be found in all ages; only they have changed their names. That is why the play has never lost its popularity. Rather, its popularity has been increased with the passing of time.

Macbeth deals with kingly ambition. It concerns the problems connected with a nation. A king is murdered and a villain usurps the throne. There are witches and a ghost, things which the Elizabethan audience might have enjoyed, but a modern man of rational mind will consider childish and silly. *Hamlet* is a drama of revenge. The ghost of Hamlet's father appears before Hamlet and others and seeks revenge for his murder by his own brother. Hamlet pursues revenge and gathers evidences of his uncle's guilt. Here also we see a usurper to the throne, a ghost and murders. *King Lear* has a theme quite unusual for the modern mind to accept. A king divides his kingdom among his daughters and consequently suffers at the hands of his selfish daughters. In these plays we are always conscious of men and women who are far above the rank of common people, and although we feel pity for their sufferings, they do not touch the depth of our hearts in the same way as the sufferings of our fellow men do.

Compared to those plays, *Othello* is a play of a different type. It is a sweet tale of love, ending tragically. Love knows no race, colour, class and age. Thus, Desdemona, the daughter of a noble senator, Brabantio, falls in love with a Moor, a wanderer staying away from the society of men, belonging to a different nation and not very handsome. She is charmed by the narration of adventures Othello himself has undergone and the great sufferings he has come through. At first she feels pity for the man and this pity develops into love. Othello also falls in love with this young charming lady because of the sympathy she has shown for his sufferings. Desdemona is so much in love with Othello that despite her father's dissent she elopes with Othello and marries him. Now enters a villain who is out to destroy their happiness to gratify his personal grudge against Othello. Othello and Desdemona do not know each other properly. They have come close together because of their deep and sincere love for each other. Naturally, they will try to guard their love jealously. As both of them are simple by nature without any knowledge of the evil in the world, they are vulnerable to evil suggestions. More so is Othello, as he is rather conscious of his colour, caste and nationality. So, when Iago slowly rouses in him suspicion about the fidelity of Desdemona, he seems to be in a fix. His love for Desdemona is genuine. So, he cannot accept the charge of faithlessness against her. But as he really does not have any idea of the nature of young women, because he has no occasion to mix with the womenfolk before, he can hardly disbelieve "honest Iago" in whom he has absolute trust. And when this cunning devil sufficiently inflames his heart with the fiery passion of jealousy, and circumstances favour the hellish scheme of the devil, Othello becomes blind with passion and without investigating the truth of the accusation with a cool brain, decides to do away with his beloved Desdemona. And when reality dawns upon him, he is so shocked and bewildered that he commits suicide.

This is a tale narrating imaginary incidents, but similar situations are to be found in every age among young men and women in love, where love is turned into disaster because of misunderstanding. As we witness the play or read the drama even today, we do not remember Othello as a mighty General of Venice or Desdemona as the daughter of a powerful and rich senator of Venice. To us they appear as a common man and a common woman in love, who are 'star-crossed,' as it were. We follow the course of action. We admire the young lovers. We have bitter hatred for the devilish Iago, a "motiveless malignity," according to Coleridge. Shakespeare has so skilfully spread the net of suspicion and jealousy, that it appears quite natural. Frustration in love often leads to violence. The deeper the love the greater is the fear of losing the beloved. And the mere suspicion that the attention of the beloved is drawn to others, makes the lover almost insane. This is to be found in every age. Perhaps, it will not be out of place to refer to a real incident in my own life, that took place about half a century ago. I was then a juror in Calcutta High Court. A young boy was accused of causing hurt to a young girl by throwing nitric acid on to her face disfiguring her permanently, as he had failed to get the love of that girl. The trial continued for several days and the boy was found guilty and was punished to seven years of imprisonment.

The characters Shakespeare created are so alive and realistic that we seem to see them around us. We wonder at the cleverness and dissimulation of Iago. We feel deep pity at the anguish and distress of Othello. We cry in despair as we witness the innocent Desdemona who does not know how to protect herself or revolt against falsehood. We laugh at the foolish Roderigo who allows himself to be duped by Iago. Thus, *Othello* tells a story of the ordinary human souls surcharged by strong emotions. It is a story of men and women who have loved and are lost, in every age.

The play also has an indirect message for the young lovers. Love makes a person blind and irrational, sometimes. The play warns the lovers against being blindly credulous. Before taking any drastic step or a serious decision, they must consider the pros and cons of the matter and judge everything dispassionately. Thus, the story of *Othello* has a universal appeal and this makes it most popular in every age and it will grow in popularity as time passes.

20

A Summing-Up

"The beauties of this play *Othello* impress themselves so strongly upon the attention of the reader," observes Dr Johnson, "that they can draw no aid from critical illustrations." Various other critics have praised eloquently this unique play of Shakespeare. Yet, the Shakespearian scholars are divided in opinion as to whether any change had come upon the temper of the dramatist when he took in hand the composition of tragedies. There are some who hold that it was only for art's sake that the great dramatist made use of his knowledge of the darker side of human life, while there are others who think that the great tragedies arose out of a soul in trouble and Shakespeare was not, in the tragedies, an impersonal artist. But none will deny that in *Othello* Shakespeare has revealed himself as a master craftsman in transforming a crude story into a throbbing and pulsating drama of the human soul.

Chances and accidents play a predominant role in effecting the tragedy in *Othello*. But they have been introduced so skilfully and spontaneously that they will not strike anybody as forced or unnatural. The dropping of the handkerchief and Emilia's picking it up secretly, the appearance of Bianca with the handkerchief before Cassio while Othello has been watching the scene from his hiding place, Cassio's arrival into the presence of Othello when he was in a swoon, and such other chance happenings are so arranged that they appear quite normal.

The rush of the movement of the situations in the play is quite significant. Actually all the incidents in the drama appear to have taken place within maximum three days. But Shakespeare has not allowed his audience or the readers to pause and ponder over this short period of time and find out many inconsistencies. Scene after scene move at a great speed and just after we have confronted a scene and start analysing it, there comes another scene more intriguing and interesting.

In characterization Shakespeare has shown his keen insight into human nature and has given the different characters their distinctive features so that we are stirred to different emotions as we confront them. We admire Othello, pity Desdemona, hate Iago and laugh at Roderigo. It is, however, in the delineation of Iago's character that Shakespeare has shown his utmost skill. Actually, the entire plot of the play is guided by Iago. So subtly and skilfully he has woven his fine cobweb that he enmeshes not only Othello, but also Cassio, Roderigo and even Desdemona.

A drama differs from other forms of literary work by being presented through dialogues. So, the use of language counts for much in a drama. Earlier it was the general practice to use verse for tragedy. But, Shakespeare used both verse and prose according to need. Verse is used by him for the speeches of people of rank and position and also for expressing intense emotion. Prose speech is generally given to people of lower class, maids and servants, but when they talk to their superiors, they often use verse. This judicious use of verse and prose makes the dialogue most effective.

The use of images and symbols is a distinctive feature of the tragedies of Shakespeare. In *Othello*, too, we will notice a number of iterative imagery. The most predominant of them are the animal images which keep a general sense of pain, torture and unpleasantness constantly before us. The sea-imagery is to be found in many places, and it reminds one of the sea background of the places where the incidents happen, and it has been suitably employed to give vent to the swelling passion and emotion of the characters. The imagery of the smell has been particularly used to indicate the good and the evil in this world of ours. The good smell suggests goodness, beauty and purity, while bad smell indicates sin, vileness and foulness. The colour images, particularly of black and white, are used to indicate the blackness or foulness and goodness or purity of human nature. Thus, with the help of images Shakespeare has been able to throw bright light on the characters and on the significance of the play as a whole.

Othello has a theme that attracts people of all ages and all nations. Shakespeare deals here with the eternal themes of love and jealousy. Othello and Desdemona are not merely a Venetian General and the daughter of a Venetian senator. They are two young lovers genuinely in love with each other and become the victims of a monstrous villain, Iago, the like of whom is to be found in all ages. The play also warns young lovers against irrational credulity and rash action. It has, thus, a universal appeal and it grows in popularity with the passage of time.

Othello can be interpreted on three levels, the personal, social and the metaphysical. On the personal level we have a straightforward domestic tragedy. On the social level we have a study of contemporary problem, the clash between the 'new man' thrown up by certain aspects of Renaissance culture, the atheist-Machiavel with his principle of pure self-interest, and the chivalric-type, representing the traditional values of social order and morality. On the metaphysical level we see Othello and Iago as exemplifying and participating in the age-long warfare of good and evil.

Critics, however, are not all praise for this unique tragedy of Shakespeare. Dr Johnson, who praises the play eloquently, has also his reservations about the play. He complains that the drama is wanting "of the most exact and scrupulous regularity" because of the First Act which opens in Venice, while the rest of the play is set in Cyprus. So, Dr Johnson holds that the classical unity of place has been violated in *Othello*. Opposing this view of Dr Johnson, Hudson is of the opinion that the First Act is eminently rich in character, in life, in everything indeed for which the dramatic form is most desirable. No narration could supply the place of Othello's address to the Senate. And without defeating the proper spirit and impression of the early out-croppings of Iago's wickedness as revealed to Roderigo, it was not possible to express them in any other way. Any attempt to produce the best parts of that Act in the narrative form would have made the drama even more irregular than it is now. Thus, the violation of the rule of unity of place does not detract from the merit of the drama.

Some critics have discovered an element of unnaturalness in Desdemona's marriage with the Moor. Such critics have assumed that Othello is a black 'negro,' which he is not actually. Othello is a chivalrous Moorish chief who has earned the regard and estimation of all and sundry, and has been entrusted with a very responsible office by the Venetian senate. He has travelled extensively and has acquitted himself creditably in various battles on sea and land. To crown all, he is of royal descent as he himself reveals to Iago. So, it is not far from natural that the daughter of a Venetian senator should have fallen in love with one so esteemed and so highly placed and who lacks only a white skin. Dr Brandes defends the marriage by remarking that Desdemona "was more womanly than other women, as the noble Othello was more manly than other men. So that after all there is a very good reason for the attraction between them; the most womanly of women feels herself drawn to the manliest of men."

In the opinion of some critics Shakespeare has painted the protagonist, Othello, as a jealous husband and this constitutes one of the blemishes of the drama. But this is a wrong view taken of Othello. Othello is not really jealous. He is not in rivalry with Cassio for the affection of his wife. Professor Dowden pertinently remarks: "It is with an agonized sense of justice that he destroys the creature who is dearest to him in the world, knowing certainly that with hers his own true life must cease."

Another charge against the play is that Iago is too much of a villain to be a natural character. In the words of Stopford A. Brooke, it looks "as if a monstrous mind had arrived by chance in the body of a non-commissioned officer." But, according to Dr Brandes, Iago is not, after all, an unnatural or impossible character. Dr Brandes thinks that Iago is a natural character and Shakespeare must have met such a character in real life. Shakespeare has made him a human character, only that he is too clever and too malignant.

Some critics take exception to Desdemona's scant respect for veracity. They are of opinion that Desdemona should not have resorted to a falsehood regarding the missing handkerchief. When Othello repeatedly asks for the handkerchief, Desdemona says, "It is not lost, but what an if it were?" (III.4.81), and then "I say it is not lost " (III.4.83). Even in her death-bed she tells Emilia falsely that she herself has taken her own life. Desdemona, however, is guilty of no falsehood in the true sense of the term. It is solely due to her guiltlessness that she blunders in the matter of the lost handkerchief. "Feeling so secure in Othello's love she counts a lost handkerchief, for all its magic virtues, as a mere trifle in comparison" (Donovan). As to the death-bed utterance, it adds a vast deal to the many invaluable qualities of her heart, and her words show unmistakably the accent of a love which no ill usage can sour or dull. Generous and loving even in death, she turns away the guilt of murder from her beloved husband, even though he has met her love with death.

Another objection raised by some critics against the full and frank treatment of sexual love in *Othello*. It is true that the way in which sexual jealousy has found an exposition in the play, does indeed provoke a sense of pain and repulsion in some readers. But the feeling that is evoked is more or less personal or subjective. Moreover the full and frank treatment of sexual love has been necessary from the dramatic point of view, as it has been the prime mover of action.

It has been often argued that Shakespeare has offended against the canons of art by representing on the stage certain shocking and sensational scenes. Those scenes are where Othello strikes Desdemona in the presence of Lodovico and others, where he treats his wife as a woman of loose character, and finally in the scene where Desdemona is murdered by Othello. With regard to the first scene, there is little defence as there is not a sufficiently overwhelming tragic feeling in the passage to make it bearable. The second scene, of course, intensifies the tragic feelings of Othello who has been terribly shaken at the thought of faithlessness of his wife. In the murder scene the bed, where Desdemona is stifled, is within the curtains which are drawn together at the words: "Let it be hid" (V.2.366).

Thus, in spite of the various objections raised against the play, *Othello* is a finished piece of dramatic art. Iago's devilish plan is realized step by step with consummate certainty. All details are knit together into one firm and well-nigh inextricable knot. And the careful carelessness with which Shakespeare has treated the necessary lapse of time between the different stages of the action, has, by compressing the events of months and years into a few days, heightened the effect of strict and firm cohesion which the play produces.

21

Critical Reception of the Play

Of all the tragedies of Shakespeare *Othello* seems to be the most popular and, according to most readers, it may not be his greatest work, it is his best play. The play was first performed in 1604, "By the Kings plaiers. Hallamas Day being the first of November. A play in the Banketinge house at Whithall called The Moor of Venis. Shaxberd" (From the record of Edmund Tilney, Master of the Revels). In the early seventeenth century it was performed several times at court, and it was published thrice, which indicate the great popular demand of the play. Comments on the early performances of the play are not available, although a witness of the play, produced in Oxford in 1610 by King's Men, noticed how the audience moved to pity and wept on seeing the murder of Desdemona.

As with the case of other plays of Shakespeare, there were Quarto and Folio versions of the play. Although the First Folio of 1623 is considered the authentic version of Shakespeare's plays, the Quarto and Folio texts of *Othello* do not differ much unlike those of *Hamlet* and *King Lear*. The Folio version dwells much on sexual references in the play, Brabantio's great distress for Othello's seduction of his daughter and the importance of Emilia in the action of the drama. The popularity of the play on the stage continued even in the Restoration period because of the amorous intrigue, the exotic language and of class, race and gender relationships treated in the play, which were the social concerns of the day.

The early critical analysis of the text of the play was found in *A Short View of Tragedy* (1693) by Thomas Rymer. His approach to the play is characterized by a stringent demand of neo-classicism, that the play should obey the three classical unities. He also suggests that although *Othello* is highly regarded by many critics, it is a bad play as it refuses to observe the natural hierarchies of race, sex and class, and as its plot revolves round a silly problem of a lost handkerchief and thus fails to rise to the level of a high tragedy. Rymer is unable to accept the fact that Othello, a black warrior, could ever be a tragic hero, and that a woman of Desdemona's stature could ever fall in love with him. All this appears to him quite unnatural. Thus neither the plot nor the characters of the play maintain any sense of decorum. Rymer's criticism of the play shows that he has not comprehended the play properly and, hence, quite justly he has been ridiculed for his views.

The popularity of the play increased in the eighteenth century so much so that in London the play was staged almost every year. The attention of the critics also was drawn to the text. Samuel Johnson's enthusiasm for the play may be considered representative of the play's critical reception in the eighteenth century. Shakespeare now became the most celebrated English dramatist of all time and his violation of the classical rules was taken as a virtue. According to Johnson, *Othello* is difficult to analyse, as the play teaches the reader the inner truth of human nature. Shakespeare, with his finest imagination, produced in it recognizable human types and presented the reader with the terror of innate human experience. Johnson is definitely disturbed by Shakespeare's rough style and lack of literary polish, yet he regards Shakespeare's insight into human nature as his principal merit and to illustrate it he carefully analyses the terrifying but convincing process by which Iago undermines Othello's faith in Desdemona.

Othello continued to be one of the most frequently published plays of Shakespeare in the nineteenth century. For, the play appealed to the romantic taste for the sublime excesses of the emotions. In this century Samuel Taylor Coleridge appeared as one of the most perceptive and important critics of Shakespeare. He made a brilliant and subtle close reading of the individual lines and phrases of the Shakespearian text and gave his reasoned judgments. He appreciated the sublime tragic beauty of the play and noticed the essential human nature presented in it. He was one with Johnson to hold that the plot of ago to destroy thello was both authentic and powerful. He saw thello as a oor and not a blac frican and believed that the character of thello was so designed by ha espeare as to derive the ma imum sympathy of the audience towards him. His remar about ago the motive hunting of motiveless malignity has become almost classical.

dward owden is a far less incisive critic than oleridge but his observations on are interesting in the sense that they give us an idea of the ictorian approach to this play. He is sympathetic to thello and esdemona and sees ha espeare as the creator of a tragic love story. He analyses the characters of thello and esdemona and carefully traces the growth of love between them. He finds in the love of each a romantic element and romance acts as a luminous mist disguising certain facts leading to the doom of the lovers. He is ambivalent about thello regarding him as a strange and e otic hero of noble stature with a certain aspect which it were well that esdemona had seen though she trembled.

ne of the important critics of the twentieth century is . . radley who has helped to create the modern conception of ha espeare as the author of four of the world s greatest tragedies in his boo

. He responds to the most painfully e citing and terrible nature of the drama. He ma es significant point when he stresses the important omission of a sub plot. He refers to the unusual method of construction by which the conflict begins late and advances without appreciable pause and with accelerating speed to the catastrophe. He also points to the theme of se ual jealousy and the painful and engrossing nature of the suffering which the torment of this passion inflicts on a great soul. uch jealousy as thello s turns human nature into chaos and brings out the beast in man. he suffering of esdemona is an intolerable spectacle that ha espeare presents in the play. he spectacle is intolerable because of her passive suffering. he cannot protest or retaliate because of her sweet nature and absolute love of Othello. Referring to Iago Bradley observes that Iago's intrigue occupies a position in the drama for which no parallel can be found in the other tragedies. Bradley, thus, shows why Shakespeare has attained such a pre-eminent literary position.

G. Wilson Knight in *The Wheel of Fire* (1930) has made an effort to understand how the language of the drama, *Othello*, worked to express its tragic themes. He is more sympathetic to Othello than many other critics and has coined the term "The Othello Music." He has analysed the beautiful poetic speeches of Othello and pointed out the grand musical words like 'Propontic,' 'Hellespont,' 'Chrysolite,' 'Mandragora,' 'Anthropophagi,' that help to understand the play not as a mere text, but as performed on the stage. Thus, he moves away from a concentration on character study, which his predecessors have done, towards a study of the play's poetic metaphors and the overall sweep of its language.

E.E. Stoll also, in his criticism of Shakespeare, tries to come out of the Bradleyan influence of studying Shakespeare's plays as character studies. He is in favour of a criticism based on the theatrical qualities of the drama, as he thinks that this was what really mattered to the dramatists of the sixteenth and seventeenth centuries. In the chapter on 'Iago' in *Shakespeare and Other Masters* (1940) his analysis of Iago illustrates the elements of his method of criticism, which is to concentrate on the action and purpose of the play and the effect they may have on an audience. He holds that at least logically or poetically Iago is one of Shakespeare's most consistent characters. He tells of Iago: "He is Satan, though without a God."

While criticism of *Othello* in the first half of the twentieth century concentrated on the existential and formal questions about *Othello's* particular status as a tragedy and the tragic design it expressed, more recent criticism has been much more based on historical research and has concentrated on the questions of race, politics and sex. Of the major critics of the modern times mention nay be made of G. Wilson Knight, T.S.

Eliot, William Empson and F.R. Leavis, all considering *Othello* as having a unique place among Shakespeare's tragedies.

William Empson in *The structure of Complex Words* (1951) analyses the variety of meanings of the word "honest" in the chapter 'Honest in *Othello*.' He shows how the major themes are contained in the smallest details which are often missed by ordinary readers and also by professional critics. In his brilliant readings of the play he scrupulously analyses individual words and relate their range of possible meanings in a general context to those in the work in question. He has counted fifty-two uses of the words "honest" and "honesty" in *Othello* and observes how such words can raise large issues.

F.R. Leavis, in *The Common Pursuit* (1952), considers Othello a lesser tragic hero than Shakespeare's other major protagonists. Both Leavis and T.S. Eliot argue that Othello is largely to blame for his downfall as he is a gullible and naïve character, and they emphasize that Shakespeare's choice of a black African as a tragic hero is responsible for all this. Marvin Rosenberg, in his book *The Masks of Othello* (1961), examines the play from an actor's point of view, and shows how difficult it is to act the roles of Othello and Desdemona, particularly because the characters appear so contradictory. The previous critics like Leavis and Eliot conspicuously ignore the stage tradition of the play and consider the play as a work on the vicissitudes of human nature, to be read as a text. Rosenberg looks at the characters as they might appear on the stage. He discusses the difficulty in acting the roles of such problematic characters as Othello, Desdemona and Iago, because of some of the inexplicable behaviours of these characters. G.K. Hunter, in his article 'Othello and Colour Prejudice' (1967) included in *Dramatic Identities and Cultural Tradition: Studies in Shakespeare and His Contemporaries* (1978), makes a serious attempt, perhaps for the first time, to examine the attitude of the Elizabethan audience to race and tries to find out their reaction to the character of Othello. Many of the later critics attempted to establish the identity of Othello as a black negro. But Shakespeare, according to Hunter, seems to be sympathetic to his protagonist and perhaps wants to impress on his audience the fact that his Moor is a black man from North Africa, who may be as noble and impressive as a white man. Later critics take up this cue and engage themselves in interesting debates. Thus, for example, Karen Newman, in his interesting essay 'And Wash the Ethiop White' (1987), attempts to link the racial prejudice to the sexual ones suggesting that *Othello* might play on an audience's fear of the mingling of the races. He sees Shakespeare eager to challenge the ideologies of race and gender in his time. He finds that the real transgression of the play is its sympathetic representation of the love of a white woman for a black man—a central taboo in the Western society, with its attendant fear of the production of undesirable mixed-race children by the couple.

The feminist theory and analysis of modern times also play a significant role in inducing the critics to rethink and refigure the significance of the play. Lisa Jardine has such a feminine perspective of the play in her article, '"Why Should He Call Her Whore?": Defamation and Desdemona's Case' in *Reading Shakespeare Historically* (1996). Her essay concentrates on the women in the play. She attempts to establish the common people's attitude to women in England around the year 1600 by using evidences from the records of court at that time. She shows that Othello murders Desdemona for her supposed adultery and not out of jealousy, as is assumed by many critics and interpreters. She holds that in Shakespeare's England husbands in Othello's position felt that they had the right to humiliate their wives in public, if they were found guilty of adultery.

Andrew Hadfield, in his essay, 'The "gross clasps of a lascivious Moor": The Domestic and Exotic Contexts of Othello' in *Literature, Travel, and Colonial Writing in the English Renaissance* (1998), explores the Venetian setting of the play, *Othello*. He shows how the political system of Venice might have appealed to many English men and women at the turn of the seventeenth century. The ways in which the Venetian Government preserved the liberty of its inhabitants, have been used by Shakespeare as a means of comparing Venice with contemporary England. Venice then was a byword for liberty, a desirable quality in moderation, although a curse if it is allowed to run in excess. David McPherson, in his essay, 'Othello and the Myth of Venice' in *Shakespeare, Jonson, and the Myth of Venice* (1990) shows how the Venetian background of *Othello* is not merely an exotic backdrop, rather it has been deliberately chosen by Shakespeare as he wants to explore a number of themes in his tragedy. McPherson, unlike Hadfield, shows the darker side of Venetian setting and discusses how the myth of Venetian liberty with its attendant promise of the lascivious vice of Venetian women attracted the Englishmen during the Renaissance.

Thus, we find that *Othello* has received constant notice of the critics from its first performance till the present times. The play has been considered from different perspectives. There are historical, social, political and even feminist points of view. The focus of attention is, however, always on the three principal characters—Othello, Iago and Desdemona. We have also noticed how the musical quality of the language used in the play has not failed to attract the attention of a critic.

Some Important Questions

1. Point out the probable date of *Othello's* composition. How do you ascertain the date?
2. What are the probable sources of Shakespeare's *Othello*? How has Shakespeare utilized his sources?
3. Consider *Othello* as a domestic tragedy.
4. "We must not call the play [*Othello*] a tragedy of intrigue as distinguished from a tragedy of character." (Bradley)—Discuss.
5. Consider *Othello* as a tragedy of jealousy.
6. "In its whole constructional effect *Othello* differs from the other tragedies." (Bradley)—Discuss.
7. "If not the perfect work of art in literature, *Othello* is undoubtedly Shakespeare's masterpiece of construction." —Discuss.
8. "While *Othello* satisfies with extraordinary completeness the classical demand for structural unity and coherence, it does this in a way entirely true to the genius of Elizabethan dramatic art."—Discuss.
9. In *Othello* chance or unreason, blind and deaf, is at the centre of human life.—Elucidate.
10. Discuss with illustrations the part played by chance in precipitating the tragedy in *Othello*.
11. Shakespeare never lost his faith in goodness even though sounding the depths of evil in his great tragedies.— Explain and illustrate this remark with reference to *Othello*.

12. Shakespeare has made a liberal use of soliloquy as an instrument of character-painting in *Othello*. Illustrate this remark with reference to the soliloquies of Othello and Iago.
13. Discuss the importance of "double time" used by Shakespeare in *Othello*.
14. Discuss Shakespeare's skilful use of symbols and images in *Othello*.
15. "The central feeling in Shakespearean tragedy is the impression of waste." (Bradley)—Examine *Othello* in the light of this statement.
16. *Othello* is the tragedy of a man who "loved not wisely but too well."—Discuss.
17. "Othello's tragedy is Othello's and not the outcome of a chance association with Iago."—Discuss how far Othello is responsible for the tragic catastrophe of the play.
18. Make a critical analysis of the temptation scene (III.3) in *Othello* laying special emphasis on Iago's role.
19. Analyse the character of Othello as a tragic hero.
20. "The Ancient rather than the Moor is in reality the principal character of the play. For, it is he who determines not only the course of the plot, but also the characters in the play."—Discuss.
21. Give a critical analysis of the murder scene (V.2). Does Othello take Desdemona's life in anger, in a fit of jealousy, to avenge his wounded honour, or as an act of disinterested judgment upon her?
22. "A union based upon mutual fascination rather than mutual knowledge of character has in it all the seeds of a bitter disenchantment, a violent catastrophe." How far is this view illustrated in the marriage of Othello and Desdemona?
23. Illustrate Shakespeare's handling of the villain as a dramatic character with reference to Iago.
24. What were the real motive forces that led Iago to act as

he did? Do you think his malignity motiveless? Discuss fully.

25. Is Iago an absolute infidel?
26. Discuss the role of Iago in the development of the action in *Othello*.
27. "Desdemona is not a tragic character, although she is a pathetic one."—Discuss.
28. Consider Desdemona as a typical Shakespearian heroine.
29. How far is Desdemona responsible for her tragic end?
30. "Emilia is the instrument of Nemesis in *Othello*." (Moulton)—Discuss.
31. What blemishes have been found by critics in the play, *Othello*? Indicate your own opinion.
32. Account for the universal appeal of *Othello*.

A Select Bibliography

Different Editions of the Text

Othello. Ed. E.A.J. Honigmann. Arden 3. London: Nelson, 1997.

Othello. Ed. M.R. Ridley. The Seventh Arden Edition. 1958; rpt. London: Methuen & Co. Ltd., 1976.

Othello. Ed. Norman Sanders. The New Cambridge Shakespeare. Cambridge: Cambridge University Press, 1984.

Critical and Other Relevant Works

Alexander, Peter. *Shakespeare*. Oxford: OUP, 1964.

Bethell, S.L. "Shakespeare's Imagery: The Diabolic Images in 'Othello.'" *Shakespeare Survey: An Annual Survey of Shakespearian Study and Production*, CUP, 5 (1952), 62-80.

Bevington, David. *Shakespeare*. Arlington Heights, Ill: A.H.M. Publications, 1978.

Bloom, Edward A. Ed. *Shakespeare—1564-1964*, Providence: Brown University Press, 1964.

Bloom, Harold. "William Shakespeare's 'Othello.'" *Modern Critical Interpretations*. New York: Chelsea House, 1987.

Bradley, A.C. *Shakespearean Tragedy*. London: The Macmillan and Co. Ltd., 1904.

Brooke, Stopford A. "Othello." *Ten More Plays of Shakespeare*. London: Constable and Company Ltd., 1913, 165-96.

Brooke, Tucker. "The Romantic Iago." *The Yale Review*, n.s. vol. vii, no. 2 (January 1918), 349-59.

Bryant, J.A. *'Othello,' Hippolyta's View: Some Christian Aspects of Shakespeare's Plays*. Lexington, Kentucky: University of Kentucky Press, 1961.

Campbell, Lily B. "'Othello': A Tragedy of Jealousy." *Shakespeare's Tragic Heroes*. Cambridge, England, CUP, 1930, 148-74.

Chambers, E.K. "Othello." *Shakespeare: A Survey*. 1925; rpt. Hill and Wang, 1958, 218-25.

Charlton, H.B. *Shakespearean Tragedy*. Cambridge, England: CUP, 1948.

_____. "Shakespeare's 'Othello.'" *Bulletin* of the John Rylands Library. 31, No. 1 (January 1948), 28-53.

Clemen, Wolfgang. "Othello." *The Development of Shakespeare's Imagery*. 1951; rpt. London: Methuen and Co., 1977, 119-32.

Coleridge, Samuel Taylor. "Notes on the Tragedies of Shakespeare: 'Othello.'" *Shakespeare Criticism*. Vol. 1. Ed. Thomas Middleton Raysor. 2nd ed. London: Dutton, 1960, 40-49.

Craig, Hardin. "The Great Trio." *An Interpretation of Shakespeare*. Columbia, Missouri: Lucas Brothers, 1966.

Davidson, Peter. "Othello." *The Critics Debate*. Basingstoke: Macmillan, 1988.

Dowden, Edward. *Shakespeare: A Critical Study of His Mind and Art*. 1875; rpt. London: C. Kegan Paul & Co., 1879.

Elliott, G.R. "'*Othello*' as a Love-Tragedy." *The American Review*, Vol. 8, No. 3 (January 1937), 257-88.

Empson, William. "Honest in 'Othello.'" *The Structure of Complex Words*. London: Chatto & Windus, 1951, 218-49.

Gerard, Albert. "'Egregiously an Ass: The Dark Side of the Moor; A View of Othello's Mind." *Shakespeare Survey*. CUP, 10 (1957).

Gervinus, G.G. "Third Period of Shakespeare's Dramatic Poetry: 'Othello.'" *Shakespeare Commentaries*. trans. F.E. Bunnett. rev.ed. 1877; rpt. AMS Press, Inc., 1971, 505-47.

Granville-Barker, Harley. *Prefaces to Shakespeare*, 4th series. London: Sidgwick and Jackson Ltd., 1945.

Hadfield, Andrew. "The 'Gross Clasps of a Lascivious Moor': The Domestic and Exotic Contexts of 'Othello.'" *Literature, Travel, and Colonial Writing in the English Renaissance, 1545-1625*. Oxford: Clarendon Press, 1998.

Hazlitt, William. "Othello." *Characters of Shakespeare's Plays and Lectures on the English Poets*. London: The Macmillan Co. Ltd., 1903, 26-38.

Hibbard, G.R. "'Othello' and the Pattern of Shakespearian Tragedy." *Shakespeare Survey*, 21(1968), 39-46.

Hunter, G.K. "'Othello' and Colour Prejudice" (1967). *Dramatic Identities and Cultural Tradition: Studies in Shakespeare and His Contemporaries*. Liverpool: Liverpool University Press, 1978.

Jardine, Lisa. "'Why should he call her whore?': Defamation and Desdemona's Case." *Reading Shakespeare Historically*. London: Routledge, 1996.

Johnson, Samuel. *Johnson on Shakespeare*. Ed. Walter Raleigh. 1908; rpt. London: OUP, 1949.

Kirschbaum, Leo. "The Modern Othello." *ELH, A Journal of English Literary History*. 11, No. 4 (December 1944), 283-96.

Knight, G. Wilson. "The 'Othello' Music." *The Wheel of Fire: Essays in Interpretation of Shakespeare's Sombre Tragedies*. London: OUP, 1930, 107-31.

Lamb, Charles. "On the Tragedies of Shakespeare, Considered with Reference to Their Fitness for Stage Representation." *The Works in Prose and Verse of Charles and Mary Lamb*. Ed. Thomas Hutchinson. OUP, 1908, 124-42.

Leavis, F.R. "Diabolic Intellect and the Noble Hero: A Note on 'Othello.'" *Scrutiny*. Vol. VI, No. 3 (December 1937), 259-83.

____. *The Common Pursuit*. Harmondsworth, Middlesex: Penguin Books Ltd., 1963.

McPherson, David. "Othello and the Myth of Venice." *Shakespeare, Jonson, and the Myth of Venice*. Newark, Del.: University of Delaware Press, 1990.

Muir, Kenneth. *Shakespeare's Sources*. London: Methuen & Co. Ltd., 1957.

Murry, John Middleton. "Desdemona's Handkerchief." *Shakespeare*. London: Jonathan Cape, 1936, 311-21.

Newman, Karen. "'And wash the Ethiop white': Femininity and the Monstrous in 'Othello.'" *Shakespeare Reproduced: The Text in History and Ideology*. Ed. Jean E. Howard and Marion F.O. Connor. London: Routledge, 1987.

Nicoll, Allardyce. "The Tragedie of 'Othello,' The Moor of Venice." *Studies in Shakespeare*. Leonard & Virginia Woolf, 1927, 80-109.

Ribner, Irving. "The Pattern of Moral Choice: 'Othello.'" *Patterns in Shakespearean Tragedy*. London: Methuen & Co. Ltd., 1960, 91-115.

Rosenberg, Marvin. *The Masks of Othello: The Search for the Identity of Othello, Iago and Desdemona by Three Centuries of Actors and Critics*. Berkeley and Los Angeles: University of California Press, 1961.

Rymer, Thomas. "A Short View of Tragedy" (1693). *The Critical Works of Thomas Rymer*. Ed. Curt A. Zimansky. Yale University Press, 1956, 82-176.

Schlegel, August Wilhelm. "Criticisms on Shakespeare's Tragedies" (1811). *A Course of Lectures on Dramatic Art and Literature*. Ed. Rev. A.J.W. Morrison. trans. John Black, rev.ed. 1846; rpt. AMS Press, Inc., 1965, 400-13.

Sewell, Arthur. *Character and Society in Shakespeare*. Oxford: Clarendon Press, 1951.

Siegel, Paul N. *Shakespearean Tragedy and the Elizabethan Compromise*. New York: New York University Press, 1957.

Spivack, Bernard. "The Family of Iago," and "Iago Revisited." *Shakespeare and the Allegory of Evil*. New York: Columbia University Press, 1958, 28-59, 415-53.

Spurgeon, Caroline F.E. *Shakespeare's Imagery and What It Tells Us*. 1935; rpt. CUP, 1971.

Stoll, E.E. "Iago." *Shakespeare and Other Masters*. Cambridge, Mass.: Harvard University Press, 1940.

____. "Othello." *Art and Artifice in Shakespeare: A Study in Dramatic Contrast and Illusion*. CUP, 1933, 6-55.

____. *"Othello": An Historical and Comparative Study*. 1915; rpt. Haskell House, 1964.

Swinburne, A.C. "Third. Period: Tragic and Romantic." *A Study of Shakespeare*. 1880; rpt. AMS Press, Inc., 1965.

Tillyard, E.M.W. "The Tragic Pattern." *Shakespeare's Last Plays*. Chatto and Windus, 1938, 16-58.

Traversi, Derek. "Othello." *The Wind and the Rain*. Vol. VI, No. 1 (Summer 1949), 248-69.

Ulrici, Hermann. "Criticisms of Shakespeare's Dramas: 'Othello.'" *Shakespeare's Dramatic Art: And His Relation to Calderon and Goethe*. trans. A.J.W. Morrison. Chapman Brothers, 1846, 183-91.

Vaughan, Virginia Mason and Cartwright, Kent. *'Othello': New Perspectives*. London: Associated University Press, 1991.

Wain, John. *'Othello': A Casebook*. London: Macmillan, 1971.

Wilson, Harold S. "Othello." *On the Design of Shakespearean Tragedy*. Toronto: University of Toronto Press, 1957.

A Brief Glossary

Abilities	: resources, warlike equipment
Affin'd	: bound, under obligation
Alabaster	: a white marble-like mineral
Aleppo	: a city in Syria, the headquarters of Turkish power
Almain	: a Spanish term for a German
Anthropophagi	: man-eaters, cannibals
Antres	: caves
Bauble	: foolish worthless creature
Beer, Small	: household expenses
Besort	: companionship
Billeted	: quartered, lodged
Birdlime	: a white sticky substance spread upon twigs to catch small birds
Blazoning	: praising
Boarded	: captured
Broil	: war
Burning Bear	: the shining constellation in the northern sky; The Great Bear
Cable	: scope
Caitiff	: wretch; literally, a captive
Callet	: public woman of the lowest kind
Canakin	: a little can used as a drinking vessel
Carrack	: a large ship like a Spanish galleon fitted for fight as well as for carrying cargo. "land-carrack" refers to Desdemona

Certes	:	indeed, certainly; an old French word
Charter	:	pledge, authoritative support
Chronicle	:	keep account of
Chrysolite	:	a rare kind of precious metal of beautiful green colour
Close delations	:	mysterious pauses, secret accusations
Clyster Pipes	:	tubes used in a medical injection
Coffers	:	chests containing luggage
Cogging	:	hypocritical
Coloquintida	:	a kind of bitter apple much used for medicinal purposes
Compasses	:	annual circuits (of the sun); years
Conscionable	:	conscientious
Conserved	:	prepared
Consuls	:	councillors, senators
Counsellor	:	talker
Cozening	:	deceitful
Crusadoes	:	Portuguese gold coins stamped with the figure of a cross
Cue	:	role, part
Curl'd darlings	:	fops with curly hair; fashionable favourites
Cyprus	:	an island in the Mediterranean
Diablo	:	Spanish word for 'devil'
Disports	:	amorous indulgences
Disposition	:	arrangement
Dram	:	drug
Encave	:	hide
Enchafed flood	:	angry sea
Engage	:	pledge
Engluts	:	swallows
Enwheel	:	encircle
Exhibition	:	allowance of money
Exsufflicate	:	inflated; swollen like a bubble, hence exaggerated
Filches	:	steals

Fineless : unlimited
Foh : fie
Fopped : cheated, befooled
Forfend : forbid
Forsooth : in truth; always used in irony
Fortunes : adventures
Free : full of goodwill
Freely : sincerely
Frize : coarse woolen cloth
Fulsome : foul
Function : mental constitution
Fitchew : a polecat with a nasty offensive smell; hence, a term for a loose woman
Galleys : flat-bottomed boats driven by oars and plying formerly in the Mediterranean
Gennets : horses of Spanish breed
Germans : relations
Government : self-restraint
Gripe : grasp
Grise : step
Guardage : guardianship
Gyve : entrap
Hellespontes : The Dardanelles, a strait between Europe and Turkey connecting Aegean sea with the sea of Marmara
Horologe : clock
Howbeit : although
Hydra : a nine-headed monster, ravaging the country of Lernia, for whose every head struck off two fresh ones immediately appeared, and who was slain by Hercules
Hyssop : a herb used as medicine
Idle : wild, barren
Inclining : behalf
Incontinently : immediately

Indign	:	unworthy, base, vile
Ingener	:	artist, poet
Intentively	:	with undisturbed attention, attentively
Injointed	:	combined
Janus	:	a Roman god of the gate with two faces looking in opposite directions
Jump	:	exactly at the very moment
Lay	:	wager, bet
Learn	:	teach
Liberal	:	licentious
List	:	listen to; wishes
Locusts	:	juicy and sweet fruits of the carole tree
Lolls	:	reclines
Lown	:	a rogue, a low fellow
Magnifico	:	a Venetian nobleman
Mandragora	:	mandrake plant that acted as a sleep-inducing medicine
Mauritania	:	Morocco and Algiers; named after the 'Mauri' as the Moors were called by the Romans
Mazzard	:	head
Meat	:	dinner
Mince	:	understate
Motion	:	faculty of understanding or judgment; also, movement of the body
Mountebanks	:	quacks
Mummy	:	juice from the flesh of a dead body that was embalmed, used for magical purposes
Nonsuits	:	a legal term meaning 'rejects the suit of,' when a suit is stopped by the judge because it is not drawn up according to the strict form of law
Offices	:	rooms or places in the castle at which refreshments are prepared or served out
Olympus-high	:	as high as Mount Olympus, the abode of the Greek gods in Homeric myth

On't	:	of it
Opinion	:	censure
Ottoman	:	The Turk
Ottomites	:	Turks
Outsport	:	overstep the limits
Paddle	:	caress, play fondly with
Paragons	:	surpasses
Pate	:	head
Pith	:	strength, vigour
Pontic Sea	:	The Black Sea, inland sea between Russia and Turkey
Potations	:	drinks
Potting	:	drinking, emptying pots of liquor
Pottle-deep	:	to the bottom of a half-gallon wine-pot
Portance	:	conduct, behaviour
Prefer	:	advance, promote (a cause)
Probal	:	probable
Probation	:	proof
Promethean heat	:	the spark of life-giving fire; Prometheus, the titan, stole fire from heaven and gave it to mortals, for which he was punished by Zeus by being chained to a peak of Caucasus, while his heart was preyed upon by a vulture. He was eventually liberated by Hercules.
Propontic	:	the sea of Marmara separating Europe from Anatelia (former Asia Minor)
Puddled	:	muddled
Quat	:	a young pimple, a term of contempt
Qualification	:	pacification, appeasement
Quillets	:	quibbles, quips
Quirks	:	conceits
Relume	:	rekindle
Rhodes	:	an island in the Aegean sea
Rouse	:	a large glass in which drink is given; deep drinking

Sagittary	:	an inn of that name
Salt	:	lewd, licentious
Sated	:	cloyed
'Sblood	:	a disguised form of 'God's blood;' an oath
Scant	:	neglect
Scurvy	:	vulgar, abusive
Seel	:	a term from the sport of falconry, meaning to hood or close up the eyes of a hawk by sewing the lids together; here it means, 'close'
Sequent	:	following one upon the other
Servitor	:	servant
Shambles	:	butcher's slaughter-house
Shrewd	:	well-founded
Sibyl	:	a prophetic woman believed to be in direct touch with the gods
Signiory	:	senate, the governing body of Venice
Sith	:	since
Skillet	:	a small kettle
Slubber	:	obscure, darken
Snipe	:	a stupid game-bird; hence, a fool
Snorting	:	sleeping soundly; obsolete form of 'snoring'
Stead	:	help
Stow'd	:	kept concealed
Strings	:	purse-strings for opening and closing the mouth of a money-bag
Suborn'd	:	corrupted, falsified
Sympathy	:	similarity
Thyme	:	a shrub used for cookery
Tinder	:	an inflammable substance like a scorched linen that readily catches fire from the spark produced when flint is struck against steel
Toged	:	clad in 'toga,' a loose outer garment worn by ancient Roman citizens

Trash	:	restrain, as though by means of a trash, a strap attached to an over-eager hound in hunting to restrain its speed
Tush	:	pshaw; an exclamation of impatience and incredulity
Twiggen bottle	:	wine bottle cased in a network of straw or twigs
Unbitted	:	unbridled, unrestrained
Unbonneted	:	without taking off the cap by way of showing respect, that is, without the feeling of being too humble or low
Veronesa	:	a vessel fitted out by Verona, a dependency of Venice
Voluble	:	inconstant, fickle
Wheeling	:	wandering from place to place with no fixed home
Whipster	:	one no bigger or bulkier than a whip; hence, a contemptible fellow
Work	:	fortifications
Yerk'd	:	stabbed
'Zounds	:	an oath; a corruption of 'God's wounds'

Index

Abdullah, 11
Accounts of the Revels at Court, 76
Aeneid, The, 83
Aguecheek, Sir Andrew, 24, 84
Al-Gaddafi, Muammar, 11
'And Wash the Ethiop White,' 198
Angelo, 82
Antony, 101
Antony and Cleopatra, 13, 77, 95-96, 99
Arden, Mary, 14
Ariosto, 81
Aristotle, 104
Arnold, Matthew, 1-2

Bacon, Francis, 11, 13
Baconian Theory, 11
Baker, G.P., 107
Baldwin, T.W., 83
Bergson, 110
Blackfriar's House, 16
Blackfriar's Theatre, The, 16
Blackwood's Magazine, 164
Boas, Guy, 149
Bodenstedt, 121
Boiardo, 81
Bradley, (A.C.), 52, 56, 64, 89, 110, 116-117, 128, 130, 136, 142, 146, 159, 195-196
Brandes, Dr., 190
Brooke, Stopford A., 105, 118, 144, 158, 180, 190
Bruno, Giordano, 12

Calvin, John, 12
Cassandra, 81
Chamberlain, John, 17
Characters of Shakespeare, The, 108
Cinthio (Giovannibattista Giraldi), 6, 78-79, 81-82, 84-88, 129, 149, 167
Cleopatra, 110
Coleridge, (Samuel Taylor), 110, 129, 139, 180, 194-195
Common Pursuit, The, 197
Commonwealth and Government of Venice, The, 83
Contareno, 83
Cordelia, 61, 65, 142, 145-146
Coriolanus, 77
Coriolanus, 101
Cresinus, (C. Furius), 82-83
Crollalancia, 11
Crollalanza, Guglielma, 12
Crollalanza, Michelangelo Florio, 11
Cunningham, Peter, 76

Dalecampinus, 83
Dekker, 76
Discorso, 81
Disdemona, 79-87
Dowden, 77, 110, 190, 195
Dr. Forman's *Diary*, 17
Dramatic Identities and Cultural Tradition: Studies in Shakespeare and His Contemporaries, 197
Dramatic Technique, 107
Drayton, 16
Dryden, 3
Dyer, Sir Edward, 13

Edmund, 110, 139
Eliot, T.S., 197
Empson, William, 197
Essential Shakespeare, The, 3

Florio, Giovanni, 12
Folio, 20, 75, 81, 193
Furness, 73

Goneril, 85
Granville-Barker, 114
Greene, Robert, 15
Groatsworth of Wit bought with a Million of Repentance, A, 15

Hadfield, (Andrew), 198-199
Halliwell, 77
Hamlet, 3-4, 13, 75, 77, 95-96, 99, 118, 159-160, 184, 193
Hamlet, 72, 82, 101, 145, 184
Hamnet, 14-15
Harrington, 81
Harris, Frank, 118
Hart, H.C., 76
Hathaway, Anne, 14
Hazlitt, 90, 108, 182
Hecatommithi, 78, 81-82
Hector, 81
Henry V, 17
Henslowe, Philip, 76
Herbert, William, 12
Herford, (C.H.), 54, 72, 129
Heywood, Thomas, 100
Hoffman, Colvin, 11
Holland, 82-83
Honest Whore, The Part I, 76
Horatio, 149
Hudson, 139, 189
Hunter, (G.K.), 197

Imogen, 61, 142
Iuvara, (Martino), 11-12

James, 110
Jardine, Lisa, 198
John, 110
Johnson, Dr. (Samuel), 8, 90, 180, 187, 189, 194-195
Jonson, Ben, 3, 16, 109, 160
Judith, 14

Kent, 149
King Lear, 4, 13, 75, 77, 95-96, 99, 159-160, 184, 193
"King's Players, The," 15
Knight, G. Wilson, 196

Lady Macbeth, 110
Lady Macduff, 65
Laertes, 72
Lear, 65, 145
Leavis, F.R., 197
Leila and Majnoon, 11
Lewkenor, (Sir Lewes), 83-84
Literature, Travel, and Colonial Writing in the English Renaissance, 198
Looney, J. Thomas, 12
Lord Chamberlaine's Company, 14
Lorkin, Thomas, 17

Love's Labour's Lost, 13, 15
Lucy, Sir Thomas, 14

Macaulay, 9, 180
Macbeth, 4, 11, 13, 73, 75, 77, 95-96, 99, 158-160, 184
Macbeth, 101
Malone, 75-76, 180
Manningham's *Diary*, 17
Marlowe, (Christopher), 11, 13, 109
Marston, 160
Masks of Othello, The, 197
McDougall, 110
McElroy, 72
McPherson, David, 199
Measure for Measure, 13, 77, 81-82, 96, 160
Merchant of Venice, The, 96
Metamorphoses, 83
Michelangelo, 12
Middleton, 76
Miranda, 61, 142
Mirror of Martyrs, 17
Moulton, 98, 134
Much Ado About Nothing, 96
Mystery Play, 106

Natural History, 82
Newman, Karen, 198
Nicoll, Allardyce, 90

Oedipus Tyrannus, 96
Olivia, 84
Ophelia, 65, 145
Orlando Furioso, 81
Orlando Innamorato, 81
Otello, 12
Ovid, 83

Pierce, William, 13
Pliny, 82-83
Poetics, 104
Poetic Justice, 5-6
Prefaces to Shakespeare, 114
Puckering, Sir Thomas, 17

"Quamar Al-Zaman and His Mistress," 11
Quarto, 20, 75, 193
Quys and Lubna, 11

Raleigh, (Sir Walter), 33-34, 158, 181
Rape of Lucrece, The, 18
Reading Shakespeare Historically, 198
Reese, M.M., 109
Regan, 85
Ribner, (Irving), 70
Richard, 110, 139
Ridley, M.R., 96
Roberts, James, 77
Romeo and Juliet, 11, 17
Rosenberg, Marvin, 197
Rylands, George, 171
Rymar, (Thomas), 193-194

Schucking, 110
Shakespeare and Other Masters, 196
Shakespeare, Jonson, and the Myth of Venice, 199
Shakespeare's Mature Tragedies, 72
Shakespearean Tragedy: *Lectures on 'Hamlet,' 'Othello,' 'King Lear,' 'Macbeth,'* 195
Sheikh Zbir, 11
Short View of Tragedy, A, 193
Spurgeon, Caroline, 174
Stanley, William, 13
Stationers' Registers, 17, 77
Stoll, E.E., 110, 196
Strachey, Lytton, 129

Structure of Complex Words, The, 197
Susanna, 14, 16
Swinburne, 85

Thousand and One Nights, 11
Tilney, Edmund, 193
Times Literary Supplement, 76
Toby Belch, Sir, 84
Twelfth Night, 24, 84
University Wits, The, 15

Venus and Adonis, 18
Vere, Edward de, 12-13
Viola, 61

Ward, Reverend John, 16
Weever, 17
Wheel of Fire, The, 196
"Why Should He Call Her Whore?" 198
Wilson, 164
Wilson, J. Dover, 3
Winter's Tale, The, 13
Winwood, Sir Ralph, 17
Woman Killed with Kindness, A, 100
Wriothesley, Henry, 15, 18
Wundt, 110